CATFISH, YAZ, AND HAMMERIN' HANK

The Unforgettable Era That Transformed Baseball

Phil Pepe

TRIUMPH
B O O K S
CHICAGO

Library of Congress Cataloging-in-Publication Data

Pepe, Phil.
    Catfish, Yaz, and Hammerin' Hank: the unforgettable era that transformed baseball / Phil Pepe.
    p. cm.
    Originally published: Talkin' baseball. New York: Ballantine Books, 1998.
    ISBN-13: 978-1-57243-839-2
    ISBN-10: 1-57243-839-8
      1. Baseball—United States—History—20th century. I. Pepe, Phil. Talkin' baseball. II. Title

    GV863.A1P45 2005
    796.357'64097309047—dc22   2005052942

This book is available in quantity at special discounts for your group or organization. For further information, contact:

Triumph Books
542 South Dearborn Street
Suite 750
Chicago, Illinois 60605
(312) 939-3330
Fax (312) 663-3557

Printed in U.S.A.
ISBN-13: 978-1-57243-839-2
ISBN-10: 1-57243-839-8
Design by Wagner/Donovan Design, Chicago IL
Photos Courtesy of AP/Wide World Photos

CONTENTS

Hammerin' Hank Aaron

FOREWORD

It's amazing how one telephone call can change a person's life so dramatically and so completely. I know, it happened to me.

In my case, the telephone call in question came on April 5, 1977. I was at home, packing for the first road trip of the season two days later, opening day of the American League season in Toronto. At the time, I was a member of the Chicago White Sox. I had joined them for 40 games in 1973, and I was preparing for the start of my fourth full season as the White Sox shortstop when the phone rang.

It was George Steinbrenner, owner of the Yankees. I had met him briefly three years earlier at a Chicago Bulls basketball game, but I really didn't know him, had never even talked to him except for a few words at that brief meeting in 1974, but I certainly knew enough about him.

After some pleasantries, George told me that he had agreed with the White Sox on a trade that would bring me to New York. Although there had been rumors that I might be going to the Yankees, rumors are rumors and very often nothing comes of them. So I wasn't counting on anything. I just tried to put the idea of going to the Yankees out of my mind so I wouldn't be disappointed if it didn't happen.

Despite all the rumors, when Steinbrenner said he had a deal for me, my heart still jumped with excitement. As a kid, I had been a Yankees fan and I had always dreamed of playing for them, and now there was a chance that my dream would come true.

George said the trade was contingent on my signing a contract, so I asked him to contact my agent and work it out with him. As far as I was concerned, there was not going to be a problem. I wasn't going to play hardball and hurt my chances of becoming a Yankee, but, then, you never know about these things.

In about an hour or so, my agent called me and said it was all worked out. I was going to the Yankees. And just like that, with one phone call, my life was changed forever.

I don't even like to think about what might have happened if that telephone call never came, or if I wasn't home to receive it, or if there had been some snag in the contract negotiations. I'm just glad things worked out as they did.

I enjoyed my time in Chicago. I would have been happy to spend my entire career there. But let's face it, the Yankees are the Yankees, and New York is New York, and going there, wearing the uniform of the most famous team in baseball . . . in any sport . . . well, that was the best thing that ever happened to me in my professional career.

For one thing, I was going from a team that had won only 64 games in 1976 and finished last in the American League West to a team that had won 97 games and went to the World Series. In other words, professionally speaking, I was going from the outhouse to the penthouse, as they say.

In my five and a half years with the Yankees, I would play in many big games, including two World Series, and enjoy some great times and thrilling moments, especially one on the afternoon of October 2, 1978, in Boston, when I was fortunate to be in the right place at the right time.

I saw Reggie Jackson hit three home runs on three consecutive pitches in the 1977 World Series, played alongside Graig Nettles when he made all those great plays against the Dodgers in the 1978 World Series, was on the bench watching when Ron Guidry struck out 18 California Angels, and witnessed the near fight between Jackson and Billy Martin in the Fenway Park dugout in 1977.

Looking back, I feel I was especially fortunate to have been a major leaguer during the decade of the seventies. It was a magical time for baseball, and in New York.

I got to play for two of the most famous, most flamboyant, and most legendary owners in the history of baseball, Bill Vicki in Chicago and George Steinbrenner in New York, and for storied managers like Chuck Tanner and Paul Richards in Chicago, Billy Martin and Bob Lemon in New York.

And I was privileged to play with great players like Dick Allen, Ron Santo, Jim Kaat, Wilbur Wood, and Goose Gossage in Chicago; Reggie Jackson, Dave Winfield, Catfish Hunter, Graig Nettles, Thurman Munson, Willie Randolph, Lou Piniella, Chris Chambliss, Tommy John, Roy White,

Ron Guidry, Bobby Murcer, Mickey Rivers, Sparky Lyle, and Goose Gossage in New York. Along the way, I formed meaningful, lasting, lifetime friendships.

This is not to say that my time in New York was always pleasant. Those were the days of the "Bronx Zoo," and we had more than our share of controversy, disagreements, and brawls in the clubhouse and in the dugout. And I also experienced the saddest of days, when Thurman Munson was killed in that terrible plane crash.

All in all, I have no regrets about my time in New York, and none about having played in the major leagues so many years ago.

I have heard it said that the seventies were the most exciting, most eventful decade in the history of baseball. I can vouch for that. It was exciting and eventful for me. Especially one afternoon in Boston.

—*Bucky Dent*

ACKNOWLEDGMENTS

A friend told me that he was reminiscing one day with his peers and together they decided that their interest in baseball had reached its peak in the decade of the seventies, when they were in their teens. To them, those were the "good old days," a time when going to the ballpark was filled with wonder and excitement and awe.

My friend said he thought the decade would make an interesting subject for a book, an oral history, with observations and recollections from many of those who had made prominent contributions to the events of the decade, and he urged me to take on such a project.

At first I hesitated. To one who grew up in Brooklyn, rooting passionately for the Brooklyn Dodgers in the forties and fifties, it was difficult to conjure the thought of the seventies as the good old days. It seemed too current.

Then it occurred to me that we were talking about, in some instances, more than a quarter of a century ago, and I began to reflect on all the historic and momentous events that took place in the decade, the broad, sweeping changes that came over the game in that period, and the idea of getting involved in such a project became intriguing.

I had spent the entire decade of the seventies as a beat writer covering the New York Yankees for the *New York Daily News,* and I estimate I covered almost 1,500 games, including preseason and postseason, and every World Series in that 10-year period, and that I knew, or interviewed, most of the principals who made news during the decade. This project gave me the opportunity to renew acquaintances with many of them and to bring back many pleasant memories.

I am indebted to the more than 60 players, managers, executives, and baseball writers, many of whom welcomed me into their homes, for giving so generously and graciously of their time.

In some instances, where more than one individual is quoted discussing a particular event, there may be conflicting views of the same subject, which, of course, can be attributed to how several individuals, on opposing sides of an issue, perceived the same incident differently.

It must also be pointed out that the author does not necessarily agree with the opinions and observations of those individuals quoted, but I believe it to be fair to allow them to have their say on the issues as they perceived them.

In order to include every event of the decade, and quote every significant individual who contributed to those events, this book would have to be three times as thick as it is. Some individuals were unreachable, some offered little embellishments to what already was included. In many cases, the best reporters were those who witnessed events rather than the participants in those events. As Yogi Berra once said, "You observe a lot by watching." I am grateful for their attentiveness to these details, and for their willingness to share them.

When I started on this project, my greatest concern was that delving into the past would be a painful reminder of how much time has gone by, and that it would make me feel old. On the contrary, reliving this glorious age of baseball helped me to feel young again.

—*Phil Pepe*

LIST OF INTERVIEWEES

Listed are the seventies affiliations.

Maury Allen: baseball writer, *New York Post*

Sparky Anderson: manager, Cincinnati Reds, Detroit Tigers

Marty Appel: director of public relations, New York Yankees

Stan Bahnsen: pitcher, New York Yankees, Chicago White Sox, Oakland Athletics, Montreal Expos

Yogi Berra: manager and coach, New York Mets

Ron Blomberg: first baseman, New York Yankees, Chicago White Sox; baseball's first designated hitter

George Brett: third baseman, Kansas City Royals; two-time American League batting champion

Johnny Briggs: outfielder, Philadelphia Phillies, Milwaukee Brewers, Minnesota Twins

Buzz Capra: pitcher, New York Mets, Atlanta Braves

Bernie Carbo: outfielder, Cincinnati Reds, St. Louis Cardinals, Boston Red Sox, Milwaukee Brewers, Cleveland Indians

Chris Chambliss: first baseman, Cleveland Indians, New York Yankees

Bucky Dent: shortstop, Chicago White Sox, New York Yankees

Al Downing: pitcher, Los Angeles Dodgers

Dock Ellis: pitcher, Pittsburgh Pirates, New York Yankees, Oakland Athletics, Texas Rangers

Mark "the Bird" Fidrych: pitcher, Detroit Tigers

Ray Fosse: catcher, Cleveland Indians, Oakland Athletics, Seattle Mariners, Milwaukee Brewers

George Foster: outfielder, San Francisco Giants, Cincinnati Reds

Jim Gantner: infielder, Milwaukee Brewers

Wayne Garrett: infielder, New York Mets, Montreal Expos, St. Louis Cardinals

Goose Gossage: pitcher, Chicago White Sox, Pittsburgh Pirates, New York Yankees

Ron Guidry: pitcher, New York Yankees

Bud Harrelson: infielder, New York Mets, Philadelphia Phillies

Fran Healy: catcher, San Francisco Giants, Kansas City Royals, New York Yankees

Whitey Herzog: manager, Texas Rangers, Kansas City Royals

Ralph Houk: manager, New York Yankees, Detroit Tigers

Al Hrabosky: pitcher, St. Louis Cardinals, Kansas City Royals

Reggie Jackson: outfielder and home-run hitter extraordinaire, Oakland Athletics, Baltimore Orioles, New York Yankees

Tommy John: pitcher, Chicago White Sox, Los Angeles Dodgers, New York Yankees

Davey Johnson: second baseman, Baltimore Orioles, Atlanta Braves, Philadelphia Phillies, Chicago Cubs

Hub Kittle: pitching coach, Houston Astros, St. Louis Cardinals; spent more than 60 years in baseball, mostly in the minor leagues

Bowie Kuhn: fifth commissioner of baseball; commissioner during the entire decade of the seventies

Jack Lang: baseball writer, *New York Daily News;* longtime secretary-treasurer, Baseball Writers Association of America

Tommy Lasorda: manager, Los Angeles Dodgers

Sparky Lyle: pitcher, Boston Red Sox, New York Yankees, Texas Rangers

Lee MacPhail: general manager, New York Yankees; president, American League

Bob Mandt: vice president, Stadium Operations, New York Mets

Mike Marshall: pitcher, Houston Astros, Montreal Expos, Los Angeles Dodgers, Atlanta Braves, Texas Rangers, Minnesota Twins

Billy Martin: manager, Minnesota Twins, Detriot Tigers, Texas Rangers, New York Yankees

Tim McCarver: catcher, Philadelphia Phillies, Montreal Expos, St. Louis Cardinals, Boston Red Sox

Matt Merola: business manager for Reggie Jackson

Gene Michael: infielder, New York Yankees, Detroit Tigers; coach, scout, New York Yankees

Marvin Miller: executive director, Major League Players Association

Mickey Morabito: director of public relations, New York Yankees

Diane Munson: widow of Thurman Munson

Bob Murphy: broadcaster, New York Mets

Graig Nettles: third baseman, Cleveland Indians, New York Yankees

Joe Pignatano: coach, New York Mets

Willie Randolph: second baseman, Pittsburgh Pirates, New York Yankees

Brooks Robinson: third baseman, Baltimore Orioles

Pete Rose: infielder, Cincinnati Reds, Philadelphia Phillies; baseball's all-time hit king

Tom Seaver: pitcher, New York Mets, Cincinnati Reds

Bud Selig: owner, Milwaukee Brewers

Reggie Smith: outfielder, Boston Red Sox, St. Louis Cardinals, Los Angeles Dodgers

Bob Stanley: pitcher, Boston Red Sox

Rusty Staub: outfielder/first baseman, Montreal Expos, New York Mets, Detroit Tigers

George Steinbrenner: "The Boss," New York Yankees

Rennie Stennett: infielder, Pittsburgh Pirates

Clyde Sukeforth: coach and scout, Brooklyn Dodgers, Pittsburgh Pirates

Jeff Torborg: catcher, Los Angeles Dodgers, California Angels; coach, New York Yankees; manager, Cleveland Indians

Mike Torrez: pitcher, St. Louis Cardinals, Montreal Expos, Baltimore Orioles, Oakland Athletics, New York Yankees, Boston Red Sox

Earl Weaver: manager, Baltimore Orioles

Bill White: broadcaster, New York Yankees

Bump Wills: infielder, Texas Rangers

INTRODUCTION

To chronicle baseball in the decade of the seventies properly, it is necessary to go back to the final months of the previous decade, specifically to the afternoon of Thursday, October 16, 1969.

Shea Stadium, Flushing, New York. With the gathering darkness and the slight chill of a late autumn afternoon in the air, Baltimore Orioles second baseman Davey Johnson sent a lazy fly ball to left field. New York Mets left fielder Cleon Jones camped under it, and the ball nestled softly in his glove, setting off a wild celebration from the 57,397 fans in attendance.

The Mets beat the Orioles 5–3; they beat them in the 1969 World Series, four games to one, in one of the most stunning upsets and most amazing reversals in baseball history.

The New York Mets had been born just seven years earlier, the product of a shotgun wedding designed to right the wrong of two New York teams—the Brooklyn Dodgers and New York Giants—who picked up stakes and moved three thousand miles away to California.

Those original Mets lost a record 120 games, finishing last in a 10-team league in four of the next five years. In 1968 they finished ninth, but it hardly offered any omen of what 1969 would bring. The Mets would become the first expansion team to win a world championship, and they would be, for all time, the symbol of hope for the downtrodden and all other expansion teams to come.

Perhaps we should not have been so shocked by the Mets' rise. Barely three months before Jones' catch of the final out of the World Series, man walked on the moon for the first time. And if man could walk on the moon, the Mets, or any other team, could win a World Series.

The Mets' championship ushered in baseball's space age, and the succeeding 120 months would bring more changes than the game had known in the first seven decades of the 20th century, the beginning of baseball's modern era.

Even the language of baseball was changing. New words had already entered the game's lexicon: *expansion, domed stadium, artificial turf.* More would come. *Arbitration. Designated hitter. Free agent.* And the word *strike* would take on a new meaning.

Becoming obsolete were words such as *doubleheader, complete game,* and *reserve clause.*

The relief pitcher, or closer, would flourish in the decade of the seventies. Of the top 97 all-time save leaders, 37 of them pitched in the seventies and 70 of them began their careers after 1969.

The decade of the seventies would produce the first strike in baseball history, the first free agent, the first night World Series game, and the first $1 million player. It would also bring George Steinbrenner, the Reggie Bar, Mark "the Bird" Fidrych, the split-fingered fastball, "We Are Family," Tommy Lasorda bleeding Dodger Blue, "You gotta believe," Marvin Miller, and "It ain't over till it's over."

The decade was only 16 days old when Curt Flood daringly and courageously tested the game's reserve clause by suing baseball, perhaps the single most important act in the game's history.

Yes, the game of baseball was changing, and it never again would be the same.

CATFISH, YAZ, AND HAMMERIN' HANK

Curt Flood was traded at the end of the 1969 season by the Cardinals to the Phillies (for Dick Allen, Cookie Rojas, and Jerry Johnson), but he refused to report, choosing instead to make the unprecedented move of challenging baseball's reserve clause. He never did play for Philadelphia, ending his career, after a trade, with the Senators in 1971, for whom he played only 13 games.

CHAPTER 1

1970

THE FIRST INNING

TOM SEAVER: Anytime you win, especially the way we won, with a good corps of pitching, which would lead to consistency, and, of course, Gil Hodges as the manager . . . I think we felt we were a club, not necessarily a dynasty . . . when you say *dynasty,* you think of clubs like the Yankees, clubs that win for long stretches of time . . . the Dodgers . . . that we would be competitive and be a good club for a number of years.

I don't think we talked about it openly, but the goal was to be competitive and maybe win two or three times in a five-year stretch. If that constitutes the definition of a dynasty, then fine. That's what our thoughts were. But, because of circumstances, those things change.

Change was the operative word for baseball as the decade of the seventies was ushered in against a backdrop of unrest and rebellion in the nation that would reach its nadir with the Kent State tragedy. National Guard troops would fire on a horde of protesting students, killing four of them. Later, two more students would be killed during a demonstration at Jackson State University.

By the start of spring training in 1970, baseball had expanded from 20 teams to 24, divisional play and postseason playoffs had begun, the Seattle franchise had moved to Milwaukee after one season, and the Bowie Kuhn era was about to enter its second year.

THE COMMISH

Kuhn, the longtime National League attorney with the prestigious law firm of Wilkie, Farr & Gallagher, had become commissioner of baseball on February 4, 1969, a compromise choice when neither of the two leading candidates, San Francisco Giants vice president Charles "Chub" Feeney and New York Yankees president Mike Burke, could garner the necessary votes from team owners for election.

Kuhn accepted a one-year term to serve as interim commissioner. He would stay on the job for 16 years, presiding over the greatest growth and the most sweeping changes in the game's history.

———

BOWIE KUHN: Baseball was in a big slump, had been slumping from 1950 on. It was not holding its own against the other professional sports and the entertainment world, and there was a desperate need to refocus it, rejuvenate it. The popularity had slipped, and that was my challenge.

My reservations about taking the job were professional. I was a lawyer; I was doing well. It wasn't a job I needed, so I had reservations. Once I got into it, it seemed to work well. The things I did all seemed to work. I had a sense that I was accomplishing a lot, and obviously the game felt the same way, because at the end of the year, they reelected me.

———

In another bizarre move, Chub Feeney accepted a mandate to succeed the venerable Warren Giles as National League president on the condition that he be allowed to move the league offices to San Francisco, where he resided, a nonsensical and incomprehensible request.

———

BOWIE KUHN: My plan was to centralize both league offices with the commissioner's office in New York. I was willing to hold off and let the American League office stay in Boston as long as Joe Cronin was league president, and the National League office stay in Cincinnati as long as Warren Giles was president. But once they retired, the idea was to move the league offices under the same roof as the commissioner's office.

I wasn't happy when Chub insisted on moving the National League office to San Francisco. That didn't go along with my plan. I thought it was a step backward. We ultimately got it done.

THE BREW CREW

Montreal and San Diego had been added to the National League, Kansas City and Seattle to the American League in 1969, with each league divided

Hold That Tiger

The Detroit Tigers had been the Orioles' toughest competitors in the two previous years. The Tigers finished 12 games ahead of the Orioles in 1968, when Denny McLain won 31 games, the first pitcher in 34 years to win 30. In 1969, Earl Weaver's first full season as Baltimore manager, McLain won 24, but the Orioles beat out the Tigers by 19 games.

The Tigers were dealt a severe blow on April 1, just a few days before Opening Day 1970, when McLain was suspended from baseball for 90 days for associating with known gamblers, frequenting a bar that housed a bookmaking operation, and investing in a bookmaking operation.

BOWIE KUHN: It was never clear just exactly what the depth of his involvement was, but McLain's involvement in a bookmaking operation in Flint, Michigan, the Long Horn Saloon, was all it took to warrant some substantial penalty. There was no indication he was betting on baseball, although a lot of members of the media felt he was, but we never generated any evidence that he was betting on baseball. But the involvement in a bookmaking operation was so obviously out of bounds that it drew a half-year suspension and probation.

McLain returned to the Tigers on July 1, but it was soon apparent he wasn't the same pitcher who had won 55 games in the previous two seasons. Then McLain violated his probation with such acts of misconduct as dousing Detroit sportswriter Watson Spoelstra with a bucket of water and as a result he was suspended for the remainder of the season.

Without their star pitcher, the Tigers quickly dropped out of the race and finished a distant fourth in the American League East.

into six-team East and West divisions. The division champions were to play a best-of-five series to determine the league champion and World Series opponents.

The Seattle Pilots, inept on the field and struggling at the turnstile, were purchased by a group headed up by an automobile dealer named Allan H. "Bud" Selig, a native Milwaukeean who had grown up idolizing the Milwaukee Braves of the fifties. Selig's plan was to move the team to Milwaukee, which had been out of major league baseball since the Braves moved to Atlanta in 1966.

BUD SELIG: I had been trying for five and a half years to bring major league baseball back to Milwaukee. We tried expansion. We thought we had a deal to buy the Chicago White Sox, but that fell through.

I went to the 1969 World Series, and I was in Memorial Stadium in Baltimore when I learned that the Seattle club might be available. They were having financial problems and the team was up for sale, but the owners were intent on keeping the team in Seattle.

But the interest was less than enthusiastic in Seattle, so we looked into the Seattle situation. Fortunately for us, no Seattle group came forward to buy the team. Early in March, I got a call from American League president Joe Cronin, who said, "Are you still interested in buying the Seattle club?" I said I was.

We got all the necessary documentation, and on March 31, at 10:50 at night, in the middle of a snowstorm, we got word that the deal had gone through. Opening Day was a week away.

———

Selig and his staff worked feverishly, night and day, to prepare for the new American League team in Milwaukee, which would assume the Seattle schedule for 1970 and play its games in old County Stadium. Tailors were called in to remove the P-I-L-O-T-S from the Seattle uniforms and replace it with B-R-E-W-E-R-S, and the season opened in Milwaukee on April 7 against the California Angels.

———

BUD SELIG: Andy Messersmith beat us, 12–0. It's the only game I didn't give a damn if we won or lost. That first day I looked up at the scoreboard, and it was the greatest thrill of my life.

THE FLOODGATES ARE OPENED

The most far-reaching event of the decade occurred on the 16th day of the new decade when St. Louis Cardinals outfielder Curt Flood, in baseball's version of the Dred Scott decision, filed a lawsuit against Major League Baseball, challenging the game's reserve clause.

The reserve clause was the lifeblood of the game for major league owners, the instrument by which they controlled their employees—the players—like pawns. It meant that a player, once signed by a major league team,

Marvin Miller, a former economist with the United Steelworkers of America, became head of the major league baseball players union in the sixties and went to work almost immediately, turning the union into one of America's strongest.

belonged to that team in perpetuity. It was stronger than the marriage vow—till death do us part or until that player was sold, traded, released, or retired—all at the owner's whim, with no voice from the player.

In 1922 Supreme Court Justice Oliver Wendell Holmes ruled that baseball was immune from antitrust laws, in effect leaving the players as mere chattel of the owners. Justice Holmes' decision remained unchallenged for three decades, until 1953, when a farmhand for the Yankees, George Toolson, frustrated by being stonewalled by the wealth of Yankees talent and hoping for his release so that he might advance to the major leagues with another team, sued baseball.

The case went to the Supreme Court, which upheld Justice Holmes' original decision by a 7–2 vote. In its decision, however, the court said it was standing by the original ruling only as a matter of precedent and suggested that any change in baseball's status should come from Congress. In that opinion, the high court intimated that the reserve clause was illegal and that change was imminent. But there was no one courageous enough to state it outright, and the players were not strong enough to mount another challenge for almost two decades. Then along came Curt Flood and Marvin Miller.

In the fifties, major league owners, becoming increasingly aware of players' discontent and recognizing the need for a players union to deal with such matters as a pension fund, helped form the Major League Players Association. It would be headed by Robert Cannon, a county judge in Milwaukee, who would be paid by the owners.

More than a decade later, the players, realizing this arrangement was not in their best interests, formed a four-man search committee consisting of Robin Roberts, Bob Friend, Harvey Kuenn, and Jim Bunning to find a new leader for their union. Their search led to a professor at the Wharton School of Business, George William Taylor, who recommended Marvin Miller, an economist with the United Steelworkers of America, who was available because his boss had been voted out as the Steelworkers' president.

MARVIN MILLER: The Players Association had been created by the owners. It fit the definition of a company union, so you would think it was a prototype. But it was dominated by the owners. It had no staff of its own. It had no office of its own. It had no continuity from one month to the next. It had no accomplishments. It had no written agreements. Their so-called adviser was paid by the owners. It was illegal. Everybody involved could have gone to jail.

The Players Association got into conflict with the owners almost immediately, even before we got into collective bargaining. The first collective bargaining was on the pension plan in the winter of 1966–67. The first Basic Agreement was negotiated in 1968. Both were accomplished without any kind of job action.

The first conflict of a serious nature occurred in the winter of 1968–1969. We were renegotiating the pension plan. The owners had decided they didn't really like having a union there. Some of them were concerned that while so far the first Basic Agreement didn't impinge too much on their control of the game, nor did the first pension agreement, they could look down the road and see an organization that would get stronger and was going to be a problem to them.

So they took this position that, even though they were expanding again in 1969, they were not going to increase their contribution to the pension plan. They were going to bring in four new teams, and all these new players, to be covered by the pension and insurance plan, and this was going to be done with the same amount of money. We said, "No, you can't do that." There's no way to do that without cutting benefits, and there wasn't the slightest basis for cutting benefits.

So we ran into what I considered an irrational position. Here they were in the flush of prosperity. They were adding four new teams and the money that brought in, and they were going to do this by curtailing benefits. That led to the first real confrontation.

The players adopted a policy of not signing contracts until the pension agreement was concluded. There had been individual holdouts before, but this was the first time you had what amounted to a mass holdout.

All of this is a backdrop to what happened the following year. General William Eckert was fired in the middle of this pension imbroglio. Bowie Kuhn had been appointed commissioner and was facing his first Opening Day with a threatened strike. So the pension agreement got settled pretty fast, and I've always given Bowie credit for the turnabout, because no sooner was he elected than the owners' position changed drastically.

By February 25, 1969, we had a new pension agreement with a vastly increased contribution from the owners, more than covering the increased number of players owing to expansion. That left us the problem of negotiating a new Basic Agreement before the 1970 season. The first Basic Agreement was a two-year agreement, covering 1968 and 1969. We had raised some very important issues in negotiating that agreement, but without the strength to follow through on them. We had raised the issue of the reserve clause. We had raised the issue of the season being too long—they had previously increased the number of games from 154 to 162 before I got there without ever changing the players' salaries or compensation in any way. We were asking for a cutback, back to 154 games. But we didn't have the strength to make either change in that first Basic Agreement.

We proposed two study committees, one to look into revising the reserve clause, without specifying in what way, and ditto in the case of the length of the season. All study committees were a joke. The owners' idea of a study committee was to come in and ask, "What's on your mind?" And when we suggested ideas to study, their answer was "No, we like it the way it is." It didn't matter what we proposed. The mildest kind of thing: "No, no, we like it the way it is." Of course they liked it the way it was.

As we headed toward Christmas of 1969, we were nowhere. In October or November, I got a call from a player who I had met in spring training and who I had talked to in the spring-training meetings, but who I really didn't know. It was Curt Flood.

Flood had come up with the Cincinnati Reds in 1956 and, after playing in only eight games with the Reds in two seasons, was traded to St. Louis, where he became a Cardinals star almost immediately. He moved right in as their regular center fielder and became a mainstay of a team that won three National League championships and two World Series in a five-year period. Twice he had more than 200 hits in a season. In 12 seasons with the Cardinals, he played in 1,738 games, had 1,853 hits, had a career batting average of .293, and was considered the equal of the legendary Willie Mays as a defensive center fielder.

On October 7, 1969, three months short of his 32nd birthday, Flood was traded by the Cardinals with Tim McCarver, Joe Hoerner, and Byron Browne to the Phillies for Dick Allen, Cookie Rojas, and Jerry Johnson.

McCarver, the Cardinals' regular catcher since 1963, was as big a hero and almost as much of a fixture in St. Louis as Flood was.

TIM McCARVER: At the time, I didn't understand the ramifications of the trade. I didn't think that it would be ultimately as large as it has become and as important as it has become. I was concerned primarily with my career and what I was going to do and how to prove myself. It was the first trade for me, and it was very emotional, as all first trades are.

The trade was more than just emotional for Flood. It displeased him and prompted his call to Miller.

MARVIN MILLER: Flood told me about the trade to Philadelphia and said he thought it was outrageous after his connection with St. Louis. He had moved his family there; he had started a portrait artist business. He had been with the Cardinals for 12 years.

Then he said, "I listened to what you said about the reserve clause in relation to the antitrust laws. I have consulted with my own attorney in St. Louis, and I want to file an antitrust action against Major League Baseball. I don't want to go to Philadelphia."

I said, "What I'd like to do is discuss this with you in detail before we take any action, and I'd also like you to think carefully about this. Why don't we make an appointment two or three weeks from now, and if you can come to New York, we can sit down and spend the day discussing this."

He said, "Sure. Can I bring my attorney?"

I said he could.

I said, "What I want you to think about in these few weeks is that this is a major step in your career because what you're dealing with is a bunch of very vindictive and powerful people here. It's not as if you can give this to your lawyer, file this lawsuit, and go on with your career. It's not going to happen that way. Your career is on the line, and while I think your action is justified, I don't want you to do it without realizing what the dangers and the possibilities are here."

He came to New York, and he and his attorney, Allan H. Zerman; Dick Moss, my general counsel at the time; and I spent the day together, having

Hall of Fame Sneak Preview

Several milestones were recorded in 1970 by five players who would eventually be elected to the Hall of Fame.

- On May 17, Henry Aaron collected the 3,000th hit of his career. With 570 home runs, on pace to challenge Babe Ruth's record 714 homers, Aaron was the ninth player to garner 3,000 hits, but the first in baseball history with 3,000 hits and 500 home runs. Two months and one day later, Willie Mays also got his hit number 3,000 and joined Aaron as the only players in history with 3,000 hits and 500 home runs.

- On May 10, Hoyt Wilhelm, pitching for his seventh team, the Atlanta Braves, in his 19th major league season at 46 years old, became the first pitcher to appear in 1,000 games. He would pitch until he was 49 and appear in 1,070 games.

- On May 12, Ernie Banks, "Mr. Cub," became the eighth member of the 500-home-runs club. His 500th homer was also RBI number 1,600 of his career. Banks would play 19 major league seasons, all with the Cubs, and finish with 512 homers and 1,636 RBIs.

- On September 3, Billy Williams, also of the Cubs, asked to sit out a game against the Phillies, ending his consecutive-game streak at 1,117 games, a National League record. But he was still 1,013 games, or about seven seasons' worth, short of Lou Gehrig's phenomenal major league record of 2,130 consecutive games.

lunch at the Summit Hotel, then back to the office, then dinner together and back to the office again. We talked into the night.

The gist of what I told him is that I thought the case had merit but that we would lose because they protect their rear ends. I told him about Justice Holmes' decision in 1922, a nonsensical decision, and about the Toolson case. I gave him the whole history so he would understand that while I was saying that those decisions were nonsensical, I was not saying they would overrule the decision. As a matter of fact, I would give odds they would not—that they would just go blindly on.

I did give Flood one bit of encouragement. I said you would think that by the time this gets to the court, so much time would have elapsed that they would take a good long look at other things that have happened—and the most pertinent in my mind was that between Toolson and what would become Flood—the Supreme Court had ruled that football was covered by the antitrust laws, basketball was covered by the antitrust laws, hockey was covered by the antitrust laws, boxing was covered by the antitrust laws, and horse racing was covered by the antitrust laws. All of that after Toolson. The logic of that is, you look at the real world; this is what you, the court, have done. But I said I'd still give odds that we lose.

Flood and his attorney sat there, their chins dropping further and further. But I couldn't let them think this was a winner, because I didn't believe it.

Flood, levelheaded and a principled guy, said, "Look, how else are we going to break this? We don't have the strength yet as a union, do we?"

I said, "Realistically, no. Maybe someday we will, but realistically we don't, mostly because if you were to take a poll of the players out there, my belief is, based on talking to them, that there is still a majority that thinks the reserve clause is necessary, that, somehow, it would create a terrible imbalance, that the rich would get richer and the poor would get poorer and that it was therefore necessary."

Then I told Flood a true story. In the first meeting I had with the Yankees, in 1966, one of the subjects I brought up, because I felt the players ought to know what I think, is that I thought the reserve clause was an abomination. It kept the players as pieces of property, it left them without dignity and without bargaining power, and, over time, we had to do something about it. I said I didn't want to kid anybody that we were going to do it tomorrow. Nor did I want to kid them that I believed this was an immutable part of the baseball scene. It wasn't.

Then I told Flood that one of the brightest, most aware players, Jim Bouton, came up to me after the meeting and said, "How would it work if you didn't have the reserve clause? A team with the most money would be buying up all the stars, and nobody would be able to beat them." And I said to Bouton, "You mean like the Yankees now?"

So Flood said, "All right, what else do I have to know?"

I said, "As I told you on the phone, I think it would be the end of your career. I don't see how you could continue playing after the suit was filed. Where would you play? You would have to play for Philadelphia, and you don't want to play for Philadelphia. If you did play for Philadelphia, you run the risk of the first court we get into saying the case is moot. You were traded, and you're playing. Where's the issue? So it would mean you can't play. How long? I don't know. If we're going to fight it all the way to the Supreme Court, it could take years. You're 32 now. Realistically, how could you be out of the game two, three years and come back?

"When I say these people are vindictive, I mean I would not put it past them to end any possibility you might have—I don't know what your feeling is about being a coach or a manager—but realistically, you'll have to forget that, too. They don't take kindly to people suing them. I think they would pull out all the stops. If there's anything in your background—and I'm not asking you if there is—but if there is anything in your background that you would not like to see in the sports pages, you wouldn't do this because they'll dig it out, and they have the capacity to do it."

He said to me, "I've got a brother in jail on drug charges."

I said, "Curt, I didn't ask you, but you'll see that written around. And anything else, and I don't want to know."

I was telling him these things not to scare him but to be realistic as I saw it. I said, "It's possible for us to pull off a miracle and win this case and for you not to get anything. It would be possible, in my mind, for a court to say that retroactively, no, because the owners were relying on prior Supreme Court decisions, but prospectively, this is in violation of the antitrust laws and you may not have the reserve clause anymore."

He said, "Good enough for me."

I asked Flood to go back to St. Louis, talk it over with his lawyer, talk it over with his wife, and let me know whether he still wanted to do it. A short time later he called me again and said, "Yes."

The executive board of the Players Association was having its annual meeting in San Juan, Puerto Rico, in the first week of December 1969. Among the members of the board were Jim Bunning, Steve Hamilton, Gary Peters, and Tom Haller. Miller suggested to Flood that he fly to Puerto Rico to present his case to the board, which would decide whether to back him.

TIM McCARVER: The Phillies didn't have a player representative. Cookie Rojas and Jerry Johnson were their player reps, and they were both sent to St. Louis in the trade. I was the player representative for the Cardinals, and I was the assistant National League representative, so since the Phillies didn't have a player rep, it made sense to me to go to Puerto Rico to represent the Phillies. I represented the league as much as the Phillies.

I went down to Puerto Rico, and that was the trip Curt made. He was going to ask for the blessing of the Players Association to support him through this whole thing.

I had a chance to talk with Curt before the meeting. I came from Memphis and he came from St. Louis, and I met him in Miami on our way to Puerto Rico. That's when I found out firsthand how serious he was about this thing, and that's when it first started sinking in that this was indeed a very big move that he was making.

MARVIN MILLER: Flood came to San Juan and made his presentation to the board. He told them how he felt when they told him he was traded, how he had thought long and hard about how unfair the reserve clause was. He did a good job of summarizing all of the negatives; nevertheless, he felt it was an important principle and that he needed help.

When he finished, the board members asked questions like, what kind of assistance would he want? He said he thought about it and that I had told him it would be important to get a top-notch antitrust lawyer and that he felt he could not afford that kind of fee and expenses, so he needed that to be paid for by the Players Association. He said he, of course, would have to be involved in the case as a witness, and discussions with whomever the attorney was, and he would need help with his expenses, back and forth from St. Louis, probably to New York, and he wanted nothing else. He didn't expect any remuneration, any salary.

In return for this, Flood would pledge in writing that to the extent he won damages in the case, he would reimburse the Players Association for all out-of-pocket expenses.

At one point, Tom Haller asked, "Does anything about this have to do with asserting black power?" You have to remember the timing of this. Flood just smiled and said, "There's not much power here," but added that he thought after talking with me that he realized it was a long shot to win, but he thought it was worth the gamble for the future of the game and for the players who were yet to come, and it had nothing to do with asserting black power.

TIM McCARVER: It was a wide-open discussion. Guys were encouraged, and Curt even encouraged the guys to go ahead and ask anything they wanted. And Curt answered everything in a straightforward fashion.

MARVIN MILLER: After all the questioning, Flood was excused and the board continued its discussion, and they unanimously approved (a) I should attempt to engage the most competent antitrust attorney I could, (b) the association would pay the legal expenses and Flood's expenses in connection with the case and the trial, and (c) Flood would provide a written agreement to reimburse the association if he won financial damages.

TIM McCARVER: I didn't doubt Curt's sincerity one bit. What a courageous thing he did—the money he gave up. In spring training, they still didn't believe Curt was going to go through with it, and in spring training, Phillies general manager John Quinn had lunch or dinner with him in Philadelphia. I think it was in February. And Quinn upped the offer to Flood to a salary of $110,000, and in those days that was a ton of money. I'm sure there were a lot of people who thought Curt was calling their bluff and that he would cave in for more money, but he didn't.

Miller returned from San Juan and contacted an old friend, former secretary of labor, former justice of the Supreme Court, and former ambassador to the United Nations Arthur Goldberg, with whom Miller had been associated when Goldberg was general counsel of the Congress of Industrial Organizations and the Steelworkers. Goldberg agreed to handle the Flood case pro bono.

MARVIN MILLER: At this time we were in negotiations with the owners, and we were getting absolutely nowhere. We had had these farcical study committees, and we were meeting a stone wall on the reserve clause and everything else. The agreement was expiring on December 31. We decided negotiations were hopeless on the reserve clause. The owners were never going to agree to change a comma, and they pretty much said so.

Jim Bouton had come in as part of the negotiating committee at one point, and I had made a point of the fact that if they carried this farce to its logical conclusion, you were never off the reserve list. Somebody told me that

Lefty O'Doul, who was then 72 years old, was still on the Giants' reserve list, and Bouton asked a tongue-in-cheek question of National League counsel Lou Carroll.

"Mr. Carroll," he said, "would you consider removing a former player from the reserve list when he reached age 65?"

And Carroll, without batting an eye, said, "No, because that would be a foot in the door."

Papers were served by Flood against Major League Baseball on January 16, 1970, which made the baseball powers that be furious.

BOWIE KUHN: Philosophically, I was not opposed to free agency. I was promoting, along with Cubs owner Phil Wrigley and Brewers vice president Ed Fitzgerald, the idea of seriously negotiating free agency with the players, because it was an inevitability in my opinion. But we were overwhelmed by the rank and file of the ownership on that issue.

My problem was that you were going to shake up the rosters, run them around year by year, and you wouldn't have the continuity baseball always had. And I didn't think that would be right for the fans.

On August 12, federal district court judge Irving Ben Cooper handed down his ruling on the suit of *Flood v. Bowie Kuhn et al.* He ruled in baseball's favor.

"Clearly, the preponderance of credible proof does not favor the elimination of the reserve system," wrote Cooper in his decision, but added he was impressed by Flood's arguments and said in his opinion that arbitration and negotiation might bring satisfaction to both parties, but only Congress or the Supreme Court could change baseball's immunity to antitrust.

Disappointed by their defeat, but encouraged by Judge Cooper's wavering somewhat in his decision, Flood, Miller, and the Players Association took their case to the United States Court of Appeals.

Flood had sat out a full season and had lost $110,000 in salary for his cause. He moved to Copenhagen, Denmark, but the tug of baseball, the desire to compete, remained a powerful force within him. Then he was contacted by Bob Short.

Short was a flamboyant and charming rogue of a businessman, the former chairman of the Democratic National Committee. He had dabbled in sports as owner of the Minneapolis Lakers, subsequently selling the team to a group that moved it to Los Angeles.

Short had a penchant for doing things with a flair and with an eye on the newspapers. In 1968 he bought the Washington Senators and promptly coaxed Ted Williams to become his manager.

On October 9, 1970, he made a trade with the Detroit Tigers, acquiring the celebrated and notorious Denny McLain in a spectacular eight-player swap in which the Tigers received right-handed pitcher Joe Coleman, who would win 62 games over the next three seasons; shortstop Ed Brinkman; and third base-man Aurelio Rodriguez. Together they would form a durable and productive left side of the Detroit infield for most of the seventies. The Tigers also acquired pitcher Jim Hannan.

Less than a month after making the McLain deal, Short acquired the rights to Flood from the Phillies for three minor league players. Flood was eager to return to the game but told Short he first had to consult with Marvin Miller and Arthur Goldberg to make certain his return would not jeopardize his appeal.

Told it would not as long as he wasn't going to play in Philadelphia, Flood agreed to sign with the Senators if Short would agree to several conditions:

1. Not to trade him without his consent.
2. To pay Flood his full year's salary ($110,000) if he was cut from the team before the end of the season.
3. To release Flood unconditionally if the two parties could not agree on terms for the renewal of his contract in 1972.
4. Major league owners would not argue in court that Flood's presence on the playing field invalidated his suit.

Short agreed to all conditions, and Curt Flood returned to the United States to prepare for his return to baseball.

The 1971 season was in its second day when the United States Court of Appeals handed down its decision upholding Judge Irving Ben Cooper's ruling against Flood. Although Flood was still left with one option, an appeal to the United States Supreme Court, the Court of Appeals decision was not to be Flood's only setback in the month of April.

On April 27, Flood sent this telegram to Washington Senators owner Bob Short:

> I tried. A year and a half is too much. Very serious problems mounting every day. Thanks for your confidence and understanding.

Flood played in 13 games for the Senators. He came to bat 35 times and had only seven hits, a batting average of .200, which was 93 points below his career average. He had no extra-base hits, no stolen bases, and only two runs batted in. He realized his career was over.

Curt Flood was a little more than a year into retirement when his case reached a conclusion. Having lost in federal district court and the United States Court of Appeals, Flood took his appeal to the ultimate and final arbiter, the United States Supreme Court, which agreed to hear the case on March 20, 1972.

Three months later, on June 18, the high court rendered its decision. By a 5–3 vote, with one abstention, the court upheld the owners in a long-winded and rambling opinion written by Justice Harry Blackmun. Curt Flood had lost the battle, but the war was still not over.

MARVIN MILLER: There's a book called *The Brethren,* by Scott Armstrong and Bob Woodward (of Woodward and Bernstein fame), and it has a chapter on the Supreme Court dealing with the Flood case. I have no way of knowing the validity of any of this, but what it says basically is that in the discussions leading up to the decision in the Flood case, the court was 5–3 in favor of Flood. The other one, Powell, disqualified himself.

The case was coming up at the same time as *Roe v. Wade*, the abortion case, and there was a lot of jockeying going on. Blackmun hadn't written an opinion on any kind of significant case—this is according to Woodward. As a result, Blackmun changed his vote, so the 5–3 for Flood became 4–4. Then somebody else changed his vote, and 4–4 became 5–3 against Flood.

You can't write an opinion for the Supreme Court unless you're in the majority, so Blackmun changed his vote and got to write the opinion in the Flood case, again according to Woodward. It was one of the most stupid opinions on record—and Blackmun was a bright guy who later transcended his role in the Flood case. But his opinion started with the names of about 100 ballplayers—George Sisler, Rube Marquard, Three Finger Brown, a pantheon of baseball heroes—that was the nature of his opinion.

I never before saw a majority opinion that ridiculed the decision like this one did. It said this decision we recognize as an aberration and goes on to give all the reasons why the opinion is stupid.

For that reason, and because it went all the way to the Supreme Court, even though Flood lost, it was something of a moral victory. Everybody told us that the court would never accept jurisdiction, that it would take one look at the docket and say we ruled on this in 1922, we ruled on this in 1953. It takes four votes for the court to accept jurisdiction, not a majority, at least four votes, and very knowledgeable people told me that we didn't have a chance. But they were wrong, and the court accepted the case for appeal.

The amazing thing is that the whole procedure—coming to trial in district court, the trial itself, the filing of an appeal to the circuit court, the circuit court hearing, the circuit court decision, filing an appeal to the Supreme Court, the Supreme Court holding a hearing to determine whether to take jurisdiction and then deciding to take jurisdiction, and then the Supreme Court making a decision—from beginning to end, that was record time. Two and a half years. It's just unheard of, and I don't know why. Was it because it was baseball and the judges liked to get involved in something like this? I don't know.

Offhand, and I'm no authority on this, I'd say that if you file a case in federal district court and carry it through to all the appeals, you're more likely talking about four, five, six, seven years. This took two and a half years, and, to this day, I don't know why.

WAIT 'TIL NEXT YEAR

With enmity between players and owners, stonewalling by the owners on the reserve clause, determination by the players to fight the reserve system as the backdrop, the new decade, and spring training, 1970 began as the upstart New York Mets and the powerful Baltimore Orioles set out to defend their league championships.

BROOKS ROBINSON: I didn't see a whole lot of difference in our attitude in spring training. We knew we had a good ballclub. When we played the Mets, it was the second time we had been in the World Series. We won the first time, against the Dodgers in 1966, a four-game sweep. We went into the Series against the Mets and won the first game, like we were supposed to. Then we lost four in a row.

My thought during the winter was, you got a Tom Seaver, you got a Jerry Koosman, you got a Gary Gentry, hey, these guys are big-time pitchers. It was just one of those things. I don't know how you can explain it. When something gets started like that, it's hard to turn it off. The thing that affected us most was that we had never had our backs to the wall like that, and we started trying to do things we were not capable of doing.

It was a little embarrassing, I think, because that was one of the biggest upsets in the history of the game, but there wasn't a whole lot of difference in our attitude in spring training. There was no rah-rah, let's prove we're the best team. We were pretty professional about it.

EARL WEAVER: We knew we were going to win again. I told my players, "Lookit, last year we won 109 games." We lost the Series, which to me was nothing, losing the Series, because that's a tremendously successful year. And you kept the team together in those days. We had everybody coming back, at the right age, even more mature and better.

We knew what we did the year before, and we knew we were going to do it again in 1970. It just wasn't a problem. I told them, "Let's not bring up last year at all. Not because of the Series, but because you have to do it all over again if you want to get back to the Series." And it was just a talented ballclub. Sure, we wanted to win the World Series in 1969, but we knew we had had a successful year, and we knew we were going to have another one.

The Orioles, buoyed by three 20-game winners—24 each for Mike Cuellar and Dave McNally, 20 for Jim Palmer—and with a cast of all-stars including Brooks and Frank Robinson, Boog Powell, Davey Johnson, Mark Belanger, and Paul Blair, won 108 games (217 wins for Weaver in his first two full seasons as a manager) and beat out the surprising New York Yankees by 15 games.

For the second straight year, the Orioles faced the Minnesota Twins in the American League Championship Series, and for the second straight year, the Orioles won in a three-game sweep. And for the second straight year, the Orioles made it to the World Series, eager to avenge their embarrassing defeat by the Mets the year before.

The Mets, however, were having problems of their own.

———

BUD HARRELSON: No doubt everybody thought it wasn't lucky when we won in 1969. We won 100 games. We had Gil Hodges. I think we felt very secure that we were the National League counterpart to the Orioles, knowing that they were kind of a dynasty through that era and that it should carry on for us in 1970.

When we got to spring training, it wasn't a matter that we had different personnel. It was a matter of everybody's attitude toward us. They were very aggressive against us, even in spring training. Everybody probably said, "Yeah, those guys are good, but we took them lightly." No one thought we could win in 1969. The oddsmakers didn't. Probably the only people who figured how good we were from the start were Hodges and the coaching staff. Hodges was good at telling us what we could do with our abilities.

So it was a letdown to see how up everybody was against us in spring training. Not that we were sleeping after we won in 1969, but everybody had a different approach to us. First pitch, they might brush you back. When we didn't win in 1970, sure, it was disappointing.

———

On April 18 against the Phillies, Nolan Ryan gave up a leadoff single to Denny Doyle, then set the Phillies down without a hit the rest of the way, striking out 15 in a 7–0 victory. Four days later, Seaver struck out a major-league-record 19 Padres, including the last 10 batters, another major league record, in a 2–1 victory, and the National League was put on notice that the Mets' young arms were primed for another world championship. But by May 11 the Mets had fallen to 14–16, and they would never get back on track.

———

TOM SEAVER: I had a subpar year. For the first time in my life, I had shoulder problems. Overall, we didn't perform to the level we did in 1969. Realistically, you can't be expected to do that. In hindsight, because you have a lot more information to draw on, you realize things just don't work out that way.

From the standpoint that we were a year older and we were world champions, I thought we would be competitive for a number of years, and when we were not, it was disappointing. Definitely.

Sparky Anderson, a career minor leaguer who spent one year in the majors as the Phillies second baseman in 1959, became the Cincinnati Reds manager before the 1970 season at the age of 36. He guided the Reds to five first-place finishes and two championships.

After posting a record of 25–7 in 1969, Seaver slipped to 18–12 in 1970. Jerry Koosman fell from 17 wins to 12, Gary Gentry from 13 to 9. Cleon Jones, who had batted .340 in 1969, batted .277 in 1970. The Mets, who had won 100 games in 1969, won only 83 in 1970 and finished third in the East, 6 games behind the Pirates, who got a big year from Willie Stargell (31 homers, 85 RBIs), Bob Robertson (27 homers, 82 RBIs), Dave Giusti (nine wins, 26 saves), and the irrepressible Roberto Clemente (a .352 average).

BIRTH OF THE BIG RED MACHINE

The big noise in the National League, however, was being made in Cincinnati, baseball's oldest franchise. Slowly, the Reds had built a potential dynasty. Lee May, Tommy Helms, Tony Perez, Pete Rose, Bobby Tolan, Johnny Bench, and Jim Merritt were already in place, but the Reds had finished fourth, fourth, and third in the previous three seasons under manager Dave Bristol.

The 1970 season brought two notable additions. The first was an inanimate object, a brand-new ballpark called Riverfront Stadium, which opened on June 30 when the Reds hosted the Braves before a crowd of 51,050. Fittingly, Aaron hit the first home run in the new ballpark.

Johnny Bench was the anchor of the Big Red Machine. Named Rookie of the Year in 1968, Bench hit a league-leading 45 home runs in 1970 and was named league MVP, helping to launch the Reds' most successful decade.

The second most feared hitter in a Reds lineup full of terror was Tony Perez, shown here after hitting a grand slam. Perez hit 40 home runs in 1970.

The second addition was a new manager for Cincinnati. His name was George Lee Anderson, and he had been a scrappy second baseman who spent a decade in the minor leagues, so scrappy that when he was playing in Fort Worth in 1955, the team's radio broadcaster pinned the name "Sparky" on him.

SPARKY ANDERSON: That was my third year in pro ball. I was a wild man. I was thrown out of 16 games in my first year in Class C ball. I don't know how many my second year. In my third year, I was wild. I was arguing all the time. I ran in from right field where I went out on a pop fly, I threw it to third, and I thought, from where I was in right field, he was out. That's pretty good eyesight. So I ran in and I was screaming and yelling, and the radio announcer says, "There goes Sparky again." And that's how it started.

When Anderson finally got to the majors, it was with Philadelphia in 1959. He played in 152 games for the last-place Phillies, batted .218 without a home run and had only 12 extra-base hits among his 104 hits. The following year, he was back in the minors, never to play another game in the major leagues.

Instead, he embarked on a career as a successful minor league manager, which led to a job as third-base coach for the expansion San Diego Padres in 1969. But he left after the season to join the California Angels as third-base coach for manager Lefty Phillips.

SPARKY ANDERSON: Lefty Phillips was my second father. I learned a lot of baseball from so many people: Rod Dedeaux [longtime University of Southern California coach], George Kissell [St. Louis Cardinals coach and instructor], and Lefty.

Buzzie Bavasi and Preston Gomez [Padres general manager and manager] had gone to the 1969 All-Star Game, and when they came back, they told me Lefty wanted me to go over to the Angels as his third-base coach and they had given their permission, which I appreciated because Lefty had done so much for me.

So I was going to coach third base for California, and after the season, I went to the Angels office to sign my contract. I was sitting there with Dick Walsh [Angels general manager] and Lefty, and we were discussing Alex Johnson. The Angels were interested in acquiring him. The phone rang and Dick was talking on the phone and I wasn't paying attention to what he was saying. Me and Lefty were going back and forth on Alex Johnson.

Then Dick hung up the phone, and he called his secretary and said, "Bring us some coffee." She left to get the coffee, and Dick said, "That was Bob Howsam [Reds general manager] on the phone, and he wants you to manage the Cincinnati Reds."

I said, "Dick, don't joke about something like that. That's a serious thing."

He said, "No, I'm serious. He wants you to call him. But I want you to have some coffee, settle down. I don't want you to kill my manager on the freeway."

On the way home, Lefty said, "You're calling from my house. I want to know before you leave my house."

So I called Bob Howsam from Lefty's house, and it wasn't like Dick had said. I didn't have the job. I could tell by the conversation. Then he asked me a question: "What would you do if a guy like Jim Maloney [the Reds' ace pitcher] decided he wasn't going to run that day?"

I said, "Mr. Howsam, I could make up a story for you. But I have no idea what I would do until I'm in that clubhouse. The only thing I can assure you is this: I'm not scared of nobody."

I no more said that than he said, "Would you take the Cincinnati job?"

I said yes, and I know to this day if I would have answered that question, "Well, I'll do this and I'll do that," I would have been out the door because I know that was a setup question to find out what my bullshit was.

Later Dick Walsh said, "I would like you, if you want, to keep your Angels contract as a souvenir." It was for $17,000. I still have it.

––––––––––

He was just 36 years old, the youngest manager in the major leagues, the 49th manager in Cincinnati history. George Lee "Sparky" Anderson. To the people of Cincinnati, he was "Sparky who?"

They would soon find out.

Sparky's Reds broke quickly from the gate and ran away with the National League West. Even when the team's pitching broke down in the second half and the Reds began to flounder, he held things together, won 102 games, and finished 14½ games ahead of the Dodgers.

Johnny Bench, developing into a full-fledged superstar in his third full major league season, led the league with 45 homers and 148 RBIs. Tony Perez belted 40 homers and knocked in 129 runs. Pete Rose, Bobby Tolan, rookie Bernie Carbo, and Perez all batted over .300. Jim Merritt won 20 games. Gary Nolan improved from 8 wins to 18. Wayne Granger saved 35 games to lead the league.

If there was a defining moment for the Reds, it came on the night of July 14 in the 1970 All-Star Game in front of 51,838 fans in Riverfront Stadium and another 60 million watching on national television. The game was tied 4–4 going into the bottom of the twelfth. After the first two National League hitters, Joe Torre and Roberto Clemente, were retired on infield grounders, Rose ripped a single to center against left-hander Clyde Wright. A single by Billy Grabarkewitz sent Rose to second.

Jim Hickman followed with a single to center. Rose, off and running with the crack of the bat, knew he was not going to stop at third. No way. He rounded the bag as the ball was fielded by Amos Otis, whose throw to the plate was strong but slightly up the third-base line.

As catcher Ray Fosse of the Indians came out to get the throw, Rose, two-thirds of the way to home, lowered his left shoulder like a fullback hitting the line. As the ball reached Fosse, so did Rose, who jarred the young catcher with a shoulder-to-shoulder collision. Fosse was knocked onto his back by the force of the blow. Rose sprawled on all fours but managed to roll toward home plate and touch it with his outstretched right hand. As a flattened Fosse lay in pain in the dirt, a dazed Rose got to his feet and asked the catcher if he was all right.

————————

EARL WEAVER: I can still see the collision today. You're rooting to win the gol-darned ballgame, the base hit comes, and there's going to be a play. Leo Durocher was coaching third, and Rose came around and Durocher was wav-ing him in. It looked like he was going to be out, but the throw was up the line and Rose just whacked Fosse. Well, that's the way the game should be played.

SPARKY ANDERSON: I was sitting about 20 rows up behind the screen, and it was so hot, I thought I was going to pass out. It wasn't anything malicious. That's just the way Pete is, he's going to hit you hard. Fosse was in the way of a freight train, and that showed people that Pete will take no quarter and give none. I think that set the tone for Pete's reputation and for our ballclub.

————————

After the game, Rose was asked about the collision. "I play to win," he said. "Period."

Ray Fosse was at the beginning of a promising career with the Indians, in his first full season as their regular catcher and a budding star in the American League. By the All-Star break, he had hit 16 home runs, was batting well over .300, and was being touted, along with Carlton Fisk of the Boston Red Sox and Thurman Munson of the New York Yankees, as one of the league's bright young catchers of the future.

————————

RAY FOSSE: As a catcher, you set up where the ball is coming. I wasn't trying to block the plate; all I was doing was positioning myself to catch the ball and apply the tag. One thing you try to do as a catcher, you never try to look at the runner or be concerned with the runner. You try to concentrate on the baseball.

I can still remember standing there, reaching for the ball thrown by Amos Otis. I was up the line a few feet, but not in the base path to try to block anybody. Simply put, you never try to slide headfirst into a catcher or home plate anyway, and Pete always slid headfirst. He started to slide head-first, and that was it. It was there. I think had he slid the conventional way, hook slide, history would have been changed and I wouldn't be talking about that play right now, almost 30 years later.

The thing that disappointed me the most was after the fact, and I mean two or three years later. I like to think that someone would not try to intentionally hurt somebody, but I read, and I continue to read, where Pete is quoted as saying, "I wouldn't have been able to talk to my father had I not hit him, Ray Fosse, the way I did in the All-Star Game." That was a blow to me, because 27 years later, my shoulder hurts more now than it ever did, just from the fact that it was fractured and separated.

I continued to play, and when you play and you don't get the things taken care of like they do now, it's a much different situation. It didn't shorten my career, because I did play eight years after that, but it damaged my career productivity-wise. I altered my swing, because I continued to play even though I couldn't lift my arm above my head. It was just one of those things. I needed somebody to say, "Hey, you're hurt, don't play." But in 1970 it was much different times.

After having a total of 16 home runs at the break, Fosse hit just two more the rest of the season and never hit more than 12 in a season thereafter. In the spring of 1973 he was traded to Oakland. He wound up playing 12 seasons with the Indians, the Athletics, the Indians again, the Mariners, and the Brewers. He finished with a lifetime batting average of .256, 61 career homers, and 324 RBIs and never reached the stardom predicted for him before the collision.

RAY FOSSE: Pete never made any bones about it from that point on, that was in front of the world, that "Charlie Hustle" image, and that was the beginning. And it expanded from that point.

The one thing that bothered me was reading stories with Pete saying we were always friends and that we were together the night before until 3:00 A.M., which is not the truth.

The night before the game, Sam McDowell and I, with our wives, and Pete and his wife all went to dinner. I had never met Pete. Sam and I were with our wives, and we ran into Pete. Sam knew him, and Pete said, "You guys doing anything tonight?" We said no, and Pete said, "How about going to dinner?"

So we went to dinner, the six of us. Sam and his wife, Carol; me and my wife, Carol; and Pete and his wife, Karolyn. After dinner we went to Pete's house and we were talking baseball. I was interested in Johnny Bench because he was the star catcher in the other league. So we talked baseball, and at 1:00 A.M. the party was over. We went back to the hotel.

Now Pete says, "Well, heck, Ray and I were out till 3:00 in the morning." And I'm saying, "Hey, Pete, get the story right," because I'm still married to my wife, but he's not. Now everybody says, "Ray and Pete were out till 3:00 in the morning, where were the wives?"

That, and the fact that we're friends. I had just met the guy, and I have spoken to him a total of three times in 27 years. In San Francisco in 1980, 10 years after the fact—Buddy Bell was with the Reds at the time—I went over to see Buddy because we were teammates in Cleveland. Pete was there and we kind of rehashed the incident, and Pete said, "Yeah, I started to slide head-first, I saw you, tried to go around you, and I hit you." And that's not what happened.

The year after the incident, we were playing an exhibition game against the Reds in Cleveland. It was early in the season and I was off to a bad start. I wasn't even hitting .200. I had just gone to have my shoulder x-rayed again and the x-rays showed the fracture and separation. Pete was running in the outfield, and he said, "Hey, you're off to a slow start, how come?"

Those were the only words I heard from him between the All-Star Game and that exhibition game in April, eight months later.

But a funny coincidence was that when he went to prison [for filing false income tax returns], he went to the federal penitentiary in Marion, Illinois. I grew up in Marion, Illinois.

Pete Rose was Charlie Hustle, and his collision with Fosse, scoring the winning run in the All-Star Game, became a rallying cry for the Reds as they charged into the National League Championship Series, swept the Pirates in three games, and faced the Orioles in the Reds' first World Series in nine years.

THE BIG BAD BIRDS

SPARKY ANDERSON: At that time the National League was so arrogant. I will admit, we never paid any attention to the American League. It was kind of like our propaganda. Then I saw them and I said, wait a minute.

Jim Palmer, ace of the 1970 Orioles staff, pitched the Birds to a win in Game 1 of the World Series that year against the Big Red Machine. At only 24 years old in 1970, Palmer won 20 games for the first time in his career.

I saw this guy Mark Belanger picking up everything there is. I saw Frank Robinson, and I said, "My God, this guy can whack." I looked at Paul Blair in center field, playing so shallow and getting everything. I looked at that big horse Powell on first base who covered the batter's box when he stepped in there. Andy Etchebarren, a fine receiver and thrower. And three 20-game winners. I said, "Wait a minute, boys. This is a good ballclub."

And then Brooks Robinson opened up right away on us. The first two games, he made about four or five plays. Really, he took us out of the games himself. I felt that Series should have gone longer. We had three pitchers down going into it, and it was rough, but we were whacking on their three 20-game winners. That's right in the box score. But Robinson, every time we got it going, bam, he made a play. Afterward I said, "This guy, he doesn't throw. Look how he throws." And it would be a strike. Just boom, there.

I asked Earl Weaver. And Earl said, "You know something, everybody is saying how wonderful he is. We see this day in and day out." And I said, "Earl, you mean to tell me he plays like this?" And he said, "Sparky, there's nobody that can play third base like he plays it."

A magician at third base, Brooks Robinson made spectacular play after spectacular play in the 1970 World Series to kill many potential Reds rallies.

Mike Cuellar pitched a complete-game 9–3 victory in Game 5 to clinch the Orioles' second championship in five years and establish Baltimore as the premier franchise in the American League.

Then I realized, this guy wasn't making no great plays against us. This was what he always did. I got to know him that winter because we were at a lot of things together, and I realized this guy couldn't only do that, he did the off-field stuff just as well. And I said, "My God, this guy's got the whole package."

The Series opened in Cincinnati's Riverfront Stadium, the first time a World Series game was played on an artificial surface. The Reds took a 3–0 lead after three innings, but the Orioles battled back to tie after five innings. In the bottom of the sixth of a 3–3 game, the Reds' Lee May led off with a smash inside third that had two-base hit written all over it. But Brooks Robinson moved swiftly to his right, backhanded the ball, and threw May out with a spectacular play.

Suddenly, the World Series had a theme. It would be Brooks, "the Human Vacuum Cleaner." He had been doing this sort of thing for years, dazzling American League opponents and fans, but his defensive brilliance had never before been paraded on a national stage. And he dominated the Series not only with his glove but also with his bat.

His solo homer in the seventh won Game 1 for the Orioles, 4–3. He drove in a run in Game 2, a 6–5 victory for the Orioles, who again wiped out an early 4–0 Reds lead.

In Game 3, back in Baltimore, Robinson made three more outstanding plays, in the first, second, and sixth, to blunt the Reds' attack. He also doubled twice and drove in two runs in a 9–3 Baltimore rout.

BROOKS ROBINSON: I went into that Series thinking, "Boy, we're gonna get a lot of work," because they had guys like Perez and Bench and Lee May, and they got one thing on their mind and that's to hit it as far as they can.

I remember telling Belanger, "We're gonna get a lot of ground balls, a lot of work in this Series." We had Cuellar and McNally. We had Palmer, who threw a straight change, a big curveball, and a great fastball. I just thought we'd get a lot of work.

The big thing is our team scored a lot of runs. We even outscored the Reds during the regular season (792–775), and in the Series we took advantage of their pitching. They had terrible pitching, and they were all banged up. They really didn't have a guy who could go out and shut you out. It was like the year before in reverse. When they hit something hard, someone would be there. When it was all said and done, I told people I played 23 years professionally, that's 162 games a year, and I don't ever remember having five games in a row like that. Plus, I was hitting, too. It was like a once-in-a-lifetime five-game series, and it happened to be the World Series, when people who are not even baseball fans tune in.

The Reds managed to win Game 4, 6–5, on Lee May's clutch, three-run homer in the eighth, ending the Orioles' 17-game winning streak—the last 11 in the regular season, 3 in the playoffs, and 3 in the World Series.

The Orioles wrapped up the world championship in Game 5, overcoming a three-run deficit for the third time and crushing the Reds, 9–3. The Orioles outhit the Reds, .292 to .213; outhomered them, 10–5; and outscored them, 33–20. Brooks Robinson led the O's with a .429 average, drove in six runs, and had two homers. And there was that brilliant defense.

EARL WEAVER: They had a lot of strong right-handed hitters; Perez, Bench, May, and Brooks got an awful lot of chances. We knew they were going to pull Cuellar and McNally. Not Palmer so much.

The amazing thing was the chances he got. The plays he made we had seen throughout the course of the season. But you might see one of those spectaculars—and he made them all through the season—but they're not that frequent. He was the best, but throughout his career, he would average only 3.5 chances per game. Third basemen just don't get that many chances, and the amazing thing was all the chances he had in that Series.

CHAPTER 2

THE SECOND INNING

A SWASHBUCKLING PIRATE

In 1971 Roberto Walker Clemente, 36 years old, entered his 17th major league season. In his previous 16 seasons, he had won four National League batting championships, collected more than 200 hits in a season four times, amassed 2,704 hits (eleventh on the all-time list), and had a lifetime batting average of .316. Still, he was relatively unknown, grossly unrecognized, and greatly unappreciated, the least-heralded superstar in the game. A variety of reasons accounted for his lack of recognition.

- He played in Pittsburgh, hardly a communications capital.
- Only once before did he have the opportunity to display his enormous talents in the World Series, in 1960, when he was overshadowed by Bill Mazeroski's sudden-death home run in the bottom of the ninth in the seventh game.
- He was born in Carolina, Puerto Rico, and had difficulty conversing in English.
- He came across to outsiders as surly, brooding, and uncommunicative, largely because of his difficulty with the English language.
- He was labeled, unjustly, a hypochondriac who often sat out games with assorted mysterious ailments.
- He was not a big home-run hitter (his highest single-season output was 29 in 1966, and he surpassed 20 homers in a season only three times in his career) or a big-run producer (he topped 100 RBIs in a season just twice, with a high of 119 in 1966).

But he was the complete ballplayer, a dangerous hitter who could slash the ball to all fields, an acrobatic fielder possessed of blazing speed and a cannon for an arm. And if he didn't enjoy widespread recognition from the casual fan, especially those in American League cities, he had the respect and admiration of his peers.

Few players were as exciting to watch as the Pirates' Roberto Clemente, shown here making a highlight-reel catch against the Mets.

TOM SEAVER: You go through the game of baseball—your relationship with the game starts at an early age, and there are different levels in the relationships you have with the game and the players within the game. As one who went inside the clubhouse, who went inside the game, I had a relationship with Roberto Clemente, facing him as a competitor and watching him play as a professional. But when I was at the University of Southern California, I sat in my uncle's seats by the Dodgers dugout and watched him play before I was even a professional.

So I had a kind of dual relationship with Roberto Clemente, Henry Aaron, Willie Mays. You watch them and you appreciate their professional approach and their God-given expertise of the game.

Then you're competing against them. Then you're competing with them in an All-Star Game. Now you've gone from the young college kid sitting behind the dugout watching them to one of their teammates. And you're dressing next to them, and they're patting you on the back and congratulating you when you're a rookie in 1967 in Anaheim, California, and just 18 months before, you were a student at USC.

That's a real strata of relationships among individuals, and Roberto Clemente is one of them. He and Mays and Aaron. These are guys who, when you weren't pitching, you just sat there and watched them play, watched what they did. Anybody who watched the ball when Willie Mays was on the field was crazy. And Clemente was very much the same.

In 1954 the major leagues were just awakening to the wealth of talent coming out of the Caribbean, and word had filtered up about a 19-year-old sensation in Puerto Rico. The Dodgers, then in Brooklyn, dispatched veteran scout Al Campanis to the island to evaluate the youngster, and before long Campanis was reporting to Brooklyn with raves for the teenager, Roberto Clemente.

"He was the greatest natural athlete I ever saw," Campanis said.

Campanis was authorized to sign Clemente for a $10,000 bonus and a salary of $5,000 for the 1954 season. Clemente would begin his professional career in Montreal, the Dodgers' highest minor league team in the Triple A International League. But there was a catch.

Montreal manager Max Macon was under strict orders from the Dodgers' front office to play the young Clemente occasionally in order for him to gain some experience, but not to overexpose him for fear he would be spotted by a scout from a rival team and lost in the draft.

A teammate of Clemente's on that Montreal Royals team was a young left-handed pitcher with an engaging, outgoing personality who was himself attempting to catch the eye of the Dodgers' brass in the hope of being promoted to the big club. He would make it to Brooklyn, but his major league playing career would consist of 26 games, of which he would win none. However, he was to make his mark in major league baseball in another role.

TOMMY LASORDA: In 1954 when Al Campanis went to Puerto Rico, he had a try-out down there and he worked out a lot of players. One of the players he saw was a youngster about 16 or 17 years old by the name of Roberto Clemente. [editor's note: Clemente was 19 years old.]

Al signed him, but in those days there was the ruling that if you gave a player more than $4,000, you had to keep him on the major league club for two years. If you didn't keep him on the major league club for two years, he was susceptible to be drafted for the price of $8,000.

The Dodgers gave Clemente more than $4,000, but they decided that because they were battling for the pennant, they couldn't carry a 19-year-old youngster for two years. So they decided to send him to Triple A, but the manager there was told he had to hide him. Don't let anybody see him. If you see scouts coming into the ballpark, take him out of the lineup immediately.

Well, we were playing one day and Clemente was in the lineup. He was batting seventh. We got a good inning going in the bottom of the first. The manager was coaching third base, he looked up into the stands, he saw about four scouts sitting up there, and he pinch hit for Clemente before he'd had an at-bat. Clemente was furious. I had to go in and I had to calm him down, because where did you ever see a player being pinch hit for when your team is coming to bat for the first time?

Clemente had no idea what was going on. He was just a kid. I used to take care of him. He'd wait for me every day so he could get something to eat. He didn't speak one word of English.

One day Clyde Sukeforth came to me. I had played for him in the minor leagues, but he was working for Pittsburgh then and he told me, "Tommy, you guys might as well play him, because we're going to take him. If you never play him one inning, we're still going to take him. If you want to play him, fine, but if you're not going to play him, we're still going to take him."

By July the Pittsburgh Pirates, then being run by that sly, old farm-system guru Branch Rickey, seemed certain to finish last in the National League and gain the desirable first pick in the draft. With that in mind, Rickey dispatched the venerable scout Clyde Sukeforth to Richmond, Virginia, for a five-game series between Richmond and the Montreal Royals.

Sukeforth, 52 years old at the time, was Rickey's most trusted lieutenant. He had played 10 seasons in the major leagues, as a catcher with the Cincinnati Reds and Brooklyn Dodgers. In 1945, when World War II had stripped the major leagues of talent, Sukeforth, who had last played for Brooklyn in 1934, returned to the Dodgers at age 43 to appear in 18 games and bat .294.

Despite a mediocre career in which he had a lifetime batting average of .264 and hit only two home runs in 1,237 major league at-bats, Clyde Sukeforth's place in history is secure.

It was Sukeforth whom Rickey dispatched to scout the Negro Leagues, with particular emphasis on a young shortstop named Jackie Robinson. The scout brought back glowing reports of Robinson as a player, and as a man of courage and determination, which helped convince Rickey that young Robinson was the proper choice to break baseball's color barrier in 1947.

Four years later, it was Sukeforth in the bullpen as a Dodgers coach during the third game of the 1951

Clyde Sukeforth, who played 10 seasons as backup catcher for the Reds and Dodgers, earned a permanent place in baseball lore by scouting and signing Roberto Clemente.

National League playoff against the New York Giants when manager Charlie Dressen called down to inquire which of the two pitchers warming up—Carl Erskine or Ralph Branca—was ready to relieve starter Don Newcombe.

"Erskine's bouncing his curveball," Sukeforth said.

"All right," Dressen replied. "Give me Branca."

So Dressen brought Branca into the game, and into baseball ignominy when he served up Bobby Thomson's famed shot heard round the world, a game-winning, pennant-winning, three-run, ninth-inning home run.

When Rickey left Brooklyn and took over operation of the Pirates, Sukeforth went with him. Now he was being asked to send back reports on pitcher Joe Black.

Black had been Rookie of the Year in the National League in 1952, when he won 15 games for the Dodgers and saved 15 others. Control problems caused the Dodgers to ship Black to Montreal, and, at age 30, he was still young enough to make a comeback. Rickey wanted Sukeforth to determine if Black could help the pitiful Pirates and was worth using their draft pick on him.

Instead, Sukeforth found himself mesmerized by the young outfielder named Clemente who played sparingly in the five games Sukeforth watched. But the cagey old scout was in the habit of arriving early to the ballpark to watch batting practice and infield practice, and what he saw dazzled him.

CLYDE SUKEFORTH: The Montreal club was taking infield and outfield practice, and I saw this kid out there throwing in the outfield. I couldn't take my eyes off him. Real great arm. You couldn't help but notice that. He wasn't playing though.

Max Macon was the manager, and Max had played for me in Montreal. 'Long about the seventh inning they're behind and they have a left-handed pitcher out there, and who should go up to pinch hit? This boy in right field. I didn't even know what his name was then. I didn't have a scorecard.

He hits a routine ground ball at the shortstop, and the play at first base was just bang-bang. I mean, they just did get him. So he's showed me he could throw and run right then.

The next four nights I was out there watching him in batting practice and his form was a little unorthodox, but he had a good power stroke. I mean, he was a pretty good-looking hitter, and you just can't miss that kind of talent.

So I wrote Mr. Rickey. I said, "Joe Black hasn't pitched yet, but I have you a draft choice." We were finishing last by a big margin, and the National League had first draft. And I told Macon when I left, "Take good care of our boy, Max. Don't let him get in trouble. Treat him like you would your own son."

And Max said, "Oh, you don't want him."

I said, "Max, we've been friends for quite a while, but don't give me that."

We had our draft meeting, and one of the scouts had a candidate, an infielder in the Southern League, and another one had a pitcher someplace else. And Mr. Rickey said, "Do you have a candidate, Clyde?"

And I said, "Yeah, Clemente with Montreal."

"Any of the rest of you fellows seen Clemente?" Mr. Rickey asked.

One fellow said, "I did. I didn't like him."

"What didn't you like?"

"Well, he wasn't playing, for one thing, and I didn't like his arm."

I didn't say anything. I didn't want to embarrass the guy, but I knew very well he didn't get a look at the arm. The boy may have been pouting or something because he wasn't playing. I told this fellow afterward, "You didn't see his arm. He probably just didn't feel like throwing, but don't think he can't throw."

Well, you've got one guy that says he's got a great arm, another doesn't like it. First choice is very important to us, so Mr. Rickey sent George Sisler and Howie Haak to Montreal to see him. Naturally, we drafted him. For $8,000, it wasn't a bad deal.

Clemente was the cornerstone for the reconstruction of the Pirates. When he arrived, they had finished last four out of the previous five years. In 1958 they would challenge the Braves for the pennant. In 1960 they would win their first world championship since 1925.

In 1955, his rookie year, Clemente batted .255. The Rookie of the Year in the National League was Bill Virdon of the St. Louis Cardinals, who batted .281 and later would become Clemente's teammate in Pittsburgh and his last manager.

In 1970, at the age of 35, Clemente batted .352, his highest average in three years, but 14 points behind the National League batting champion, Rico Carty of Atlanta.

DOCK ELLIS: Clemente was very much misunderstood. They said he was a hypochondriac, but he wasn't. He was doing what the Pirates told us. Danny Murtaugh often told me, "Dock, I don't want you pitching if there's something wrong with you." He told Clemente the same thing, but it was magnified when he sat out. He was always saying something was wrong with him, but the guy had a bad nerve in his neck. And he played.

They said he was surly, and the writers didn't like him. They didn't take the time to get to know him. He was a good dude, and he was very proud. He showed me how to wear my socks. "No," he said. "You can do all the crazy things you want to do, but never wear your socks down, never wear the high stirrups, always show some gold with the Pirates." And if you ever saw me pitch, you saw that I always wore my socks high.

I played with him long enough to see him do things I never saw other guys do. Not to say other guys could not do those things, but I saw Clemente day in and day out and I can't say anything about anybody but him. He was the best I ever played with. He did things I never saw done before in base-ball—as a hitter, a runner, an outfielder, throwing the ball, running the ball down, going up on the wall, up on the screen, throwing to all four bases. I saw him throw guys out at all four bases.

Being in Pittsburgh didn't help him, and it wasn't until the 1971 World Series that people realized how great he was and what he was all about, because in the World Series, you're under the magnifying glass. People had a desire to know who he was, and members of the press made sure that people knew who he was with a lot of in-depth interviews and investigation as to what he did in Puerto Rico, what he meant to the Puerto Rican people, how he cared about baseball.

His love for the game came out. The way he played came out. How he got in shape. All that came out. The Pirates didn't want to pay him money one year because they said he didn't hit home runs, so he went and hit home runs [29 in 1966, the only year from 1964 through 1967 he failed to win a batting title] just to show he could do that.

ALL-STAR HEROES

A new powerhouse was emerging in the American League in 1971. After finishing second in their division in each of the previous two years, the Oakland

Athletics hired as their manager Dick Williams, who had led the Boston Red Sox to a pennant in 1967, only to lose the World Series to the St. Louis Cardinals in seven games.

In Oakland, Williams inherited a group of outstanding young players, including the best young home-run hitter in the game, Reggie Jackson, who had crushed 47 out of the park two years earlier at the age of 23.

In 1971 Jackson would finish second in the league in homers with 32, one behind Bill Melton of the Chicago White Sox, and would combine with Sal Bando for 56 homers and with Rick Monday and Joe Rudi to form a potent outfield. Two 20-game winners headed an impressive pitching staff—Vida Blue, 24–8 with a league-leading 1.82 ERA, and Jim "Catfish" Hunter, 21–11—as the Athletics won 101 games, a total matched by the Baltimore Orioles, and won the American League West by 16 games over the Kansas City Royals.

Outstanding pitching was the key to the success of the Orioles, who captured the American League East for the third consecutive season, each time winning more than 100 games. For only the second time in major league history (the first was the Chicago White Sox in 1920), four 20-game winners pitched for one team—Dave McNally, 21–5; Mike Cuellar, 20–9; Jim Palmer, 20–9; and Pat Dobson, 20–8.

At 22 years, Catfish Hunter had thrown a perfect game against the Twins. By the time he was 25, he had collected his first 20-win season, helping lead the Athletics to American League prominence in the early seventies.

EARL WEAVER: Palmer had outstanding talent, McNally came through our farm system, and we made a tremendous trade for Cuellar. He kind of went unnoticed, but I had seen him when I was managing in the Puerto Rican Winter League. I had Tony Perez, Orlando Cepeda, Davey Johnson, and Paul Blair on my team, and this little guy was coming in and making them look like fools with that screwball, so the first chance we had to get him [from the Astros for Curt Blefary after the 1968 season] we jumped on him.

Our pitching coach, George Bamberger, could get in pitchers' heads, and he handled Cuellar. Those guys just rubbed off on each other. Palmer was a physical guy. He ran, and they tried to keep up with him. Cuellar didn't want to run, and Bamberger made him run. And we used to make them throw a lot between starts. In those days, they wanted to pitch every four days, because they're pitching for next year's contract.

Bamberger's theory was the more you throw, the stronger your arm's gonna get. It's just like lifting weights. Bamberger would walk them through it, and they were masters. Cuellar and McNally, they were like Greg Maddux. He's an artist going to work. Palmer had the high fastball, and we came up with Dobson, who was just a mediocre pitcher in Detroit. But Bamberger and I both loved his curveball.

I said, "George, we gotta make him cut the curveball down, so he could throw it for strikes whenever he wanted." Somehow, George could make them do that.

The Orioles and Athletics helped the American League end an eight-year dominance in the All-Star Game by winning the 1971 game in Detroit, a game made memorable by Jackson's titanic home run against the Pirates' 19-game winner, Dock Ellis. It came with one on in the bottom of the third and the National League leading 3–0—a blast that hit the light tower in the upper deck in right-center field, some 500 feet away.

REGGIE JACKSON: I made the team as an alternate. I was picked to replace Tony Oliva, who got hurt. I remember my teammate Sal Bando telling me, "Don't embarrass us and strike out."

The National League had a starting outfield of Roberto Clemente, Henry Aaron, and my all-time hero, Willie Mays. Three of the greatest players ever to play the game, and I was there with them.

The 1971 All-Star Game, won by the American League, 6–4, featured six home runs, all by future Hall of Famers. Johnny Bench, Hank Aaron, and Roberto Clemente went deep for the National League, and Harmon Killebrew, Frank Robinson, and Reggie Jackson did the same for the American League. Jackson's home run (above) was the most memorable, hitting the light tower at Tiger Stadium.

Bando's words were on my mind when I was sent up by Earl Weaver to pinch hit against Dock Ellis in the third inning. I figured Earl must have wanted to get rid of me early.

Jackson remembered taking two strikes, then hearing Bando's words reverberating in his ear: "Don't embarrass us and strike out." He choked up slightly on the bat and crushed the next pitch, sending it riding into the great beyond.

REGGIE JACKSON: People thought I was hotdogging it around the bases. In fact, I just wanted to watch where it landed. I wasn't sure it was going out at first. When I was, then I hotdogged it.

Jackson's titanic shot launched the American League to a 6–4 victory in a battle of home runs. Johnny Bench hit a two-run shot for the National League in the second. Henry Aaron hit a solo shot in the third, his first All-Star Game home run. Ten weeks earlier, on April 27, Aaron had joined Babe Ruth and Willie Mays as the only players with 600 home runs in their careers.

Jackson and Frank Robinson of the Orioles hit two-run shots for the American League in the bottom of the third, Robinson becoming the first player to hit a home run in the All-Star Game for each league.

Harmon Killebrew, who would hit the 500th home run of his career less than a month later, hit a two-run homer in the sixth, and Roberto Clemente belted a solo homer in the eighth. Vida Blue of the Orioles was the winning pitcher and was followed to the mound by a pair of Orioles, Jim Palmer and Mike Cuellar.

GIANT KILLER

As the season was winding down to September, with the Pirates in command in the National League East and the Giants and Dodgers battling in the West, the teams out of the race called up recruits from the minor leagues to evaluate their future talent.

On September 5, in Candlestick Park, San Francisco, the Houston Astros sent a 21-year-old, 6'8", right-handed flamethrower from Vienna, Louisiana, named James Rodney "J.R." Richard to the mound to face the Giants. Richard, who had been the nation's number two pick in the June 1969 free agent draft, had shown enormous promise in little more than one minor league season. Fortified with a fastball that was clocked at 100 miles per hour, he completely overmatched minor league hitters.

The Astros were eager to see him pitch against major leaguers, especially such formidable opponents as the Giants, with Willie McCovey, Bobby

Dave McNally, shown here pitching against and beating the New York Yankees in late September, won 21 games in 1971. In so doing, he joined three other Orioles who won 20 that year—Mike Cuellar, Jim Palmer, and Pat Dobson—and led the Orioles back to the World Series.

Bonds, and the legendary Willie Mays, who had turned 40 years old in May but was still a productive hitter.

Richard consistently fired his high, hard one past the Giants' bats, beating them 5–3 and striking out 15, including Mays three times.

FRAN HEALY: They called me out of the bullpen to pinch hit. I go out and I strike out and I come back to the dugout, and [Giants manager] Charlie Fox said, "We have his pitches." [Richard was tipping off his pitches.] And I said, "So do I." Jeez, he was throwing 100 miles an hour.

HUB KITTLE: It was unbelievable the way J.R. handled those big bombers. He just blew them away with that overpowering fastball and one of the greatest hard sliders I've ever seen.

The first time Mays came to bat, J.R. just threw that fastball by him. I was coaching first base, and as Willie passed me on his way to the outfield, he said, in that high-pitched voice, "Man, where'd they get that big black dude? He scared me half to death."

Five years later, Richard had become a star in the National League, a 20-game winner for the mediocre Astros in 1976, and the most intimidating pitcher in the league. In 1978 he would strike out 303 batters, joining Sandy Koufax and Steve Carlton as the only National League pitchers to strike out 300 batters in a season. Richard would strike out 313 in 1979, but the following season he complained of a fatigued arm. Doctors could find nothing wrong with his arm, and Richard was accused of malingering.

Later, the mysterious ailment would prove to be an aneurysm. Richard never pitched in another major league game.

BIRDS VS. BUCS

The 1971 American League Championship Series paired the flamboyant Oakland Athletics against the red-hot Baltimore Orioles, who had finished the season with 11 straight wins and stormed right through the playoffs. With McNally, Cuellar, and Palmer at the top of their games and the second two pitching complete games, the Orioles scored their third straight ALCS

Willie Stargell, shown here hitting home run number 48, led the National League in home runs and powered the Pirates to the pennant in 1971.

sweep. In three years, they had played nine league playoff games and won them all.

In the National League, the Cincinnati Reds slumped to fourth place in the West with a record of 79–83, while the San Francisco Giants and Los Angeles Dodgers battled to the final day of the season before the Giants prevailed to win by a game and face the Pirates in the NLCS.

Willie Stargell had emerged as the National League power king, leading the league with 48 homers and driving in 125 runs, but the Pirates' heart and soul remained Clemente. Having passed his 37th birthday, he batted .341, fourth in the league behind Joe Torre, Ralph Garr, and Glenn Beckert, and his 11th time over .300 in his last 12 seasons.

The Pirates dropped the first game of the best-of-five National League Championship Series to Gaylord Perry. After that, it was all Pittsburgh.

Bob Robertson hit three homers in Game 2 and another in Game 3 as the Pirates swept the last three games and were in the World Series for the first time in 11 years.

Robertson was the hitting star of the Series with a .438 average, four homers, and six RBIs, while Clemente was a typical, if undistinguished, .333 hitter for the four games. But his time had not yet come.

With their four 20-game winners and their 14-game winning streak, the Orioles were heavy favorites to win their second straight world championship, and they looked as if they would do so in a walk as they took the first two games in Baltimore. Clemente had two hits in each of the first two games, but the Orioles managed to minimize his damage.

EARL WEAVER: Clemente played in Puerto Rico when I managed there in 1966 and 1967. He was a star in the big leagues already, and he would come in after the Winter League season had started and play his first game without batting practice and make plays you couldn't believe, make throws you couldn't believe.

He played for San Juan, and I managed Santurce. So when we faced him in the World Series, I knew Clemente well. I knew what he could do, and nothing he did surprised me. We handled Stargell in that Series [no home runs, one RBI, a .208 average], but we didn't handle Clemente.

Back in Three Rivers Stadium, the Pirates got it going in Game 3. Clemente knocked in the first Pittsburgh run, and Bob Robertson belted a three-run homer to give the Bucs their first win, 5–1.

Game 4 was a historic event, the first night game in World Series history.

Roberto Clemente hit two home runs in the 1971 World Series, batted .414, and was named the Series MVP.

BOWIE KUHN: For me, it was just promotion of the game. People said, "Aw, he's selling out to the television interests," and I certainly was not indifferent to the fact that you can generate more money with a night game. But what I was concerned with was regenerating the interest in the game, and I wanted to put the big event on when people could see it.

We did one All-Star Game at night before I was commissioner, and I was the National League attorney, and I was very impressed with the numbers. So when we had to make a decision about putting World Series games on at night, I said, "Let's go."

There's no question in my mind that that decision was a pivotal one in the game beginning to turn around and move.

In that historic first World Series night game, the Pirates spotted the Orioles three runs in the first, then came back to win 4–3 and tie the Series at two games each before a crowd of 51,378 and a television audience of 61 million.

Bob Robertson and Steve Blass (jumping above) celebrate the final out of the 1971 World Series, which was won in seven games by Pittsburgh, the fourth championship in Pirates history.

The experiment was such a success that commissioner Kuhn announced that all weekday games would be played at night in the 1972 World Series.

The Orioles had the decided advantage in the pitching matchup for Game 5, 21-game winner Dave McNally against 8-game winner Nelson Briles. But Briles pitched the game of his life, a two-hit shutout to give the Bucs a three-games-to-two lead.

Back in Baltimore the Orioles evened the Series with a 3–2 win in 10 innings, as McNally came back to get the win in relief by retiring Al Oliver with the bases loaded in the top of the tenth. But in Game 7 Clemente put the Pirates ahead with a home run in the fourth and Steve Blass outpitched Mike Cuellar 2–1 on a four-hitter, and the Pirates reigned as world champions.

Clemente hit safely in all seven games and led all hitters with a .414 average. He also hit two homers, drove in four runs, and made brilliant, acrobatic plays in the field and lightning strikes on throws from the outfield. Finally, in his 17th major league season, he was getting the accolades he had long deserved.

BROOKS ROBINSON: The thing that impressed me most, you hear about someone who can do all these wonderful things and then in the showcase of baseball, he goes out and does this. It was unbelievable. He did those things in the World Series.

I had seen him in spring training and in All-Star Games, and you know he's a great player. But then having him do those very things in the World Series against you, that's what it's all about.

WAY OFF SEASON

Baseball's annual winter meetings were held that year in Arizona in December, where a series of blockbuster trades were pulled off that would have wide-ranging ramifications. On December 2 the Los Angeles Dodgers traded slugger Richie Allen to the Chicago White Sox for left-hander Tommy John and acquired veteran Frank Robinson from the Baltimore Orioles.

Then 36 years old, Robinson was coming to the end of a Hall of Fame career. He had spent six years in Baltimore, during which the Orioles had reached the World Series four times. While Robinson's career and production were dwindling and the Orioles felt the need to replace him with younger players, they had not calculated how much they would miss his leadership and his desire to win.

Eight days later, the New York Mets and California Angels made a trade that would have an impact on baseball for the next two decades.

Since coming into the league, the Mets had been unable to come up with a quality third baseman, except for the 279 games they got out of "the Glider," Ed Charles. Two years earlier, they traded a young prospect, Amos Otis, to the Kansas City Royals for Joe Foy, who played 99 games for the Mets, batted .236, and hit six homers, then was dumped. Otis, meanwhile, had 14 productive seasons in Kansas City.

The Mets were again in search of a third baseman. They settled on veteran Jim Fregosi, a former All-Star shortstop for the Angels whom the Mets believed could move over and solve their third-base problem. To acquire Fregosi, the Mets gave up four young players: Don Rose, Francisco Estrada, Leroy Stanton, and a 24-year-old right-handed pitcher from Alvin, Texas, who in five seasons in New York had failed to live up to his potential and had a record of 29–38. His name was Nolan Ryan.

JACK LANG: It was my trade. We had the winter meetings in December in Phoenix, Arizona. We were staying at the Arizona Biltmore Hotel. A lot of trades were made. Every other hour, another trade was made. The Mets, who had won in 1969, did nothing in 1970, and Hodges needed a third baseman because they let Ed Charles go after the pennant-winning season.

Bob Scheffing was the general manager, Donald Grant was the chairman of the board, and Gil Hodges was the manager, and all week long, while everybody else was making trades, Scheffing and Grant were out on the golf course, playing golf every day at the Arizona Biltmore. Friday night, Grant came in from the golf course in his golf outfit, and I met him in the lobby, and I remember sitting in one of the lounge chairs and I said to him, "Don, you gotta make a trade."

Everybody else had made a trade. The Yankees made their big trade for Rich McKinney. I think of the 24 clubs, 18 of them had made a trade. But the Mets hadn't made one, so I said to him, "Don, you gotta make a trade. You've got all your writers here, sitting here all week long."

And he said, "We're talking while we're out on the golf course. We'll make a deal."

Now, the meetings ended on a Friday night and we went home on Saturday morning, and nothing had happened. We were back from

The Mets pitching staff was brimming with young talent at the end of the sixties. The youngest, and the one with the most electric stuff, was Nolan Ryan, shown here pitching against the Dodgers. On December 10, 1971, the Mets traded him to the Angels for Jim Fregosi, a move questioned by many at the time and one that looks even worse in hindsight.

the meetings, and on Monday we got a phone call. The Mets had just made a deal. Nolan Ryan to the California Angels along with four other guys for Jim Fregosi.

Fregosi came over and was out of shape and overweight, and he wasn't used to playing third base because he had been a shortstop in California. They thought they could make a third baseman out of him. He turned out to be a total flop. Now it was the following May, or June, and he was in and out of the lineup, and he wasn't hitting. And one night Grant came through the press box, and I'd been criticizing them in the paper for the deal, and I looked up at him, he looked at me, and he said, "What are you staring at?"

"Nothing," I said.

"All you do is knock us for that deal," he said.

"It was a lousy deal."

We were in the back row, and we were shouting at each other over near the radio booth. It got so loud, and our language got so bad, that Lindsey Nelson got up and closed the door.

He said, "You made us make that deal."

I said, "I told you to make a deal, I didn't tell you to make that deal."

That went out over the air. And after the game, Lindsey Nelson came up to me and said, "I'm going to have to start showing you more respect. I didn't know you had the power to make deals."

BOB MURPHY: In hindsight, it was one of the worst deals in Mets history. The Mets had a desperate need for a third baseman. Casey Stengel had tried to get Amos Otis to move to third, and Otis refused to do it. They just never had a third baseman, so they had a chance to trade Ryan for a third baseman.

At that time, Nolan was so wild. He was having a lot of trouble throwing strikes, so there wasn't a hue and cry like, "Oh, don't do this." Ryan was not a steady, consistent guy in the rotation, although he had that great arm and he had some good moments as a Met.

In the 1969 playoffs against Atlanta, Ryan relieved Gary Gentry in the third inning of Game 3 with two on and none out and the Braves leading 2–0. He struck out Rico Carty and went on to finish the game, a 7–4 Mets victory.

BOB MURPHY: Striking out Carty was one of the highlight moments in Mets history. Paul Richards told me Ryan was the only pitcher who could strike out Carty.

JACK LANG: Not to blame Hodges, but he made the decision to trade Ryan. The Angels desperately needed a pitcher, and Hodges felt that was the one pitcher he could afford to give up because he was never sure Ryan was ever going to get control. When Ryan got over to the American League, he was getting those high fastball strikes over there that he wasn't getting in the National League. He also got to work every fourth day, which he couldn't do with the Mets because he was in and out of military service on weekend calls. He was never in the regular rotation, and as a result, his control suffered.

Also, Nolan never liked it in New York. He was afraid for his wife, Ruth, who was a beautiful woman, and every time he went on the road, Ruth stayed with Nancy Seaver. They were good friends. Nancy knew her way around New York, and she liked to go to the theater and museums and to dinner and shopping, so they would go to New York City all the time. But Nolan, who was a country boy, was worried that his beautiful wife was not safe in the city, and he had told the Mets that he wanted to be traded because he wanted to get out of New York. He just was worried about his wife when he was on the road.

The Mets farm director at the time of the trade was Whitey Herzog, but he was not in on the mix when the trade discussions were held. He found out about it in a telephone call from general manager Bob Scheffing.

WHITEY HERZOG: We got back from the meetings and I got a phone call from Scheffing, and he said, "We just traded Nolan Ryan to the Angels for Jim Fregosi."

I said, "What? I would never make that deal."

Scheffing said nothing and just hung up. I didn't know until the next day that we also gave them three other guys. I wouldn't have traded Ryan for Fregosi even up.

CHAPTER 3

THE THIRD INNING

STRIKE ONE

At first it seemed like some April Fool's joke.

April 1, 1972, five days before the start of the season, as teams were getting ready to break training camp in Arizona and Florida, the Major League Players Association called the first strike in professional sports history. Players walked out of camp. Many headed home. Others waited around, hoping for a quick settlement.

At issue was renegotiation of the players' benefits plan that had been first settled two years before. While some within the baseball establishment argued that this was hardly a strike issue, others viewed it as gamesmanship on the part of the players, a strategic ploy aimed at attempting to intimidate the owners for the following year when the Basic Agreement, including the reserve system, was scheduled to be negotiated.

The strike lasted 13 days. Settlement was reached when the teams agreed to contribute an additional $490,000 to the benefit plan in 1972 and to use $500,000 of the plan's profits for additional benefits. It was, according to Players Association executive director Marvin Miller, "an honorable agreement," but it was merely a starting point. The players had sent the owners a message by demonstrating the unity and courage to strike, which would result in greater gains in the not too distant future.

When the season commenced on April 15, a total of 86 games had been lost. It was decided they would not be made up, resulting in an imbalance in the number of games played among teams, which would prove to be a factor in determining the winner of one of the four divisions.

Major league baseball's first strike ended on April 13, 1972. Joe Torre (right) and union head Marvin Miller meet with the press.

THAT FATEFUL DAY

With no work to do, no players to oversee, New York Mets manager Gil Hodges decided to take advantage of his unscheduled day off, Easter Sunday, April 2, to get in a round of golf with three of his coaches, Joe Pignatano, Eddie Yost, and Al "Rube" Walker. The Mets had broken camp in St. Petersburg on Florida's Gulf Coast. They were scheduled to conclude spring training with a series of games on Florida's east coast and were housed at the Ramada Inn in West Palm Beach.

JOE PIGNATANO: Gil and I went to mass together, then we had breakfast together, and we met up with Rube and Eddie on the golf course, which was behind the inn, just across the street from the ballpark. We played 18 holes, then Gil left us because he said he had to send some fruit home. He was gone about 15 minutes, and when he came back, we played nine more holes.

When we finished, we went into the clubhouse and had a few beers with the club pro, Jack Sanford, the old San Francisco Giants pitcher. We spent about 20 minutes, a half hour with Jack, just chewing the fat and reminiscing, then we decided to walk back to our rooms. By then, it was about 5:30.

I grabbed my clubs and Gil's clubs, and he said, "Give me my clubs. What do you think I am, a cripple?" I said, "No, I'll carry both sets. The weight on both sides will make me balanced." And he said, "Give me my clubs back."

So we started walking to our rooms on the walkway that leads from the golf course to the inn. Rube and Eddie peeled off, because their rooms were on one side of the inn and Gil and I were on the other side. As we left Rube and Eddie, Gil said, "We'll see you at 7:00 for dinner," and they said, "OK."

I was walking a little ahead of Gil, and all of a sudden I heard the sound of his clubs rattling on the ground. I turned around and he was laying on the ground, on top of his golf clubs. I rushed to him and took the clubs out from under him, and his head was bleeding. A few seconds later, the bleeding stopped. His heart stopped pumping. Later, the doctor said he was dead when he hit the ground.

Hodges was two days short of his 48th birthday when he died. He was a strapping 6'2" and a muscular 220 pounds, without an ounce of fat on him.

Gil Hodges was born in Princeton, Indiana, and came through the Dodgers' farm system as a catcher. When the Dodgers signed Roy Campanella, they converted Hodges into a first baseman. In 1948, when Jackie Robinson was shifted from first base to second, Hodges took over as the Dodgers' first baseman and became one of the most beloved Dodgers ever. He married a Brooklyn girl, Joan Lombardi, and lived in Brooklyn until his death.

In the 1952 World Series against the Yankees, while Hodges was enduring the agony of going hitless in 21 at-bats, a priest in a Brooklyn church ascended the pulpit one Sunday and told his flock, "It's too hot for a sermon today. Just say a prayer for Gil Hodges."

When the Dodgers left Brooklyn for Los Angeles in 1958, Hodges went with them. In 1962, when the New York Mets came into existence, they brought Hodges back home by selecting him in the expansion draft. He was 38 years old and in the twilight of a magnificent career during which he would belt 370 home runs and set a standard for defensive excellence at first base.

In 1963, after he had played 11 games for the Mets, the Washington Senators asked for permission to talk with him about their manager's job. He took over the worst team in the American League and in five seasons improved it from tenth place to a tie for sixth.

The Mets brought Hodges back in 1968 to become their manager, replacing Wes Westrum. He finished ninth in his first season, then a year later pulled off one of the biggest miracles in baseball history by leading the Mets to the 1969 world championship.

With Hodges in place as manager, the Mets looked forward eagerly to other championships.

BUD HARRELSON: I was back home. I don't remember who the call came from, but whoever it was said, "Your boss just died," and I said, "Joan Payson?" He said, "No, Gil Hodges."

Wow! We were all devastated. Everybody loved him. Scared shitless of him, but respected and loved and . . . scared. That was devastating for everybody.

He had had a heart attack in 1968, the last week of the season, but he came to spring training in 1969 fairly mild after the heart attack. He was generally mild anyway. Soft-spoken, but he got his message across, sometimes just with a look.

He knew how to handle the press. He was well respected. He handled the players well; he handled the front office. After his heart attack, he took better care of himself—got his rest, walked a lot, and you never thought about him dying. He was . . . Superman.

TOM SEAVER: It's one of those moments in time that you're never going to forget. I was sitting in my office at my home in Connecticut, and I was paying bills at my desk. The phone rang, and it was Buddy Harrelson.

My desk sat facing the window. It was at night and I had the window in front of me, and when I picked up the phone and heard his voice I got very excited because I thought the news would be that the strike was over and that we would go back to work. You have a thousand thoughts in a heartbeat—"Thank God the strike is over and we can go back to work"—and all of a sudden his voice got very sad, and he said, "No, Gil died."

There was almost disbelief. You just didn't believe it. I said, "What?" He said, "Yeah, he had a heart attack and died immediately. He was dead before he hit the ground." That's what I remember him saying. At least that's what I think I remember him saying.

Maybe I don't remember the words exactly, but I remember the emotion, which was total disbelief. In the flash of an eye, he was gone.

Gil was invincible. He had had a heart attack, but that didn't mean a thing, because he was a pillar of strength. He was, what, 48 years old? *He was 48 years old.* Terrible. *Terrible.*

With Gil gone, the whole organization changed, because there was no pillar of strength to give the organization direction. Gil was the individual that gave the organization direction, that the people, even though they had positions higher than Gil, they would listen to him and he would tell them when they were wrong. As soon as Gil was out of the picture, the thing began to implode. Decisions were being made by the owner, or the individual that the owner put in place who was a mouthpiece for the owner, and it just disintegrated.

JOE PIGNATANO: That night, I ran into Mets general manager Bob Scheffing and Yogi, and Scheffing told me that Yogi had been named the manager, and I said, "That's fine."

Berra was the logical choice among the Mets coaches to take over the manager's job. He was a New York hero for 18 seasons as a Yankee, a Hall of Fame catcher, and a lovable character. He was well liked by the other coaches, the players, the press, and the fans. And he was the only member of Hodges' coaching staff with experience as a major league manager, having led the Yankees to the American League pennant in his only season as a manager, 1964.

Lawrence Peter Berra was born in "the Hill" section of St. Louis and nicknamed Yogi by a boyhood pal who had watched a travelogue about India in the local movie theater. Depicted in the travelogue was a Hindu fakir called a yogi who sat with his arms folded, his legs crossed, and a look of solemnity and sadness on his face. The fakir reminded the boy of his friend, and from that day on, Larry Berra was Yogi.

The Yankees signed Berra for a bonus of $500 and sent him to Norfolk, Virginia. A tour in the U.S. Navy interrupted Berra's career, but when he returned in 1946 he was called to New York. Three years later he became the Yankees' regular catcher. In Berra's 17 full seasons, the Yankees won 14 pennants and 10 world championships. When he retired after the 1963 season, he had accumulated 2,148 hits, 358 home runs, and 1,430 RBIs and was the all-time leader in World Series games played, at-bats, hits, and doubles.

After one season as player/coach, Berra was named manager of the Yankees in 1964. He rallied the team to the American League pennant, but when he lost the World Series to the Cardinals in seven games, he was fired.

In 1965 Berra was brought to the Mets as a coach by his old mentor, Casey Stengel, and remained a Mets coach under Stengel, Wes Westrum, and Hodges. With Hodges' untimely death, Berra was getting a second chance to manage, eight years after his first chance.

The Yankees were scheduled to fly by chartered plane from their training base in Fort Lauderdale, Florida, to New York the day after Hodges' death. Because most of the players had gone home, the plane would be more than half empty. In a neighborly gesture, the Yankees offered to stop off in West Palm Beach to pick up the remaining Mets and take them home.

The trip home was a solemn one. On board were coaches, front-office personnel from both teams, and reporters. There were women and children on the plane and, in the rear, the wooden coffin with the body of Gil Hodges.

ESCAPE FROM WASHINGTON

Also delayed by the strike was the first major league game ever to be played in Texas. Frustrated in his effort to get a better lease for his Senators in Washington's RFK Stadium and caving in under the weight of declining attendance, Bob Short had negotiated a deal to move his team to the fertile and virgin Dallas–Fort Worth territory in the town of Arlington, midway between the two Texas metropolises.

It was a move fought by Bowie Kuhn, not just because he had worked at old Griffith Stadium as a boy and had grown up a fan of the Washington Senators, but also because he was fervently against franchise removal and believed it was important to have a team in the nation's capital, which had already lost one team when the original Senators moved to Minnesota in 1961 and became the Twins.

Kuhn did see the merits of a team in the growing Dallas–Fort Worth area, and the American League, eager to get the jump on the rival National League, was all for Short moving his team to Texas. Kuhn worked hard to find a buyer who would keep the team in Washington, but he was unsuccessful. Meanwhile, in a long-winded telephone conversation with the commissioner, as reported in his book with Marty Appel, *Hardball: The Education of a Baseball Commissioner* (Lincoln: University of Nebraska Press, 1997), Bob Short was adamant about the move:

> No one can keep me in Washington, not Nixon, not Cronin, not Kuhn. I will cannibalize the club if necessary. I own it . . . and I will move wherever I want. I'll go to St. Paul, Dallas, or Toronto.
>
> No place in Washington is safe at night, and Nixon can't do anything about it. I may sell Ted Williams to Boston or Darold Knowles or Frank Howard or Mike Epstein. Ted says Washington is a horseshit town and I've gotta get out. I'll go elsewhere before I'm forced into bankruptcy like Seattle. I know I had my eyes

wide open when I went to Washington, but I told the American League I wouldn't keep it there forever. If we're to save Washington, everybody has to give something: me, the players, TV, and the federal government. . . . Maybe things will work out in a Cinderella way, but that's not likely.

In the end, Kuhn ran out of options, and, unable to find a buyer who would keep the team in Washington, he had no choice but to approve, reluctantly, the transfer of the franchise to Arlington, midway between Dallas and Fort Worth. Thus were born the Texas Rangers.

SAY, HEY

On May 11, the Mets and Giants pulled off a two-player trade that made banner headlines, especially in New York. The Mets were bringing back another beloved New York hero, the illustrious Willie Mays, five days after his 41st birthday, to the city where he had had his greatest triumphs. In return, the Mets would send pitching prospect Charlie Williams and $50,000 to San Francisco.

FRAN HEALY: Charlie Fox wanted to get rid of him. They didn't know what to do with him because Giants owner Horace Stoneham loved him, but he wasn't very productive anymore and they wanted him out of there.

Mrs. Joan Payson, who had been a Giants fan when they were in New York, loved Willie, and the Mets were going to be able to carry his salary, but it was a downer for the Giants players. Willie Mays leaving the team! Even though he was 40 at the time, everybody was in awe of him.

At first, it was seen as nothing more than a sop to Mets fans, a ploy to help sagging attendance. But three days after the trade, Mays made a triumphant return to New York with a game-winning home run against his former team. He would appear in 69 games for the Mets and bat a respectable .267, finishing the season with eight home runs and 22 RBIs.

Hit number 3,000 for Roberto Clemente, on September 30, 1972, was the legend's last. He joined nine others with 3,000 hits.

By midseason the Pirates were well on their way to a return trip to the National League Championship Series, paced again by the power of Willie Stargell, the leadership of a now-aging Roberto Clemente, and a solid, if unspectacular, pitching staff that included 19-game winner Steve Blass and relief specialist Dave Giusti.

The Chicago Cubs stayed close for a while, but when they began to fade, manager Leo Durocher resigned and was replaced by Whitey Lockman.

The Mets were no worse and no better under Berra than they were under Hodges. In fact, they would win the same number of games in 1972, 83, as they won in 1971, and finish a notch higher. But their great third-base gamble fizzled as Jim Fregosi struggled at the plate and in the field. A series of nagging injuries reduced him to only 101 games, 85 at third, and he batted just .232, with five home runs and 32 runs batted in.

Meanwhile, Nolan Ryan finally realized his potential with the California Angels. He won 19 games and lost 16, had an earned run average of 2.28, and led the American League in strikeouts with 329 in 284 innings.

JOE PIGNATANO: Gil didn't want to get rid of Nolie. He liked his arm and his stuff. We all did. But Nolie wasn't happy in New York, and neither was his wife. He begged Gil to send him someplace else. Gil hated to do it, but he did it for Nolie. He didn't want an unhappy player on his hands. Besides, we desperately needed a third baseman.

In the National League West, the Cincinnati Reds rebounded from their 1971 slump to win the division going away as Johnny Bench led the league in home runs with 40 and RBIs with 125.

The races in the American League, in both divisions, were much more competitive.

HAIR

If the Cincinnati Reds became the dominant team of the seventies, no team better exemplified these changing times than the Oakland A's, with their gaudy double-knit uniforms of green and gold and their experiments prodded by an innovative owner, Charles O. Finley, who proposed orange baseballs and automatic ball dispensers and urged his players to grow facial hair.

Styles were changing in the seventies. It was the hair generation, given impetus in large measure by the enormously successful Broadway musical of the sixties, *Hair*, and the black power movement that was characterized by the Afro hairdo. But baseball continued to live in the Dark Ages, forbidding players from sprouting facial hair while in uniform, until Finley, ever the showman, always the maverick, offered his players $300 each to grow handlebars, Fu Manchus, and walruses.

RAY FOSSE: I remember playing a game with Cleveland and then going back to my house, and I was watching *The Game of the Week* on television and it was the A's. And I called to my wife, "Carol, look, those guys are wearing mustaches." I couldn't believe it, because that was the first time ever that guys were wearing mustaches.

That kind of opened the door, and the Indians allowed us to wear mustaches. And everybody else started doing it, too. The next spring, I had just started growing a mustache, and with 10 days to go in spring training, I got traded to Oakland. I remember playing against the Cubs in Mesa, Arizona, and I got on third base and I had about a seven- or ten-day growth of mustache, and Ron Santo said, "You knew you were going to get traded, didn't you? You started growing your mustache."

But I was too late to collect the $300 bonus.

BOWIE KUHN: I didn't have any strong feelings against mustaches. A lot of what Finley did I supported, which is hard to believe in hindsight. Charlie did some good showmanship stuff. The game needed some showmanship. I was doing things to try to change the way we marketed the game.

Maverick owner of the A's, Charlie Finley (center), with third baseman Sal Bando (right), outfielder Alan Lewis (left), and the 1972 World Series trophy after Oakland beat Cincinnati four games to three. It was the Athletics' first championship since 1930, when they were still in Philadelphia.

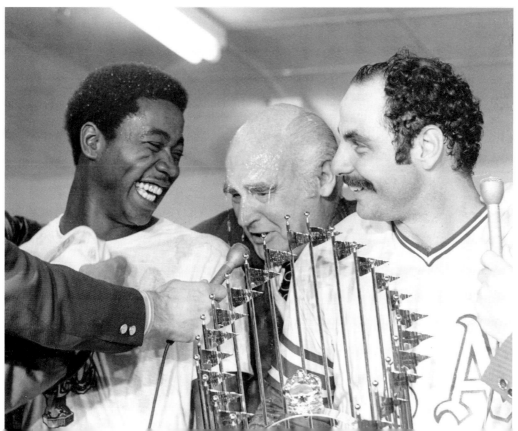

So what's wrong with mustaches? We always had mustaches in the game historically [at the turn of the century]. So they weren't in vogue at the time Charlie got involved in it, but they were getting in vogue, so what's wrong with it?

As long as ballplayers didn't make fools of themselves, I had no problem with it. As distinguished from Dock Ellis in Pittsburgh, who had hair curlers on. I said get rid of them. That was embarrassing. That's a very simple test—it was embarrassing.

I never did anything about Afros. I didn't find them offensive or embarrassing like hair curlers. That's a different thing. I didn't have a problem with reasonable things that people did with their hair. They're lucky to have some.

———

As the decade proceeded, mustaches, Afros, and long, flowing locks became prevalent in baseball, although some owners, like the Yankees' George Steinbrenner, forbade beards and constantly monitored the length of their players' hair.

When Oscar Gamble joined the Yankees in 1976, his Afro sat majestically atop his head like a crown. It was so huge, it made one wonder how he managed to keep his hat on his head. (When the uniquely coiffed Gamble was charged in a paternity suit, his laughable defense was "mistaken identity.") Ultimately, Steinbrenner ordered Gamble to trim his proud mane.

DICK ALLEN

The Athletics were in control in the American League West in 1972, although they had to fight off a surprising challenge from the Chicago White Sox, who stayed in contention up to the final week by the sheer force of one man.

Richard Anthony "Dick" Allen was something of an enigma. One of the most feared sluggers of his time, Allen put up Hall of Fame numbers year after year. In six full seasons with the Philadelphia Phillies, he belted 177 home runs and drove in 542 runs. But he was regarded as a troublemaker and a malcontent, and he soon became the object of Philadelphia's notorious boo birds.

One day, while awaiting a pitching change at his first-base position, Allen scrawled a message in the dirt with his spikes: "BOO!"

After the 1969 season, Allen was traded to St. Louis in the infamous Curt Flood deal. After one year in St. Louis, he was traded to the Dodgers. After one year with the Dodgers, he was traded to the White Sox. Four teams in four years.

In Chicago he was welcomed with open arms by manager Chuck Tanner, who recognized not only Allen's ability but his individualism. Tanner was to be the only manager who left Allen alone and just let him play. And Allen responded with his greatest season—a .308 average and a league-leading 37 homers and 113 RBIs. He was practically a one-man offense for the White Sox, who also had a pair of 20-game winners, knuckleballer Wilbur Wood, 24–17, and former Yankee Stan Bahnsen, 21–16.

———————————————

STAN BAHNSEN: In my rookie year, I played with Mickey Mantle, and he was the best player I ever played with, but that was his last year in the big leagues. As far as the best player I ever played with at the peak of his talent, Richie Allen in 1972, when he was the MVP, was the best. He had an incredible year. I won 21 games, and Richie won at least 10 of them for me with his bat.

He was such a clutch hitter and such a winner. I never saw him make a mistake running the bases. He was one of the most feared hitters in the league by pitchers. I talked to pitchers, and they hated to see him come up in a game-winning situation. He was the kind of hitter that managers would say, "Don't let this guy beat you."

As a teammate he was great. He was very misunderstood. His teammates loved him, but to the public and the press, he was pretty much standoffish, which probably had its roots in Philadelphia.

Chuck Tanner idolized him. Because of Richie, we had a lax-disciplined team, because Chuck didn't want to have a lot of different rules for different guys. If you were a regular and you were doing the job, if you didn't want to take batting practice that day, you didn't have to.

Richie Allen didn't hit that much. His theory was "When I'm swinging the bat well, I don't want to take batting practice, because then I'm going to be seeing a guy throwing 60 miles an hour instead of 90, and it's just going to mess me up."

It wasn't because he didn't want to work, because in spring training, he would hit almost until his hands were bloody. He wore a weight belt, and he would hit and hit and hit. He got ready.

Behind Mickey Lolich's 22 wins, the Tigers returned to postseason action after holding off the Boston Red Sox on the next-to-last day of the season.

I was traded to the White Sox on the same day Richie was. I wasn't excited about going to the White Sox, but I picked up the paper the next day and saw that Richie Allen was traded there, too, and I said, "Oh, man." As a pitcher, you see a guy like Richie Allen on your side, you know you've got a chance to win.

Richie held out that spring, and he finally signed on the day the strike started. We were all leaving the clubhouse, and he was coming in shaking everybody's hands. Then the season started and he had no spring training, and on Opening Day he hit two home runs. It was, like, this can't be fair. The guy was just, like, bionic.

GOOSE GOSSAGE: I had the privilege of playing with so many great players, but Dick Allen was the best player I ever played with.

In 1972, it was the greatest year I've ever seen a player have. I would have loved to have seen him if he just set his mind to "I'm going to put up numbers." The numbers would have been staggering. But if we had a four- or five-run lead, it was like, "Hey, boys, I'm out of here. You've got to take it on in from here. You guys can hold them from here."

He'd take himself out if we had a big lead, so every RBI he had that year was serious damage. There was no padding. Defensively, he was unbelievable. And running the bases. To this day, I have never seen anybody that could run the bases like he did. He was phenomenal—the shots that I saw him hit throughout all the ballparks in the American League.

And what a great guy. He took me under his wing. What a wonderful guy. There never was an ounce of phoniness in Dick. What you see is what you get. He was his own man, and he still is. I saw him recently, and to this day I still love the guy.

He started on Opening Day and never stopped hitting, but alone, Allen could not help the White Sox overtake the Athletics, who won the division by five and a half games.

In the Eastern Division, the Orioles felt the effect of losing the competitive fire of Frank Robinson. A team that had won more than 100 games for three consecutive seasons won only 80 and tumbled to third place.

The surprise team of the American League was the Detroit Tigers, under manager Billy Martin in his second year with Detroit. Mickey Lolich, who had never won 20 games before, won more than 20 for the second straight season under Martin and pitching coach Art Fowler. Joe Coleman, whose previous high in wins was 12, followed up a 20-win season under Martin and Fowler with 19 victories.

The Boston Red Sox battled the Tigers down to the wire in the American League East. Because of the games lost by the strike, the Tigers would play 156 games and the Red Sox 155. Each team lost 70 games, but the Tigers won their extra game, were division champs, and faced the Oakland Athletics in the best-of-five American League Championship Series.

REGGIE SMITH: We had an opportunity to win it outright when we went into Detroit for the last three games. We had our chance, so playing one less game wasn't a factor. All we had to do was win two out of three in Detroit and we'd win the division, so it was right there for us to win it. We lost the first two games, and that clinched it for them, so we had nobody to blame but ourselves.

CLEMENTE'S 3,000th HIT

While the Tigers and Red Sox were staging their photo finish, the Oakland Athletics, Cincinnati Reds, and Pittsburgh Pirates, having disposed of the competition, were merely getting ready for the postseason. There was, however, one race of interest in the National League—Roberto Clemente's bid to become only the 11th player in baseball history to record 3,000 hits in his career.

Hit number 2,999 came in Philadelphia against Steve Carlton in the Pirates' final road game of the season. Clemente was immediately removed from the game so he could hit number 3,000 in front of the home fans. In the next-to-last game of the season, against the Mets, Clemente faced Tom Seaver, who held Roberto hitless in three at-bats.

TOM SEAVER: I used to pound Clemente inside, pound him inside, pound him inside, and he liked the ball out over the plate, and he'd hit the ball to right center. I threw a slider down and away and it was a damn good pitch, and he

The Phillies lost 97 games and finished in last place in 1972, but Steve Carlton, shown here winning his 25th game, won 27 games that year, representing a staggering 46 percent of all Phillies wins for the year.

hit a line drive right down the right-field line. It must have been 10 feet fair. And Rusty Staub was standing right there. He had him played perfectly. He never moved and he caught it, and that would have been Clemente's 3,000th hit. The next day I watched from the dugout, the last day of the season. A double into left center off Jon Matlack for his 3,000th hit. I watched that, because you knew he was in line for it and he was one of those guys that I had this different level of relationship with, you know, watching him as a kid, and now you've got a chance to see him get his 3,000th hit. You want to pull for Matlack, but you'd love to see the 3,000th hit. Boom, he gets a double, a line drive off the left-center-field wall. You're there, and you remember it because of what he meant to you before you were a professional.

DOCK ELLIS: I pitched that game. He got his hit, and he walked off the field—he was getting ready for the playoffs—and I told Bill Virdon [Pirates manager], "I'm finished, too." It was the sixth inning, and I said to Virdon, "I got to go now. I got to get ready for the playoffs." So he let me come out of the game, and I was in the clubhouse drinking champagne with Clemente.

The press was driving him crazy about the 3,000th hit, but to him it was no big deal, because he knew he was going to get it, if not this year, then next year.

1972 PLAYOFFS

Both League Championship Series went the full five games. In the National League, with the series tied at two games each, the Pirates took a 3–2 lead into the bottom of the ninth of Game 5. Johnny Bench led off with a homer off Dave Giusti to tie the score. After Tony Perez and Denis Menke followed with singles, Virdon brought in Bob Moose to pitch to pinch-hitter Hal McRae. Moose uncorked a wild pitch to let in the winning run, and the Reds were back in the World Series.

In the ALCS, Oakland won the first two games at home, but an incident in the second game ignited the Tigers. Relief pitcher Lerrin LaGrow, mopping up for the Tigers in a 5–0 defeat, threw one close to the head of Oakland's spunky shortstop Bert Campaneris, who retaliated by throwing his bat toward the mound.

By adding second baseman Joe Morgan, who came in a trade from Houston, the Reds found a spark plug for the top of the order. The next seven years the Reds finished either first or second in the National League West.

When the melee subsided Campaneris was thrown out of the game. He would be suspended for the remainder of the Championship Series. He would be allowed to play in the World Series, if the Athletics got there, but he was suspended by Bowie Kuhn for the first seven games of the 1973 season.

The Tigers came back to win Game 3 at home, then snatch victory from defeat in Game 4. With the score tied at 1–1 after nine, the Athletics apparently left the Tigers for dead with a pair of solo homers in the top of the tenth. But the Tigers rallied for three in the bottom of the tenth to force a sudden-death fifth game.

Oakland won Game 5, 2–1, but it was a costly victory. The Tigers scored in the bottom of the first, but the A's came back to tie the score in the second inning when Reggie Jackson stole home. But he pulled his hamstring in the process and was removed from the field on a stretcher, his season at an abrupt end.

Catcher Gene Tenace of the Oakland Athletics goes deep in Game 5 of the 1972 World Series against the Reds.

Oakland scored the winning run in the fourth on an RBI single by Gene Tenace, and Vida Blue pitched four scoreless innings in relief for the save. The single was Tenace's only hit of the series. He was saving his best stuff for later.

THE SWINGIN' A'S

Fury Gene Tenace (born Fiore Gino Tennaci) shared Oakland's catching duties with Dave Duncan. He had completed his fourth major league season in 1972, appearing in 82 games, 49 behind the plate, batting only .225 with five home runs and 32 runs batted in. But in Game 1 of the World Series, he wrote his name into the record books by becoming the first player in history to hit home runs in each of his first two World Series at-bats, four days after his 26th birthday. His two-run shot and solo homer knocked in all his team's runs as Oakland took Game 1 in Cincinnati, 3–2.

SPARKY ANDERSON: By the scouting reports, he surprised us. We knew he was a high-ball hitter. We made a mistake and got the ball up.

But it did surprise us that he attacked us the way he did. As the Series went on we got so much respect for him, because we knew if we made mistakes with him, he could really hurt us.

Game 2 was historic for another reason. Before the game, baseball commemorated the 25th anniversary of Jackie Robinson's entry into the major leagues with a ceremony at second base.

His debut with the Brooklyn Dodgers on April 15, 1947, which broke baseball's long-standing color barrier, not only was the most significant event in baseball history, but it also was among the most significant in 20th-century American history. But since his retirement from the game following the 1956 season, Robinson, displeased with baseball for dragging its feet on the hiring of blacks in management and front-office positions, had staged a one-man boycott of the game.

Bowie Kuhn urged Robinson to return for the 1972 World Series with the promise that he, the commissioner, would continue to fight for minority hirings. Robinson accepted the invitation. His hair had turned snow white and diabetes had impaired his eyesight, yet his voice retained its youthful timbre as he made an impassioned plea in front of 53,224 people at Riverfront Stadium for baseball to hire a black manager.

BOWIE KUHN: He could barely see, but he was still sharp. I remember him commenting that he could make out Bobby Tolan's batting stance and he didn't like it.

The Athletics won Game 2 behind Catfish Hunter and Rollie Fingers, who had the help of some spectacular Oakland defense. The Reds trailed 2–0 going into the bottom of the ninth when Tony Perez led off with a single to left. Denis Menke then hit a rocket headed for the left-field wall, but the A's brilliant left fielder, Joe Rudi, raced back to the wall, leaped, and made a spectacular backhanded catch, crashing into the wall as he did.

Cesar Geronimo then ripped a smash to first that seemed headed for right field until first baseman Mike Hegan made a dive for the ball,

The Oakland Athletics turned baseball on its head by donning loud green and yellow uniforms, wearing flashy white cleats, and, as in the case of relief pitcher Rollie Fingers (above), sporting flamboyant mustaches.

smothered it, picked it up, and raced Geronimo to the bag for the second out, Perez taking second. Hal McRae, batting for Darrel Chaney, singled to left to score Perez to make it 2–1.

With Julian Javier sent up to pinch hit for reliever Tom "the Blade" Hall, Rollie Fingers, with the magnificent handlebar mustache, was called in from

No More Rainouts

The real Big Red Machine in action at Riverfront Stadium. The Zamboni-like device sucked up 100 gallons of water per minute from soggy AstroTurf and spewed it over the fence, cutting down the time to get the field in shape after rain delays.

the bullpen. Fingers got Javier to foul to first, and the A's, thanks to their brilliant defense, had taken a two-game lead in the Series.

The Reds came back to win the third game 1–0, but Tenace hit his third home run in the Series in Game 4 and singled in the middle of a two-run rally in the bottom of the ninth as the A's came from behind to take a 3–2 victory and a three-to-one lead in the Series.

The Athletics trailed 2–1 going into the bottom of the ninth. With one out, rookie Gonzalo Marquez, who had had only 21 at-bats during the regular season, was sent up to pinch hit for George Hendrick against the Reds' ace reliever, Clay Carroll. Marquez set the tone for the winning rally by lining a single to center after fouling off several of Carroll's pitches.

As the victory's hero, Marquez was summoned to the postgame interview area to talk with reporters. Since the Venezuela native's English was spotty, teammate Bert Campaneris was asked to accompany him to serve as an interpreter.

The questioning went as follows: a reporter asked a question in English, Campaneris translated it in Spanish to Marquez, who answered in Spanish, after which Campaneris translated the answer into English for the reporter.

Reporter: "Gonzalo, how many foul balls did you hit before your single?"

Campaneris: *"Gonzalo, cuántas pelotas foul pegastes antes de obtener tu primer sencillo?"*

Gonzalez: "I theenk I heet fi or seex."

Campaneris: "He say he theenk he heet fi or seex."

Down three games to one, the Reds were not finished. They won the next two games to tie the Series and force a decisive seventh game in Cincinnati.

Again it was Tenace who provided the spark for the Athletics, with two hits and two RBIs in a 3–2 victory that gave the Athletics their first world championship since 1930. Tenace batted .348 for the World Series, with four home runs and nine RBIs.

Two days after the final game of the 1972 World Series, nine days after he had addressed the crowd at Riverfront Stadium, Jackie Robinson died. He was 53.

BOWIE KUHN: The touching and emotional thing about Jackie's death was that it came just a few days after he had come back to the World Series. But I take pride in the fact that I got him to come back, and I feel I kept my promise to him. I worked very, very hard to see that minorities were properly treated. I felt very strongly on that issue. I didn't think baseball had done enough. Anybody who knows anything about the Hall of Fame will tell you that I opened the door for the old Negro Leaguers.

I think Rachel Robinson will tell you today that in her book—and probably in Jackie's, although I couldn't say that for sure—I got good marks on that score.

TRAGEDY

It was New Year's Eve in Puerto Rico. Party time. Pittsburgh pitcher Bob Johnson had planned to celebrate the New Year, and he invited the members of his San Juan team in the Puerto Rican Winter League to his apartment in the fashionable tourist area of Condado, overlooking the Atlantic Ocean.

Manny Sanguillen was there. So were Richie Zisk, Milt May, Tim Foli, and Rennie Stennett.

RENNIE STENNETT: The only reason I was in Puerto Rico was because Roberto Clemente was supposed to play for San Juan, as he did every year, but after the World Series, he decided to take a rest. So they gave me his contract to take his place. It was my first year in the big leagues, and the Pirates thought it would be good for me to play in Puerto Rico to gain more experience.

Clemente would not be at Bob Johnson's party. He had other plans—an errand of mercy. He was scheduled to fly to Nicaragua with a plane carrying food and clothing for the thousands of Nicaraguans who had lost their homes in the recent earthquake.

A compassionate man, Clemente had accepted the position of honorary chairman of the Nicaraguan Relief Committee, but there was nothing honorary about the position as far as Clemente was concerned. As he did with everything, Clemente threw himself completely into the job.

RENNIE STENNETT: That day, somebody told Manny Sanguillen that Roberto was trying to get in touch with him for something. Manny had a rental car that had something wrong with it, and he had to return it. He asked me to follow him in my car. Roberto had an office across the street from the ballpark [Hiram Bithorn Stadium]. We were going to stop to see Roberto, then I would follow Manny so he could drop off his rental car and drive him back.

It was after our game, about 4:00 in the afternoon, and we drove around for about an hour and we couldn't find a place to park. So Manny never saw him. Instead, he drove to return his car, and I followed him.

That night we went to Bob Johnson's apartment for the New Year's Eve party. Sometime during the night, somebody said, "Look out the window, there's a ship on fire." We all looked, and we could see flames coming from the water.

It was about 2:00 A.M. I know it was after the old year went out and the new year came in. We all left the party and went home, and at about 4:00 in the morning, we all got a call that woke us up to tell us that Roberto's plane had crashed.

Everybody got up and went over to Clemente's house. It was sad. We just couldn't believe it.

I'm not saying the flames we saw were Roberto's plane, but when you put everything together, that's what you have to think.

Roberto didn't want to go, but he heard that people were not getting the stuff he was sending them. They said guards were taking it. So Roberto went to make sure the people got the stuff, and everybody was thinking the reason he was looking for Manny was to ask him to go with him. Knowing Manny, if he had been able to find a parking space and got to see Roberto and Roberto asked him to go, Manny would have gone.

DOCK ELLIS: I was in a motel room in Los Angeles with my wife, now my ex-wife. It came on the air. They just broke into everything. When I heard it, I just broke down crying. He meant a lot to me. Before, I could never talk about it. Roberto and my father—I'd talk about them dying and I'd break out crying. I just let them go about three years ago.

Investigators said the DC-7 carrying Roberto Clemente and food and clothing for the Nicaraguan earthquake victims took off at 9:22 P.M. on December 31, 1972. One engine exploded immediately, causing the pilot to attempt to return to the airport. He never made it.

For 11 days, divers searched the waters off Isla Verde for survivors. Each day hundreds of people stood on Piñones Beach, waiting, looking, hoping.

Roberto Clemente's body was never found.

CHAPTER 4

1973

THE FOURTH INNING

ROBERTO

News of Roberto Clemente's tragic death hit the baseball community hard. It was difficult to fathom the loss of such a vibrant, seemingly indestructible, larger-than-life hero. There was anger that he should have been snuffed out so senselessly when he was embarked on an errand to aid his fellow man. If there was any consolation, it was that he had managed to get his 3,000th hit in his final game, but that was small solace for the grief.

JACK LANG: It was the morning after New Year's, and I was driving into the baseball writers' suite in the New York Sheraton Hotel when I heard a news bulletin on the car radio that Clemente was killed in a plane crash while taking relief supplies to the victims in Nicaragua.

The first thing that crossed my mind was why should we wait for this guy, let's put him in the Hall of Fame. When I got to the hotel, I called Joe Reichler [retired Associated Press baseball writer then working in the commissioner's office] and I mentioned it to Joe, and he said, "That's funny, I was thinking the same thing." He said, "Let me talk to Bowie about it."

He went in and talked to Bowie, and a couple of hours later he called me back at the hotel. He said, "Bowie is all in favor of it, but we've got to convince the Hall of Fame people to do it. He thinks it would be a great thing for baseball."

About a week later—after some objections from Paul Kerr, president of the Hall of Fame, who didn't like the idea of having somebody not wait the five years like everybody else—Kerr was finally convinced that it would be a good thing for baseball and for the Hall of Fame to have this special election.

Joe Heiling [Houston baseball writer] was president of the BBWAA [Baseball Writers Association of America] at the time, and it got his approval—he was all for it. Dick Young [*New York Daily News* columnist] was violently opposed to it, and he was writing columns saying he was opposed.

Some writers wondered if this special election was setting a dangerous precedent, that there would be a rush to judgment and a groundswell of sympathy for a fallen hero. Clearly, to most members of the BBWAA, Clemente would not be elected by a sympathy vote. He was eminently qualified and would surely be elected five years after he had played his last game.

It was agreed by the officers of the Hall of Fame and of the BBWAA to send out ballots for a special election. The number of responses was 424. To be elected, Clemente would have to get the approval of 75 percent of those who voted, or 318 votes. He received 393 votes, 75 more than needed, or 93 percent. Roberto Clemente would thus become not only the first player elected to the Hall of Fame without the five-year waiting period but also the first Latin American so enshrined.

JACK LANG: Most of the no votes were not against Clemente. Many of those who voted no wrote little notes on their ballot saying they were not against Clemente going into the Hall of Fame, but they were opposed to what we were doing and the method we were using to elect him. They thought he should wait his five years. They felt we were setting a precedent, and Paul Kerr, president of the Hall of Fame, said this would be the only time we'd do it. When Thurman Munson died, there were some writers who wanted to have a special election for him, but it never even came to a vote.

THE DH

There were two notable additions to the American League at the start of the 1973 season. They arrived in controversy but with an air of excitement, hope, and anticipation that they would infuse the staid and stolid junior league with a new flair and flamboyance.

For a while they did. But as time went on, they seemed to wear out their welcome, becoming an irritant to some, an intrusion to others, but grudgingly accepted as a necessary evil.

One was the designated hitter rule, viewed by many as an aberration to the great game, an ersatz attempt to stimulate offense on the grounds that fans prefer high-scoring contests in all sports—which, in fact, was the idea. The rule called for an extra hitter in the lineup, batting in place of the pitcher.

Proponents of the designated hitter rule argued that not only would it increase offensive productivity and thereby fan excitement and interest, but it also would extend the careers of stars who were defensive liabilities either by age or by disinclination for defense. And stars meant money at the box office. The rule's critics argued that the DH would drastically alter the strategy of the game as fans had known it for three-quarters of a century. Baseball was steeped in tradition and lore, which meant resistance to change. As Bill Veeck, the maverick owner of the Cleveland Indians, St. Louis Browns, and Chicago White Sox, once facetiously but pointedly commented, "The only changes the game has made since the turn of the century was taking the collars off the uniforms and allowing players to bring their gloves in from the field."

The American and National Leagues were diametrically opposed in their positions on the DH. The American League favored it and adopted it unanimously. The National League condemned it and eschewed its use, predicting its rapid demise. The disagreement over the DH rule further widened a vast breach that existed between the two leagues, both in style and in substance.

MARTY APPEL: The American League did it because they were lagging behind the National League by almost every measure and they felt they needed a boost to generate some excitement.

LEE MacPHAIL: The designated hitter was actually suggested by Connie Mack many years ago. It came into being because the defense was gaining ascendancy over the offense. Pitchers were throwing harder and coming up with varied pitches. The relief pitcher, improved gloves, and improved defense all worked to the detriment of offense.

In the National League, this was counterbalanced to some extent by artificial turf, but the American League had less artificial turf. We in the American League turned to the DH to help offense and keep the stars in the game for a longer period of time.

Chub Feeney [president of the National League while MacPhail was president of the American League] and I argued about this all the time. He kept saying that baseball should not be played under different rules. And I kept pointing out that the American League has the designated hitter; so do the colleges, the high schools, American Legion, and all the minor leagues, so it should be up to the National League to conform.

BOWIE KUHN: Joe Cronin, president of the American League at the time, was the guy who persuaded me to support it. Others in the league had supported it, like Charlie Finley [A's owner] and Michael Burke [president of the Yankees], but they didn't carry as much weight with me as Cronin, a traditional man who loved the game very much. He persuaded me to support the designated hitter, and I did and cast the vote to put it into effect.

THE BOSS

The other addition to the American League in 1973 was George Steinbrenner.

The New York Yankees were the most glamorous, most prestigious, most successful franchise in the history of professional sports, although they didn't start out that way. The American League was in its infancy when, in 1903, president Ban Johnson, recognizing the need for a New York franchise in his upstart league, arranged for a pair of New Yorkers to purchase the Baltimore Orioles and move the team to New York.

Originally known as the New York Highlanders, they became the Yankees in 1913. Two years later, they passed into the hands of brewmeister Colonel Jacob Ruppert, who bought out his partner Tillinghast Huston in 1923, and eventually to businessmen Dan Topping and Del Webb, who presided over the greatest dynasty sports have known.

Aging and looking to scale down their activities, Topping and Webb put the Yankees on the market in 1964. Acting on the advice of Michael Burke (a CBS vice president in charge of investments), the network, looking to diversify (among its properties was the hit Broadway musical *My Fair Lady*), purchased the Yankees for $13.2 million. To reward Burke for his successful acquisition of so prestigious a property, CBS named him team president, a job he would come to cherish for its high visibility, its glamour, its excitement, and because it caused his competitive juices to flow.

Burke was charming and flamboyant. His clothes were of the latest cut, and his long, gray hair was styled in the fashion of the day. He had played football at Penn State University and served in World War II with the OSS, the predecessor of the CIA. But he knew little about baseball and less about running a baseball team.

When CBS took over, the Yankees were completing a run of 15 American League pennants and 10 world championships in 18 years. But for the next eight years, under the stewardship of CBS, the Yankees went through their longest championship drought since they won their first pennant in 1921. From 1965 to 1972 they had four losing seasons and finished higher than fourth only once. Two years after CBS bought the team, the Yankees finished 10th, with the worst record of any Yankees team in 53 years. Under CBS, attendance never surpassed 1.3 million, dropping under 1 million for the first time in 28 years in 1972.

William S. Paley, chairman of the board of CBS, ordered Burke to find a buyer for the team, but gave him the option of putting a deal together and suggested that CBS would look favorably upon any group of purchasers that included Burke.

Burke looked for New Yorkers who, aware of the team's history and tradition, would be interested in buying the Yankees. He found no takers. In a conversation with Gabe Paul, president of the Cleveland Indians, Burke learned about a group of Clevelanders who had been unsuccessful in their attempt to buy the Indians and might be interested in the Yankees.

The group was headed by George M. Steinbrenner III of Lorain and Cleveland, Ohio, a young man of 42. He was unknown in New York, but he was a businessman of estimable worth and renown in the Cleveland area, enough to have been voted by *Cleveland* magazine as one of the top 50 "Movers and Shakers" in the country before the age of 40 and to be an intimate of Senator Ted Kennedy of Massachusetts.

Although the Yankees would be his first entry into the world of baseball, Steinbrenner had a longtime involvement in, and love for, sports. He had been a hurdler in his prep and college days at Culver Military Academy and Williams College, had served as graduate assistant football coach at both

Purdue University and Northwestern, and had won championships as owner of teams in the National Industrial Basketball League and American Basketball League (ABL).

At age 30, he bought the Cleveland Pipers of the ABL and showed the foresight and courage to be the first owner of a major sports franchise to turn his team over to a black man. Steinbrenner hired John McClendon, who had led Tennessee A&I to three straight small-college national championships in the fifties.

With a team built around future Knick Dick Barnett and the fabled Bevo Francis of Rio Grande College, Steinbrenner's Pipers won the ABL championship. Steinbrenner also had the questionable distinction of being the only owner of a major sports franchise to be ejected from a game for arguing with a referee.

Less than two years after the Pipers won the championship, the American Basketball League folded. Steinbrenner tried to get an NBA franchise. When he failed, his father, growing old and contemplating retirement, urged his son to enter the family business, Kinsman Marine Transit Company, which ran cargo ships along the Great Lakes.

Within a few years after taking over for his father as chairman, Steinbrenner headed up a group that bought out the American Shipbuilding Company, merged it with Kinsman, and tripled its annual revenues to some $200 million in sales.

On January 3, the press was summoned to Yankee Stadium, where Mike Burke announced that a 12-man group headed by two "general partners," he and Steinbrenner, had purchased the Yankees for $10 million, $3.2 million less than CBS had paid for the team nine years before.

"It's the best buy in sports today," Steinbrenner said. "I think it's a bargain."

Steinbrenner and Burke were the only partners to appear at the January 3 press conference. One week later, the remainder of the group was introduced to the press at the posh "21" Club. In the group of "limited partners" was Gabe Paul, who had resigned his position with the Cleveland Indians to join the Yankees, thereby raising some intriguing issues.

Six weeks earlier, acting as operative for the Indians, Paul had traded the coveted, power-hitting, lefty-swinging Graig Nettles to the Yankees for four young prospects, a deal that raised questions of impropriety in baseball circles.

Moreover, if Burke was to continue as president and CEO of the Yankees, and Lee MacPhail was to continue as the team's general manager, what function was Paul to perform?

Addressing the question, Burke suggested that Paul, nearing retirement, would serve as an observer and consultant and that this would be a nice, cushy way for him to wind down his long baseball career.

Longtime baseball observers and acquaintances of Paul found this difficult to accept. They knew Paul as a still-energetic man who retained the thirst for the hands-on operation of a baseball team, one who would not, indeed could not, take a backseat.

At the January 3 press conference, Steinbrenner had made his intentions known. "We plan absentee ownership," he said. "We're not going to pretend we are something we aren't. I'll stick to building ships. I won't be active in the day-to-day operations of the club at all. I can't spread myself so thin. I've got enough headaches with the shipping company."

Those initial remarks would be tossed back at him many times in the years to come.

THE STRANGEST TRADE

While the George Steinbrenner years would produce many controversies, the first one in his regime was not of his making and was one of which he had no knowledge.

One day early in spring training, Yankees president Mike Burke, general manager Lee MacPhail, and manager Ralph Houk invited the reporters covering the team into Houk's office. The door was closed, and MacPhail proceeded to stun the assembled media with a story so bizarre as to defy belief.

Two members of the Yankees pitching staff, Fritz Peterson, who had won 20 games in 1970 and 69 games over the past four seasons, and Mike Kekich, who had begun to fulfill his great promise by winning 10 games in each of the previous two years—both left-handers, such close friends that they were practically inseparable—had entered into an arrangement whereby they would trade wives. Not just wives, but children, family pets, and residences.

Peterson would move in with Kekich's wife and family in the Kekich home, Kekich would move in with Peterson's wife and family in the Peterson home. Their intention, agreed to by their spouses, was to obtain a divorce and marry each other's spouse.

————————————

MAURY ALLEN: Late in the 1972 season, I believe it was in August, I had a party at my house, as I like to do every year. I usually invite some friends and other writers, and I like to have a couple of ballplayers that I enjoy being around. I invited Peterson and Kekich and their wives.

Nothing unusual happened at the party, which broke up about midnight. My wife, Janet, and I were cleaning up, it was about 2:00 A.M., and I heard voices in the driveway outside my kitchen window. I looked out, and there were the Petersons and Kekiches in a long conversation. I even mentioned to my wife that they were still out there long after they had left our house.

I didn't think anything of it until it came out that they were trading families; then I learned that what they were discussing outside my house that night were the arrangements and the details of their swap.

MARTY APPEL: You have to remember this was the first eight weeks of George Steinbrenner owning the team; the coincidence of this is incredible. Peterson had not signed his contract and was a holdout. He was on the Florida west coast. Kekich was in camp. Peterson heard that Kekich was telling the press about this, which was not true. So Peterson encountered Milton Richman [United Press International baseball writer] and spilled the beans to Milton.

Milton put it out on the wire, and we were in Fort Lauderdale and we had to scramble to deal with the press. I was not in Houk's office when the announcement was made. I was just a kid, assistant to Bob Fishel [Yankees director of public relations].

But I was involved when it was discussed what to tell the press and the decision was made to level with the press, but to tell them this shouldn't be this big a story, it's a personal matter. This was in the primitive days, when baseball writing was on the curve of changing. It was even decided to exclude Sheila Moran [covering for the *New York Post* in her first spring training]

Fritz Peterson (front), with his wife, Marilyn, and Mike Kekich, with his wife, Susan, shocked everyone when they swapped spouses in 1973.

because she was not one of the boys; she would not understand, and she would sensationalize it and put it all out of proportion. How can you put this story out of proportion?

GENE MICHAEL: I didn't believe it when I first heard about it, because it was Peterson and Kekich. These two guys were always pulling some stunt. They were big practical jokers, especially Peterson. He would order things out of a catalog, like fishing gear and hunting rifles, and have them sent to Thurman Munson at the stadium. Thurman would get these packages and he had no idea how they got there, and Fritz would be hiding around the corner watching Thurman opening the packages and Fritz would be laughing like crazy.

So when my wife told me she heard they were swapping wives, I just said, "Don't believe that stuff. Those guys are pulling some trick again." That's the first thing I thought: it's a crazy rumor that they started, because they're always pulling some trick.

They were always doing some crazy thing, one after another. It never ended. And they were always together. If one of them was walking through the lobby of a hotel on the road, he was asking where the other one was. That's how close they were.

I didn't find out the truth until I went to spring training. We were doing a clinic, and Fritz came up to me and said, "Stick, I'm sorry I didn't tell you." I said, "You don't have to apologize to me for that." But that's the first I heard of it, even though a lot of guys had known it for months.

One of those who knew about it for months was the Yankees manager.

RALPH HOUK: We were in Milwaukee, and Peterson came to me and asked me if it was all right if he went back early. His wife was there, and he said he would leave early and Kekich would drive Peterson's wife back. Well, I saw nothing wrong with that, so I gave him permission.

It was right after that that I heard about their arrangement and their plans to swap wives. It became public in spring training. That was one thing I didn't even know how to handle. I was trying to downplay it the best I could, and that was a mistake. I should have just come out and said it all, because there's no way you can keep anything from the press. The less you keep from the press, the fewer problems you're going to have, because they're going to find it out anyway.

I talked to both of them, and they were very happy with their arrangement, so what are you going to say?

In all my years in baseball, that was the biggest surprise I ever had.

———

Once the story hit the papers and the news broadcasts, it spread like wildfire. Peterson and Kekich took more than their share of shots from fans and opponents. In the Sarasota training camp of the Chicago White Sox, former Yankee Stan Bahnsen, unlike most others, was not surprised by the news.

———

STAN BAHNSEN: I knew about it four or five months before it came out, but I still couldn't believe it. Not because they were both left-handed, but this was bizarre. We were close. Me and Peterson and Kekich and Mel Stottlemyre were always goofing around. And then, when I heard about it, I talked to them, and they said this is the real deal.

When the story hit the papers, White Sox manager Chuck Tanner came to me and said, "Aren't you going to thank me for trading for you?"

I said, "Why?" and he said, "Well, I saved you a wife."

———

Out of baseball after the 1977 season, Kekich enrolled in medical school and is presently practicing medicine. He and the former Marilyn Peterson broke up soon after the incident.

Peterson fell from 17 wins in 1972 to eight in 1973. On April 27, 1974, he was traded to the Cleveland Indians. He pitched three seasons for Cleveland and Texas and won only 24 games before leaving baseball. A quarter of a century after the wife-swapping, Peterson remains married to the former Susan Kekich and is active with Baseball Chapel.

THE FIRST DH

Late in spring training, Ralph Houk approached left-handed slugger Ron Blomberg and asked him how he felt about being the Yankees' designated hitter on Opening Day. In his first two seasons with the Yankees, Blomberg, the number one draft pick in the country in the June 1967 draft, had shown a potent bat but no aptitude for defense. He was batting .326 at Syracuse when the Yankees called him up on June 24, 1971.

In 64 games he batted .322. In 1972 he batted .268 and had 14 homers and 49 RBIs in 299 at-bats and showed himself to be a charming, likable, and engaging, if somewhat naïve, young man.

Once, when he was battling a slump, Blomberg told a reporter, "I should never have become a baseball player. I should have become a doctor and a lawyer like my mother and father wanted me to be."

The Yankees thought they had struck gold with Blomberg, who was Jewish and figured to be a huge gate attraction for New York's large Jewish population. And, in fact, Blomberg, who had tremendous power and hit some of the longest home runs this side of Mickey Mantle, would become one of the most popular Yankees of his time.

Blomberg told Houk he wouldn't mind being the team's designated hitter if Houk felt that would help the team. When reporters heard about Blomberg's selection, they gathered around him to ask how he felt about being a DH.

"I don't know," he said. "I've never done it."

RON BLOMBERG: I know that sounded like a Yogiism. Nobody had ever done it. But what I meant is that I had never even done it in spring training games. Felipe Alou had done most of the DHing.

But I pulled my hamstring late in spring training, and Ralph figured I would be better off DHing because the weather up north was going to be cold in the beginning of the season.

The Yankees were scheduled to open the season in Boston on Friday, April 6, a 1:00 start. Because it was the earliest starting time in the American League, Blomberg would be the first designated hitter in baseball history.

RON BLOMBERG: I never thought anything about being the first DH, about the history and stuff. But the night before Opening Day, I was reading the *Boston Globe* and they had the starting lineups for the first game, and there was my name, batting sixth as DH.

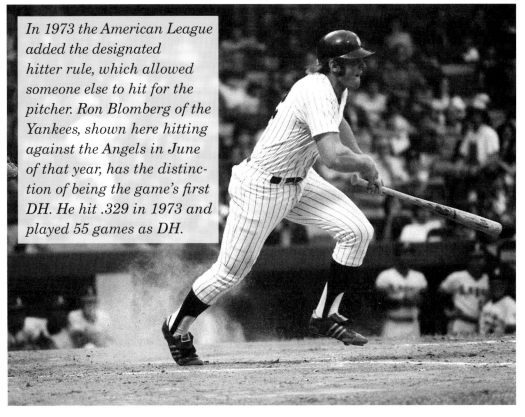

In 1973 the American League added the designated hitter rule, which allowed someone else to hit for the pitcher. Ron Blomberg of the Yankees, shown here hitting against the Angels in June of that year, has the distinction of being the game's first DH. He hit .329 in 1973 and played 55 games as DH.

The next day I talked to Elston Howard [a Yankees coach] and asked him what I was supposed to do. Ellie said, "Just stay warm until it's time to hit. Think of it as pinch-hitting four times."

As it turned out, we scored a couple of runs right away, so I got to bat in the first inning. If we didn't score those runs, Orlando Cepeda, who was Boston's DH and was batting fifth, might have been the first DH in history. I batted against Luis Tiant with the bases loaded and drew a walk.

I still didn't think much about it, never realized it was so controversial, but after the game Marty Appel [the Yankees' assistant director of public relations] asked me for my bat so he could send it to Cooperstown. The bat is there in Cooperstown. I've been there a few times, and it's on display, with my name as the first designated hitter in baseball history. It's a funny way to make the Hall of Fame.

MARTY APPEL: It's the only bat in the Hall of Fame that commemorates a base on balls.

When Houk told him he was going to be the DH, Blomberg said, "What does a DH do?" He made it seem like it was such a new phenomenon, but we had done it all spring training, so it was not that incredible a novelty.

I remember being aware of who was going to be the first DH, and since our game started earlier than any others, it was either going to be Blomberg or Orlando Cepeda, the Red Sox DH. A couple of guys had to get on for Blomberg to bat in the first inning, otherwise it was going to be Cepeda who was almost certain to bat in the bottom of the first.

We were all naïve in a sense back then, not in terms of the history of the game, but in terms of the memorabilia value, like let's grab his helmet, let's grab his shoes, let's grab everything associated with being the first DH. Today, you would see more of that. In fact, today I don't think it would automatically go to the Hall of Fame. The player would say, "Hey, wait a minute, I can get $85,000 for this bat."

RON BLOMBERG: I never got comfortable being a DH. I felt I was too young to focus on the job. A veteran player would have had it easier. And I was too muscular to sit around doing nothing until it was time to hit. But I know I wasn't the greatest fielder, and I never liked to play defense, so it was the right thing for me. But it's difficult to pinch-hit four times in a game.

Whoever realized the DH would be so controversial? The way I see it, it's a position, and with the union being so strong, they endorsed it because it means you're giving another player a chance to get a paycheck. The people who are against it have to realize that there are always going to be changes in sports. Look at the three-point rule in basketball. The DH was started as an experiment, and a lot of people thought it would last a few years, then get phased out. But now, more than 30 years later, it's still there.

Blomberg adjusted well to his new role as designated hitter. His average rose over .400 through the month of June and stayed there until June 28. He was the first player to hit over .400 that late in the season since Ted Williams and Stan Musial did it in the 1948 season.

Eventually, a series of injuries took a toll on Blomberg, and he finished with a .329 average, second best in the American League to Rod Carew's

.350. Carew would win six batting titles in the seventies, including four straight from 1972 through 1975. Blomberg, however, appeared in only 100 games for the Yankees and had just 301 official at-bats, too few to be listed among the league leaders.

It didn't take long for George Steinbrenner to renege on his promise to "stick to building ships" and stay out of the day-to-day operation of the Yankees or for a power struggle to develop between him and Mike Burke, which many had believed was inevitable. The season was not a month old when Steinbrenner, with Burke standing at his side, announced that Burke had "decided" to resign his post as Yankees president and remain as a consultant. Gabe Paul would be the new team president, and hereafter the Yankees would have one general partner, George M. Steinbrenner III.

"A lot of times, making someone a consultant is putting him out to pasture or a settlement," Steinbrenner said. "This isn't the case here."

THE BOSS

Steinbrenner began to spend more and more time with the Yankees as the season progressed, much to the dismay of manager Ralph Houk and the players. Gene Michael, the Yankees' shortstop in the first year of the Steinbrenner reign and one of the team's more fun-loving players, recalled one particular episode involving Steinbrenner's early penchant for being an "involved owner." Michael was known for an aversion to insects and other objects that crawl, ooze, or slime, a weakness that was often exploited by his more playful teammates.

GENE MICHAEL: We were playing the Rangers in Texas, and Steinbrenner was there, sitting in a box seat right next to our dugout. While we were batting, somebody had put half of a frankfurter in one of the fingers of my glove. When our inning was over, somebody gave me my glove and I went out to shortstop. I put the glove on, and I felt something slimy in there. I shook my hand and nothing came out. Then I shook my glove and a piece of a hot dog came out. So I took the hot dog and I fired it toward the dugout, but it slid over in front of a security cop who was sitting on a wooden chair right in front of George. George Steinbrenner was sitting there.

A Texas high school phenom, David Clyde was drafted by the Texas Rangers in the summer of 1973 and made his major league debut at Arlington Stadium just weeks later. He would win only 18 games over a five-year career.

I'll never forget this. Graig Nettles made this up, I know, but he said that George said, "Give me that hot dog. I want that hot dog, I want that hot dog." And Nettles said to me that he said to George, "What are you going to do, fingerprint it?"

It's blurry in my mind now, but I think I remember George saying he was going to find out who put the hot dog in there and he was going to punish him. Or he told Houk to find out who did it, but Houk just ignored him.

Houk was known as "the Major." He was a tough Kansan who had earned a battlefield commission in World War II and was a longtime Yankee as a player, coach, and manager. He ruled his team with fear and intimidation but was regarded as a players' manager who would not abide meddling from above. It seemed inevitable that he would eventually clash with Steinbrenner.

RALPH HOUK: George didn't bother me much that year, but there was one time in Texas. We had a chance to win a game. I sent Johnny Callison up to pinch hit, and he struck out or popped up. It would have been a big pinch-hit if he had made it. George called me that night and said, "Get rid of Callison."

I said, "We can't get rid of Callison. Besides, we've only got about a month to go and we're going to have to pay him anyway. And in a couple of days you could expand the roster, so there's no reason to get rid of him."

George Steinbrenner bought the Yankees in 1973 and boasted that he would restore the Yankees to glory. Three years later he had.

But George said, "You go tell him he's gone."

I decided I wouldn't do that, so I called Lee MacPhail, and I said, "Lee, I'm not going to tell Callison he's gone. I'm just not going to do it."

And Lee said, "Let me talk to him [Steinbrenner]."

A little while later, Lee called and said, "You better tell Callison."

THE RYAN EXPRESS

On May 15, Nolan Ryan, having developed into the most feared pitcher in baseball, pitched the first no-hitter of his career for the California Angels, beating the Kansas City Royals 3–0 and striking out 12. His catcher was Jeff Torborg, who had caught no-hitters thrown by Sandy Koufax and Bill Singer with the Dodgers.

JEFF TORBORG: When the trade was made with the Mets, I remember thinking that the potential that Nolan had was really exciting for me, because I enjoyed working with pitchers and I was intrigued with what Nolan brought to the club with that unbelievable arm.

The first time I met him and found out what kind of person he was, we became really good friends.

He came to us in the 1972 season, and that was the year of the strike. We were all in Anaheim. Vada Pinson and I were player representatives, and we practiced as a team on a little ballfield down on State College Boulevard, not far from Anaheim Stadium. When the workout was over, we'd take some batting practice and play a little intrasquad game, then I would take Nolan over to the side and we'd throw on this little mound and home-plate area, which was dangerous. If he bounced the ball on that mound, I could have gotten killed.

We put a lot of time in there, and he was frustrated. Also, it was a difficult time for him, because during the strike, just coming over, I don't think he had made much money at that point, and he was wondering whether he was going to have to take his family home.

But we worked like crazy. I was trying to teach him what I had learned from the Dodgers, on halves of the plate. Working low and away on the outer half of the plate. We worked a lot for those couple of weeks, and he would eat me up with balls in the dirt. Then Angels pitching coach Tom Morgan had his own way of standing in front of Nolan on the mound to make him drive out in front so he didn't spin off the ball. He had a tendency, because he threw so hard, to really grunt and throw the ball, and his front side would pull and he would be wild, up and in, on a right-hander.

Tom stood on the mound in front of him and made Nolan stride out past him so that he was reaching out toward the plate.

In 1972 Ryan won 19 games, and I felt bad about it. We were playing against Oakland, and he was going for his 20th and I had the flu. I hurt everywhere. Elbow and back and shoulder. I couldn't throw Bert Campaneris out at second base; he eventually scored, and we lost the game, 2–1. I really felt bad, because I was hoping he would get his 20th win.

———

Two months to the day after his no-hitter in Kansas City, Ryan pitched his second no-hitter, in Detroit, striking out 17, including 8 straight. He got Norm Cash on strikes in his first three at-bats. In the ninth inning, Cash came to the plate carrying a piano leg, and plate umpire Ron Luciano, a fun-loving guy but a stickler for the rules, said, "No, no, you can't do that," and sent him back for a regular bat. Cash popped out for the final out.

———

JEFF TORBORG: I caught the first no-hitter, but I got hurt in Detroit—I broke a finger. And Art Kusnyer was the catcher, and we set up a set of signs where Nolan would give Art the signs off his hat. And he pitched his second no-hitter.

———

Ryan would miss an unprecedented third no-hitter against the Yankees in Anaheim on August 29 when Thurman Munson was credited with a single in the first inning on a pop fly that fell when Angels second baseman Sandy Alomar Sr. and shortstop Rudy Meoli miscommunicated and each backed off a catchable ball that landed on the dirt behind second base. It was the Yankees' only hit of the game.

Ryan would win 21 for the Angels, completing 26 of 39 starts and recording the astounding total of 383 strikeouts in 326 innings, which broke by one the all-time major league record established by Sandy Koufax in 1965. Ryan's strikeout total was even more amazing considering he never had the luxury of pitching against a pitcher.

———

JEFF TORBORG: As the season wound down and Nolan was trying to break Sandy's record, I had a glove that I started out the season with, and he threw so hard that the glove took a beating. A start or two before his last one, we were in Boston and he threw a ball with a runner on third base, right through the webbing. I mean that's how hard he threw, he tore the webbing and the ball hit the backstop on the fly and the run scored.

I had to catch him in his last game, and you don't want to go to another glove. It's one of those things, you're really comfortable with a glove you're using, you're superstitious. This glove, which I still have, has a patch on it, it's been re-worked, restitched, reglued, everything you can imagine just to get through the last game. I don't know if there are any other pitchers in major league history you can say threw a ball through the webbing of some guy's glove.

In his last start against the Twins, he needed 15 strikeouts to tie Sandy's record, and they got to him early. Three or four runs in the first inning and we're thinking, "He may not get out of the inning, let alone take a run at Sandy's record."

We caught up, and the game went into extra innings. Nolan had 15 going into the ninth, but he couldn't get the strikeout to break the record. In the ninth he couldn't get it; in the tenth he couldn't get it. In the eleventh inning, Rod Carew walked with two outs and the pinch-hitter was Rich Reese.

The trainers had been massaging Nolan's calves. He started getting cramps from about the ninth inning, because he's a drop-and-driver. He really used his legs. He and Tom Seaver were your classic drop-and-drive power pitchers, where they really dropped down on that back leg and drove into the plate. So he got these terrible cramps, and in those days they treated you differently. We used to eat salt pills. Nowadays, they say salt pills don't do it, you have to take potassium.

So they were trying to feed him salt pills and massaging him, and by the time he got to the eleventh inning, we got two outs and Carew was on first base and Nolan threw two fastballs past Rich Reese. On the second strike, Carew took off for second base. I took my best throw I made all year, and I said, "Oh, my God, not now." I think we had him, but the umpire called him safe, and I said, "Oh, yeah."

On the next pitch, Nolan let one fly, and Reese didn't come within two feet of it. He swung in one place and the ball was in another, and that was the 16th punchout and the 383 and the record.

Vida Blue (above) and Catfish Hunter were the two best pitchers on an exceptional Oakland staff. In 1973 Blue won 20 games for the second time in his career.

The interesting thing is he was 14–16 with seven starts left that season, and we couldn't figure it out. I know we didn't have a very good team, but how can he be 14–16 with his kind of great stuff? So I suggested to him, "Nolan, let's try something. I want you to give me the signs like you did in the no-hitter to Art Kusnyer." He said, "No, no, I don't want to do that." I said, "I've got an ulterior motive. Let's change our luck—you know how superstitious baseball players are—let's change our luck and you give me the signs off your hat, then I'll relay the signs to the infield, and that way you're really thinking about what you want to do."

"No, no," he said, "I like the way you call the game."

And I said, "Let's just try it. See what happens." He would give the signs off his hat. He'd stop on the front of his hat for a fastball and the back of his hat if it was a breaking ball. It was where he stopped. And he won his last seven starts. He won 21, had two no-hitters, which really should have been three, and struck out 383. That's an unbelievable record.

Despite the DH, designed to add offense to the game, Ryan was one of 12 20-game winners in the American League in 1973 (the National League, without the DH, had one).

WILBUR WOOD

Wilbur Wood, the seemingly indefatigable knuckleballer of the Chicago White Sox, started 48 games, completed 21, pitched 359$\frac{1}{3}$ innings, started both games of one doubleheader, and had the distinction of being a 20-game winner (24) and a 20-game loser (20) in the same season.

Among them, Wood, Stan Bahnsen, and Steve Stone started 112 games for the White Sox, 69 percent of their games.

JEFF TORBORG: Wilbur could pitch a lot because of that knuckleball, and because of him, the White Sox went with a three-man rotation at times. Bahnsen started throwing overhand, and by the time the season was over, he was throwing sidearm.

Jim Palmer, 22–9, was a 20-game winner for the fourth consecutive season and led the Orioles to their fourth American League East title in five years, although they failed to win 100 games, finishing at 97–65.

Charlie Finley's mustachioed Oakland Athletics boasted three 20-game winners (Catfish Hunter and Ken Holtzman with 21 and Vida Blue with 20) and the league's home-run (32) and RBI champion (117) in one Reginald Martinez Jackson. The Athletics battled each other in the clubhouse but put all internal hostilities aside when they walked onto the field and won their third straight American League West title, then beat the Orioles in the American League Championship Series, three games to two, and went in search of their second straight world championship.

In the National League, the Cincinnati Reds won the West for the second straight year, coming from 11 games behind on July 1 to beat out the Los Angeles Dodgers by 3½ games. Pete Rose, a human hit machine, rapped out 230 hits and led the league with a .338 average, his ninth consecutive season over .300. In his first 11 major league seasons, Rose had won three batting titles, had more than 200 hits in a season six times, and had accumulated 2,152 hits.

CHANGING OF THE GUARD

The Dodgers were encouraged for the immediate future by their early run and by the steady stream of young talent coming up from their minor league system. By 1973 they had completely revamped their infield.

In the midsixties, the Dodgers had fielded baseball's only all-switch-hitting infield—slick-fielding Wes Parker at first, Jim Lefebvre at second, base-stealing king Maury Wills (the first man to steal 100 bases in a season, 104 in 1962) at shortstop, and the veteran Jim Gilliam at third.

After the 1966 season, Gilliam retired and Wills was traded to Pittsburgh. He would return to the Dodgers in 1969 and regain his shortstop position through 1971. Lefebvre lost his starting job to Lee Lacy in 1972, and Parker, only 32, retired after the 1972 season. After Gilliam, the Dodgers tried a number of third basemen—John Kennedy, Jim Lefebvre, Bob Bailey, Bill Sudakis, Billy Grabarkewitz, and a youngster out of Michigan State University named Steve Garvey, who had shown in the minor leagues that he would be a dangerous and productive run-producing hitter.

Garvey had wanted to be a Dodger for as long as he could remember. Growing up in Vero Beach, Florida, he spent most of his spare time in the spring at the Dodgers' spring training base. His father drove the Dodgers' bus and would take young Steve along on most of the trips.

TOMMY JOHN: When I got to the Dodgers in 1972, their infield was Wes Parker, Jim Lefebvre, Maury Wills, and Steve Garvey. Garvey was horrible at third base. He could field the ball, field shots, but he couldn't throw it across the infield. If it hadn't been for Parker, Garve would have had 100 errors.

Toward the end of the season, they gave Garve a first baseman's glove—Parker had announced his retirement and everybody thought Bill Buckner or Tom Paciorek was going to get the first-base job—but they gave Garvey a first baseman's glove and said, "Take it over, because we have a kid down in Triple A ball who can play third." "The Penguin," Ron Cey.

Maury, during the strike, didn't keep himself in good shape and came back from the strike out of shape. He was 39 at the time, and he couldn't get his bat going, so they put Bill Russell in at short and he started hitting the ball.

Russell and Davey Lopes were both center fielders in the minor leagues. Tommy Lasorda changed them to shortstop and second base when he had them at Albuquerque. Chuck Tanner, when he was managing the Pirates, told me, "Tommy, I saw these guys play in the minor leagues. These two guys were the best center fielders I've ever seen."

Russell had tremendous speed, and Lopes played a shallow center field and had great speed, obviously, with all the stolen bases [59, 77, and 63 in 1974, 1975, and 1976], and he could go get balls.

Remarkably, that infield would remain intact with the Dodgers for nine seasons, until Lopes was traded to Oakland in 1982 and replaced by Steve Sax. In those nine years, the Dodgers would win four pennants and one world championship.

YOU GOTTA BEE-LIEVE!

The National League East was a dogfight, open to any team that could get hot or, as it would turn out, could win more games than it lost. Through the early part of August, it was a four-team race with only the Phillies and Mets seemingly out of contention.

On Friday, August 17, the Mets were buried in last place with a record of 53–65 but only seven and a half games behind the first-place St. Louis Cardinals with 44 games to play. Manager Yogi Berra, in the last year of his two-year contract and under scrutiny from the Mets' front office and their fans, looked at the standings and said to himself, "We can still do it."

YOGI BERRA: Everybody was stumbling and fumbling like they didn't want to win. We had come off a bad West Coast trip [three wins, five defeats], but we didn't lose any ground. We were still only seven and a half games out. Everybody in our division had some kind of streak except us, and I had my whole team back. I felt if we could go on a little streak, we could make a move.

That night, the Mets lost a heartbreaker, 2–1, to the Reds in 10 innings, the only run for the Mets coming on a home run by Willie Mays off Don Gullett. It was home run number 660 of Willie's career, and it would be his last. With the loss, the Mets fell 13 games under .500, their lowest point of the season. But the next day, shortstop Bud Harrelson, the glue of the Mets' infield, came off the disabled list, and his return seemed to energize the Mets.

One night the Mets were paid a rare clubhouse visit by the team's chairman of the board, M. Donald Grant, a stately and somewhat stuffy man who had made his fortune on Wall Street.

"I just thought I should talk to them," Grant explained, "to try to get their chins off the ground. I told them there was still plenty of time, that they couldn't give up, that if they believed in themselves, they could do it. I told them they had to have faith, that they had to believe in themselves."

After Grant had delivered his message, Tug McGraw, the iconoclastic relief pitcher, climbed on a stool and exhorted his teammates. "You gotta bee-lieve," he shouted. "You gotta bee-lieve."

JOE PIGNATANO: Mr. Grant came to the locker room and gave us a big spiel because we were playing terrible. So he gave us this pep talk. "You gotta believe in yourself," he says. "You gotta believe in the fellow alongside of you. All those sitting on the bench, you gotta believe in the team." Believe, believe, believe, believe. That's all he kept saying was believe.

He was walking out the door and he got just about near the trainers' room and Tug jumped up. "You gotta believe, you guys. You gotta believe." He

Tom Seaver led the National League in ERA (2.08) and started two games in the World Series against the A's.

thought Grant was gone, but he was still there, and he heard Tug and came back into the room. Tug just looked at him and said, "You're right, Mr. Grant, you gotta believe," and everybody just shook their heads. Here he was mimicking the man, and he turns it around. Son of a gun.

The Eyes of Texas Are Upon You

The Texas Rangers didn't have much to cheer about in their early days. When the Rangers signed high school pitcher David Clyde, all of 18 years old and the number one pick in the 1973 amateur draft, owner Bob Short ordered manager Whitey Herzog to immediately put him into the starting rotation. On June 27, 1973, David Clyde made his major league debut in front of a full house at Arlington Stadium against Rod Carew and the Minnesota Twins. Clyde pitched five innings, struck out eight, and gave up only one hit—a second-inning homer. The Rangers held on for a 4–3 win, giving Clyde a W and hanging the loss on Jim Kaat.

Clyde would last five seasons in the majors, going 7–18 for Texas through 1975 and 11–15 for Cleveland in 1978–1979. Like most bonus babies, he never lived up to the hype.

TOM SEAVER: Tug is one of those rare individuals in the game—not to sound negative, because it's actually a positive—who found enjoyment even in losing. He was that kind of effervescent and positive personality; even when he lost it was still a day at the ballpark and it was still a baseball game. He wasn't overly happy when he lost, but that's what you felt about Tug in retrospect. He had a real love for the youthful exuberance that you find in the game.

I was never one for hotdogging and things like that, the slapping of his glove on his thigh. My first impression was that it was hotdogging, to a degree. But you mellow later, and you see how positive it was.

He did it, from what I understand, initially with a relationship between him and his wife in the stands. He would come off the mound, and the slapping of his glove on his thigh was a signal to his wife. Then it became something bigger, and it grew into "You gotta believe," and it became a rallying cry. It wasn't hotdogging, and that's what Tug was all about. Full of this enthusiasm, and he would let it come to the surface.

To a degree, he was mocking Grant, but there's a crossover in this. The slapping of the thigh and "You gotta believe," that's just Tug.

All of a sudden, the Mets started winning, closing in on .500, and with no team in their division stepping out and taking control, their hopes soared.

One night, they came from behind with a ninth-inning rally, an important victory and a significant moment in the season.

JOE PIGNATANO: We're down a couple of runs in the bottom of the ninth. Two outs, nobody on. All of a sudden, we get a couple of base hits, a walk, and bingo, we score four runs and the other team gets beat. After the game, Yogi tells the press, "You see, it ain't over till it's over."

That, too, became a rallying cry for the Mets, along with "You gotta believe." The press picked up on this newest Yogiism. "It ain't over till it's over" came to mean the pennant race, not just a game.

When the calendar turned to September and the pennant race moved into the stretch run, the Mets were playing their best ball of the season, closing in on first place. On September 20, they faced the Pirates in Shea Stadium, a critical game as the Pirates were leading the Mets by a game and a half.

The score was tied going into the top of the thirteenth. Richie Zisk was on first base for the Pirates when rookie Dave Augustine drilled a line drive to deep left field that looked like a home run when it left the bat. But the ball hit the wall, the point of the wood fence.

A fraction of an inch higher and the ball would have ricocheted off the wall and soared over the fence for a two-run homer. A fraction of an inch lower and it probably would have ricocheted back past left fielder Cleon Jones for an extra-base hit, allowing Zisk to score.

Instead, the ball hit the point and shot up a few feet in the air, like a "pointer" in stoop ball, and landed in Jones' glove. He whirled and threw a perfect strike to the cutoff man, Wayne Garrett, who whirled and threw a perfect strike to catcher Ron Hodges to nail Zisk at the plate. The Mets won the game in the bottom of the thirteenth.

WAYNE GARRETT: When that happened, I said to myself, "This is our year. No way we can lose now." I saw a lot of balls hit that fence in Shea Stadium, and they usually go out. I've never seen one act like that.

To Harry Walker, scouting the Mets for the Cardinals, there was a simple explanation: "You can't tell me there isn't a man up there pulling the strings."

A few days later, Walker was convinced when a ground ball hit a rock and glanced off the shoulder of Montreal shortstop Tim Foli, letting the Mets win a big game against the Expos.

"You can sense when things start breaking for a team," Walker said. "Things happen that defy explanation."

Was it divine intervention? Angels in the outfield? Or another example of what has come to be known as "Yogi Berra luck"? Good things always seemed to happen to him.

———

JOE PIGNATANO: This is when Yogi was a coach and Gil Hodges was the manager. We were in spring training. There was Gil, Rube Walker, me, and Yogi. One day we left the hotel on St. Petersburg Beach, the Colonial Inn, and we were going to drop off our laundry on our way to the ballpark.

So we stopped at the laundry, we all put our laundry in, then we went to the ballpark, did our day's work, and on our way back to the hotel, we stopped to pick up our laundry.

Gil got his laundry. Rube got his laundry. I paid for my laundry. And when they rang up Yogi's laundry, a big red star came up and he got his for nothing.

———

On September 25, 53,603 fans showed up at Shea Stadium for Willie Mays Night. Five days earlier, four months past his 42nd birthday and struggling through a season in which he would bat only .211 and hit six home runs in 66 games, Mays had said that the 1973 season, his 22nd, would be his last.

After being showered with gifts, Mays walked to the microphone to address the crowd. He thanked the fans and the Mets for his night, then, tears welling in his eyes, ended his speech with "Willie Mays, it's time to say good-bye to America," then walked off the field to a standing ovation.

As they headed for the final weekend of the regular season, the Mets were in a three-team race with the Cardinals and Pirates for the National League East title.

Three Brave Men

In seven seasons in Baltimore, Davey Johnson hit 66 homers. In 1973 he tied Rogers Hornsby's home-run mark for second basemen and combined with Hank Aaron and Darrell Evans to make the Braves the first team to have three players with 40 home runs or more in the same season.

It was attributed to bat-corking or the short fences in the Launching Pad.

DAVEY JOHNSON: There was nothing flukey about it. I could pull. If you look at 1971, I was going to hit 30 homers. I had 16 at the All-Star break, hurt my shoulder, and finished with 18.

We had a good hitting team in Atlanta—Mike Lum, Dusty Baker, Ralph Garr, Aaron, Evans, and me. Hank was the greatest hitter I've ever seen. Darrell was my roommate, and I taught him everything he knew about hitting home runs.

I actually hit one more home run than Hornsby, but it came when I was a pinch-hitter.

I hit my last homer in my 153rd game. Leo Durocher said to me, "You'll be lucky if you hit 10 homers next season," and I think he told Jerry Reuss to throw at me, because Reuss hit me on the left shoulder. I was about two or three homers ahead of Stargell, and he went to Montreal and popped a few out in that Jarry Park band box, and I lost the home-run title by one.

Because of late-season rainouts, the Mets were forced to play a double-header—in the rain—against the Cubs in Chicago on Monday, October 1, the day after the regular season was scheduled to end. The Mets needed to win one of the two games to clinch the National League East pennant, a come-back as shocking and as unexpected as their journey from ninth place in 1968 to the world championship in 1969.

AL HRABOSKY: Our [the Cardinals'] season was completed and we had to stay around, because if the Mets lost a doubleheader to the Cubs, then we would have been tied. But the Mets won their first game and that was it. They clinched and we finished second.

With their victory, the Mets had completed their remarkable comeback, finishing a game and a half ahead of the Cardinals. The Mets' record was 82–79, a winning percentage of .509, the lowest in baseball history for a champion. But what chance did they have in the National League Championship Series against the powerhouse Cincinnati Reds, who won 99 games and had a winning percentage of .611?

What chance? As Tug McGraw exhorted, "You gotta believe." Or as Yogi Berra warned, "It ain't over till it's over."

THE BRAWL

The tone of the NLCS was set in the first game. Although the Mets were beaten 2–1 on solo homers in the eighth and ninth by Pete Rose and Johnny Bench off Tom Seaver, who struck out a league-playoff-record 13 batters, the Mets showed they had the pitching to stop the Reds' vaunted attack. When Jon Matlack stymied the Reds with a 5–0, two-hit masterpiece, the Mets were all even at one game apiece and going home for the remaining three games. Their chances were looking good.

BUD HARRELSON: My misfortune was that Matlack's locker was next to mine in Cincinnati. The writers were waiting for him to get off national TV, so I was sitting there and the writers I guess were bored, so they decided to ask me some questions.

"So what did you think about the Reds against Matlack?"

I said, "They look like me hitting."

That's really all I said. I didn't say anything about Pete Rose, just the whole team, that they looked like me hitting. And they did. They couldn't hit. Not that day they couldn't. This great team. The Big Red Machine.

I think it got twisted, because somebody came back and said, "So-and-so in the other clubhouse said this and that," and I said, "What?"

I didn't think anything of it, but the next day Joe Morgan came out and grabbed me by the shirt and said, "If you ever say that about me again, I'll punch you."

Rusty Staub was standing there, and I said, "What?" I knew Joe. We grew up in the same area of northern California. Rusty got in there and said, "I don't know what's going on, but Bud didn't say anything about you or about anybody in particular."

Morgan was mad. They had this buildup, and I can't speak for them about what was actually said to them by a writer or how it got twisted.

Joe said, "OK, I'm OK with it, but Pete's not. Pete's going to use it. And Pete's going to get you. He will do anything to win."

The Mets jumped out to an early lead in Game 3—a run in the first, five in the second. When the Reds batted in the fifth, they were behind 9–2 to Jerry Koosman, and you could sense a feeling of tension and frustration from them.

TOM SEAVER: I was sitting on the bench, and you knew something was going to happen. Just as a professional, you knew Rose was going to do something. You knew somehow, somewhere Pete was going to do something, because this

See Ya, Ralph

On Sunday, September 30, the Yankees finished out their season against the Tigers, but the big news was the stunning announcement that Ralph Houk had resigned as manager.

Eleven days later, Houk signed a three-year contract to manage the Detroit Tigers.

RALPH HOUK: There are a lot of people that say I left because of George Steinbrenner, but that really isn't true. That was his first year as owner, and he didn't bother me at all that year, except a little bit toward the end when he decided we were going to change coaches. I argued about that because I always felt you had to have your own coaches as a manager. That started a little disagreement there.

Really, though, I had been in New York a long time, and we were having a rough time. We weren't winning ballgames. The losing and all the other stuff just got to me, the crowds screaming and hollering at me as they do, which is normal in New York, or any baseball city. But I think it's especially true in New York.

I discussed it with my wife, Betty, and we said maybe we'll retire.

I still had a year to go on my contract, and George tried to get me to stay. The fact is, he was quite honest with me. He said, "Ralph, you're going to make a mistake if you leave here. I'm going to go out and get some good ballplayer; I'm going to pay for them." At the time, I really didn't know George that well, and I thought, "Well, that's probably a lot of talk." But he did. He went out and he got Reggie Jackson, he got Catfish Hunter, and that's what won him those pennants, the money he spent.

But at the time, I just thought it was time to get out.

was the Big Red Machine and the most runs they scored in any one game in that series was two. Rose was totally frustrated, and you could see that.

I went to the clubhouse to get a cup of coffee, because it was cold. I opened the door, and the radio was on in the clubhouse and I heard, ". . . the fight . . . at second base . . . " I was in the clubhouse, one foot in the door, and I turned around and ran down the runway under the stands toward the dugout. Concrete steps. And I was wearing spikes. And all of a sudden, my feet went out from under me and my head went down, ba-rump, ba-rump, ba-rump, ba-rump. I hit my head about four times.

I ran out there and my head was killing me. By the time I got out there, it was after the fact. It was all done, and I had the worst headache in the world. I was the one who got hurt the most, and I never got into it.

BUZZ CAPRA: That fight was my big claim to fame in the playoffs. I got more attention for that. I hadn't been in a ballgame for a couple of weeks.

We were shellacking the Reds pretty good, and Pete Rose, the aggressive player that he was, came into second base hard on Buddy, who was a New York favorite. Everybody loved Buddy. And of course the size factor [Rose, 5'11", 195, and Harrelson, 5'11", 160], and there were some words said, Buddy got slammed to the ground, and here we go.

I was in the bullpen, and bullpen coach Joe Pignatano, leading the charge, opened up the bullpen gate. I was running out there, you got to be part of the team, but I was hoping, me and Buddy being the two smallest players on the team, whatever happens happens. I hoped I wouldn't get choked, but you got to go with your team.

There was a big pile-on at second base, and their pitchers were coming out of the bullpen, too. There was a lot of milling around, and just as things were about to come to an end, out of the corner of my eye, I saw something coming from the side. I saw an arm coming, and it punched me right in the ear. It was Pedro Borbon. I said it the next day, and I'll say it again. It was a cheap shot.

He apologized to me later on, but he punched me in the ear, that's how far from the side he came. My hat came flying off. Duffy Dyer saw it and he grabbed Borbon, and I got some good shots in on Pedro. Then we were scuffling, there were bodies all over the place, and I fell to the ground and I was trying to cover up my head so I didn't get kicked, and the next thing I knew there was somebody grabbing me by the back. It was Willie Mays. Of course, they didn't want to mess with Willie, because they had a lot of respect for him.

I got up and my shirt was hanging out, and Willie and Rube Walker were holding me, and I wanted to get loose so I could get a few more shots at Borbon. I was infuriated. My hat came off, and Borbon, in a rage on his way back to the dugout, picked my hat up by mistake and put it on his head. One of his teammates pointed to the hat, and Pedro took it off his head, looked at it, and took a big bite out of it. Ripped it into three pieces. I still have that hat.

SPARKY ANDERSON: I think Pete was a little teed off about how things were going. I don't think Harrelson meant anything. It was a tough, hard slide, maybe a little harder than was necessary. I'm glad nothing really happened between those two because of the size of them; that's not a fair fight.

It got ugly because a couple of guys did things they shouldn't have, and one of them was mine, Borbon. My God, you don't come in from the bullpen and coldcock somebody who's not looking at you. In all fairness, that wasn't done right. That poor guy, I was right near it, and I heard the splat.

JACK LANG: After the fight, the Reds were on the field and fans were throwing all kinds of garbage onto the field. Somebody threw a whiskey bottle out of the stands at Pete Rose standing in left field. It just missed his head and landed on the field. When that happened, Chub Feeney, the National League president, who was sitting near the Mets dugout, asked Yogi to go out to talk to the fans.

They made an announcement on the PA that if the fans didn't stop, the Mets would forfeit the game. So Yogi went out with Willie Mays, Tom Seaver, Rusty Staub, and Cleon Jones, and they pleaded with the fans to stop or they'd lose the game.

BUD HARRELSON: Everybody in the world, when they hear Pete Rose or Bud Harrelson, that's what they remember. It wasn't as big a thing as it became. He used it, and we've talked about it. I did call him some names, and he said I didn't know him well enough to call him those names.

I talk to kids, and they'll say, "My dad tells me you had a fight with Pete Rose. Do you want to tell us about that?" I say, "Yeah, I hit him with my best punch," and everybody says "Yeahhh." And I say, "Yeah, I hit him in the fist with my eye."

That gets them off of it, because it wasn't a big thing. It was big in the sense that we were pitching, and Pete was trying to get his team motivated. He won the next game with a home run in the twelfth off Harry Parker.

But the fight was nothing. I've always liked Pete. We disagreed then. My brother beat me up many times. Right from the beginning, Pete and Tommy Helms were kind of mentors to me. When I first came up, they watched me, they saw my enthusiasm, they saw me struggle, and they encouraged me. They said relax and they told me a couple of things to help me, and I never forgot that. Even though I'm in this with Pete, I never forgot that. I had a lot of respect for the guy, except I didn't like what was going on. I got hit after the play was over.

We did a card show together in 1995, and we signed those pictures. I signed a picture to him that said, "I'll never mess with the hit man again," and he signed one to me that said, "Thanks for making me famous."

PETE ROSE: I gave him my little pop-up slide. Buddy says to me, "You blankety-blank," and I told him, "Hey, you don't know me well enough to say that." I grabbed him, and Wayne Garrett came tumbling into me from third and all hell broke loose.

The next day I felt like I was playing the whole city of New York. I can't tell you what it felt like going around the bases that day after hitting that home run [in the twelfth inning off Harry Parker].

With the series tied at two games each, Tom Seaver, who had allowed two runs in the first game and lost, allowed two runs in Game 5. This time, the Mets supported him with a 13-hit attack and Tug McGraw got the final two outs in a 7–2 victory. The Mets had pulled off another miracle.

PETE ROSE: Right there at the end of the game, that's the most scared I've ever been in my life. Two outs, I was on first base. Dan Driessen up. The Mets fans were ready to come out on the field, because the Mets were way ahead and they were going to win the damn series. I know that if Driessen made out, I was still gonna be on the field when the fans came. I looked over at our dugout and saw seven or eight of our players on the top step with bats in their hands, just in case anything happened.

Driessen made out and I was just around second base at the time and, I promise you, the fastest I've ever run on a ballfield was from second base to the third-base dugout that day at Shea Stadium. I was thinking, "That's what they mean when they talk about running for your life."

Now the whole world was believing in the Mets. But did the Mets have one miracle left to use against the powerful Oakland Athletics in the World Series?

ONE MORE MIRACLE?

The Mets started the World Series exactly as they had started the National League Championship Series, losing 2–1 as Ken Holtzman, Rollie Fingers, and Darold Knowles combined to outpitch Jon Matlack and Tug McGraw.

With 1973 being the first season the designated hitter was used in the American League, and the National League remaining adamant against the rule, the NL refused to bend on allowing the DH in the World Series. Not until 1976 would there be a compromise, with the DH used in World Series games played in American League ballparks. But for this year, the DH was out of the World Series.

That put Oakland pitchers, who had not hit all season, at a disadvantage. But in his first at-bat, Ken Holtzman doubled in the third inning and ignited the A's game-winning, two-run rally. Oakland pitchers would get three hits for the Series; Mets pitchers would get two.

The Mets evened the Series in Game 2, an affair filled with controversy, drama, and historical significance. At the time it was the longest game in World Series history, four hours and 13 minutes, and it was decided in dramatic and bizarre fashion in the twelfth inning.

Oakland scored two in the bottom of the ninth to tie the game at 6–6. Then, in the twelfth, with two on and two out, Willie Mays lined a single to center to drive in the go-ahead run. It would be the final hit in the legendary career of the great Mays, who would retire after the Series with 3,305 hits and 661 home runs, postseason play included.

After a single by Cleon Jones loaded the bases, John Milner followed with a bouncer to second baseman Mike Andrews, who let the ball go through his legs for an error, allowing two more runs to score. On the next play Andrews threw high to first base for another error, and the Mets had their fourth run of the inning and a 10-7 victory to even the Series.

The next day, commissioner Bowie Kuhn received a letter from the Oakland team physician stating that Andrews had a chronic shoulder injury and requesting that he be replaced for the balance of the Series by Manny Trillo. Kuhn immediately saw through the ruse, recognizing that Oakland owner Charlie Finley was up to his old, cruel tricks. He wanted to "fire" Andrews for making two errors and costing the A's the game. Kuhn said he would allow the change if the Mets agreed, but Mets general manager Bob Scheffing declined to grant permission for the switch, and with good reason.

RAY FOSSE: We were on our bus at the arena getting ready to take the buses to the airport to fly to New York, and we were all sitting in the bus, family, everybody ready to go, and what's the holdup because everybody was there? Somebody said, "They just released Mike Andrews," and man, you talk about a bunch of guys getting upset. You gotta be kidding me.

We went to New York the next day for the workout, and every one of us put black armbands on the sleeves of our uniforms with the No. 19. And with the New York media, you know how that went over. And Charlie just went absolutely berserk when he saw that.

Before Game 3, [manager] Dick Williams called a clubhouse meeting, and we all figured it was just about, hey, it's one-to-one in the Series, it's going to be a tough three games in New York. But the first words out of his mouth were, "I've had it. I'm going to quit at the end of the World Series, regardless of what happens."

You talk about mouths dropping. Here's your manager who's already won one World Series and he's three games away from winning another one, and he says, "I'm quitting."

BOWIE KUHN: It [Finley trying to replace Andrews on the roster] was an attempt to circumvent the rule, and it was an attempt to embarrass the

Reggie Jackson hit a two-run home run in Game 7 to help propel Oakland to their second consecutive championship.

ballplayer. Charlie was just burned up and he was going to embarrass Andrews, and I wasn't going to have any part of it.

Andrews remained on the Oakland roster for the World Series, and Kuhn would fine Finley $5,000 for his attempt to bend the rules.

Back in New York for Game 3, the Athletics again took the lead in the Series with a 3–2 victory as Tom Seaver, once again, suffered from lack of support. He struck out 12 A's in eight innings but left for a pinch-hitter in the bottom of the eighth with the score tied, 2–2. Oakland pushed over the winning run against Harry Parker in the eleventh. A historic note was Mays' final at-bat in the major leagues. He pinch hit for McGraw in the tenth, and history will note that the last at-bat of his sensational career regrettably was a weak ground ball to short.

Again, the Mets came back, winning Game 4, 6–1, behind Matlack. In the top of the eighth, Dick Williams made a grand and compassionate gesture by sending Mike Andrews up to pinch hit for Horacio Pina.

RAY FOSSE: I don't think any manager would pinch hit Mike Andrews, because he was a good second baseman but, as a hitter, probably secondary. But Dick Williams sent him up to pinch hit, and the standing ovation he got in New York, to see those people stand and cheer, I still get goose bumps thinking about it. But that was Dick Williams.

The Mets had jumped out to a three-run lead in the first on a three-run homer by Rusty Staub, who was playing with a severely bruised elbow he had injured crashing into the right-field wall making an eleventh-inning catch against the Reds' Dan Driessen in the fourth game of the National League Championship Series. The injury kept Staub out of the final game of the Championship Series and the first game of the World Series. When he came back in Game 2, he had to toss the ball underhand. The injury didn't affect his hitting, however.

After his homer off Ken Holtzman, Staub singled home two more runs in the fourth. He would end the game with three singles, a homer, and five RBIs, and for the Series, he would lead all batters with a .423 average and 11 hits and tie Reggie Jackson with six RBIs.

Daniel Joseph "Rusty" Staub had come up to the Houston Colt .45s in 1963 as a kid of 19 years. After six seasons in Houston, he was traded to Montreal, where he became a hero in French-speaking Canada, dubbed "Le Grande Orange" because of his red hair. Three years later, on April 5, 1972, he was traded to the Mets for three prospects: Mike Jorgensen, Ken Singleton, and Tim Foli.

Staub was the missing piece in the puzzle that would push the Mets to the 1973 National League pennant, a professional hitter who would deliver a .279 average, 15 home runs, and 76 runs batted in.

After four seasons in New York, he would be traded again, to Detroit. After three and a half seasons in Detroit, he returned to Montreal for 38 games in 1979, spent a year in Texas, then returned to the Mets for the final five seasons of a distinguished 23-year career in which he amassed 2,716 hits, 292 home runs, and 1,466 RBIs in the regular season.

When his playing days were over, Staub, who was born in New Orleans, settled in New York, where he became a restaurateur, bon vivant, raconteur, television personality, and one of the most popular men about town.

BUD HARRELSON: Players used to complain about Rusty because he would get his feet wrapped. I used to hear that stuff all the time. "He can't run, why's he taping his ankles?" And I'd say, "He hits .300; maybe you should tape your ankles." He's got bad ankles, let him get them taped. As if getting them taped would make him like a racehorse and he was going to run faster.

The Mets won Game 5, 2–0, behind Koosman and McGraw, then went back to Oakland needing one win in two games to complete their second miracle in five years. But Oakland would not roll over. Again Seaver suffered from lack of support. When he left for a pinch-hitter in the eighth, he trailed 2–0 on a pair of RBI doubles by Reggie Jackson. The A's won, 3–1, behind the stellar pitching of Catfish Hunter, and forced a sudden-death seventh game.

Jon Matlack, who had pitched so brilliantly in the Championship Series and World Series, had nothing. He was tagged for a pair of two-run homers in the third by Bert Campaneris and Jackson. The Athletics wrapped up the Series with a 5–2 victory and became the first team since the 1961–1962 Yankees to repeat as world champions.

Minutes after the final out, while his players were celebrating their championship, Oakland manager Dick Williams, true to his word, announced his resignation.

Ralph Houk was replaced as Yankees manager by Bill Virdon, pictured here, who led New York to 89 victories and a second-place finish in 1974.

CHAPTER 5

THE FIFTH INNING

1974

THE REVOLVING DOOR

With the new year came a new American League president, longtime baseball executive Lee MacPhail having replaced Hall of Fame shortstop Joe Cronin, who retired. It also brought the first of what was to be a nonstop revolving door of Yankees managers during the reign of George M. Steinbrenner.

When Dick Williams announced his resignation as manager of the Oakland Athletics minutes after his team had won its second straight world championship, Steinbrenner moved swiftly to sign Williams and bring him to New York as a replacement for Ralph Houk.

As renovation had begun on Yankee Stadium, the Yankees had moved their offices to their temporary home, Shea Stadium, which they would share with the New York Mets. Just before the end of the old year, the Yankees had staged a gala press conference at a restaurant near Shea Stadium, on the site of the 1964–65 World's Fair in Flushing Meadows, Queens, where Williams was introduced as the new manager of the Yankees—it presumably having escaped Steinbrenner's notice that Williams was still under contract to Oakland. But it did not escape the notice of Charles Finley, who held that contract.

Never one to stand in a man's way—or to let an opportunity pass to get the upper hand on one of his fellow owners—Finley magnanimously said he would agree to let Williams out of his contract on the condition that the Yankees compensate him with two young players. Scott McGregor was a 20-year-old left-handed pitcher who had been the Yankees' number one pick in the June 1972 free agent draft and had won 12 games for Double A West Haven in 1973. Otoniel "Otto" Velez was a 23-year-old outfielder from Puerto Rico who had batted .269 with 29 homers and 98 RBIs, for Triple A Syracuse.

The Yankees balked at the demand. "We're not going to mortgage our future," said Yankees president Gabe Paul. "McGregor and Velez are our crown jewels, and we're not going to give them up."

But Finley held firm on his demand, and the Yankees gave up on Williams and searched for another manager. (McGregor would eventually be traded to Baltimore, where he won 138 games in a 13-year career, including 20 in 1980. Velez, the other crown jewel, would bounce around from New York to Toronto to Cleveland, batting .251, hitting 78 home runs in 11 seasons, and never living up to his potential. By 1984 he would be out of baseball.)

To fill the manager vacancy, the Yankees chose Bill Virdon. Although he had spent his entire career in the National League, Virdon was not without a Yankees connection. Originally signed by the Yankees, he was traded from their minor league system to the St. Louis Cardinals in 1954 for veteran outfielder Enos Slaughter. The Cardinals, in turn, traded Virdon to Pittsburgh in 1956, and four years later he was the regular center fielder for the Pirates when they defeated the Yankees in the 1960 World Series.

It was, in fact, a ground ball hit by Virdon in the eighth inning of Game 7 with the Pirates trailing 7–4 that hit a pebble, jumped up, and caught Yankees shortstop Tony Kubek in the Adam's apple. It opened the gates for the Pirates to score five runs, then eventually win the climactic game, and the Series, on Bill Mazeroski's dramatic home run off Ralph Terry in the bottom of the ninth.

After he retired as a player in 1968, Virdon served as a Pirates coach until 1972, when he was named to replace the retiring Danny Murtaugh as the team's manager. In his first season, Virdon led the Pirates to a division title but was beaten by the Reds in the National League Championship Series.

With the Pirates a disappointing third in September of 1973, Virdon was fired and replaced by the man he had succeeded, Murtaugh.

Still eager to manage, Virdon accepted a job with Denver in the Triple A American Association for the 1974 season, but when the Yankees called, Virdon was allowed out of his contract so he could manage in the majors.

Virdon inherited a team that had finished fourth in the American League East in 1973, but had added several new faces, most notably first baseman Chris Chambliss, in the Fritz Peterson trade with Cleveland; outfielder Lou Piniella, in a trade with Kansas City; and pitcher Pat Dobson, in a trade with Atlanta. Virdon also inherited a team that, for the next two seasons, would play in a home away from home.

Before the season started, Mickey Mantle, in his first year of eligibility, and Whitey Ford, in his second year of eligibility, were elected to the Hall of Fame; Ray Kroc, who made his fortune as originator of the famed McDonald's hamburger chain, purchased the San Diego Padres for $12 million; and pitcher Dick Woodson of the Minnesota Twins became the first player in baseball history to submit his contract dispute to salary arbitration. Woodson was asking for a salary of $29,000. The Twins were offering $23,000. In a momentous and historic decision, which would become a trend and baseball's bane for the next quarter of a century, the arbitrator ruled in favor of Woodson.

MOVE OVER, BABE; HERE COMES HENRY

We thought certain records would never be equaled, that they were forever. But Babe Ruth's single-season home-run record of 60 fell in 1961, and only 13 years later, his all-time record for home runs of 714 was also about to be surpassed.

Henry Louis Aaron of Mobile, Alabama, had been remarkably consistent, hitting more than 40 homers in a season eight times and more than 30 in a season another seven times, and he had been blessed with uncommonly good health throughout his career. As he entered his 21st season, still a formidable batsman at age 40, he needed one home run to tie the mighty Babe.

When the 1974 major league schedule was released, it revealed that the Braves and Hank Aaron would play the first three games of the season in Cincinnati on April 4, 6, and 7, then play their home opener on Monday night, April 8, against the Los Angeles Dodgers. As the season approached, word circulated through the baseball grapevine that Braves owner Bill Bartholomay had decided to keep Aaron out of the series in Cincinnati so that he could take his shot at the record in Atlanta as an accommodation to the Braves fans and for the franchise's financial well-being.

On April 4, 1974, at Cincinnati's Riverfront Stadium, the Braves' Hank Aaron, in his first at-bat of the season, hit career home run number 714 off Jack Billingham of the Reds. It tied him with Babe Ruth.

When commissioner Bowie Kuhn learned of the plan, he met with Bartholomay and ordered the Braves owner to play Aaron in at least two of the three games in Cincinnati, a number based on the pattern of Aaron's use the previous season.

BOWIE KUHN: I talked to Bartholomay, and he said, "Look, Commish, for goodness' sakes, he's a great hero in our town. He ought to break the record in our town."

He was very honest with me, and I said, "Bill, I understand; that's perfectly reasonable, but unfortunately, there's an overriding concern and that is if he's such a great hero, he ought to be playing in Cincinnati. We're not doing our best to win in Cincinnati if that's so. So the ruling is, he plays at the same ratio he played the year before, which was two out of three games."

Reluctantly, Bartholomay, fearing censure in the form of a fine or suspension or both, complied with the commissioner's edict, and Hank Aaron was in the Braves lineup, batting fourth, on Opening Day in Cincinnati, April 4.

When Reds starter Jack Billingham walked Braves leadoff man Ralph Garr to start the game, the Riverfront Stadium crowd began to buzz in anticipation of Aaron's first shot at tying the record.

There were two runners on and one out when Aaron came to bat in the first inning. He worked the count to 3–1 and, with his first swing of the season, sent the next pitch on a line over the head of left fielder Pete Rose into the seats for number 714. The crowd went wild, and the game was stopped for a ceremony at home plate with Vice President Gerald Ford, who was in attendance, participating.

SPARKY ANDERSON: Jack Billingham was pitching. The first time up, he hit a home run. He got 714. I said to myself, at least we won't see him for the rest of the series. And they took him out, and I thought, in my opinion, you're just opening the season, and I think people have to realize this, he must have that opportunity for history in front of his people.

I believe it to this day. If we were in August or September in a pennant race, that has to be thrown out the window. But we had just played our first of 162 games. And, my God, that had nothing to do with integrity. If it had anything to do with integrity, that's where they did right. The integrity belonged in his place. He belonged to Atlanta. He was the only thing they had going. My God, give them something.

GEORGE FOSTER: I didn't start that game, and for some reason, I didn't place a great deal of importance on it at the time. But as the years went by, and after watching it, you look back and you feel good for Henry for doing what he did. Then you hear some of the inside stories, like Jack Billingham saying that the fans started to boo him because it was a 3–1 count and they wanted Hank to get a chance to swing the bat. Then he hit the next pitch out. It was exciting watching it on replays later on.

After tying Ruth's record, Hank Aaron still had to play one more game in Cincinnati, according to Kuhn's edict. But Braves manager Eddie Mathews had other ideas.

"We've been fair enough," Mathews said. "My thinking changed now that he's hit the homer."

Mathews said Aaron would not play on Saturday and Sunday in Cincinnati, but Kuhn held firm and forced Mathews to back down. Aaron played on Sunday and batted three times. He grounded out once and twice was caught looking at a third strike. His next game would be against the Dodgers in the Braves' home opener on Monday.

***

AL DOWNING: I didn't find out until Saturday that I was going to pitch on Monday in Atlanta. We opened the season in San Diego, and I was told I was going to pitch Sunday against the Padres, so I was focused on them. They had a pretty good hitting team—Nate Colbert, Dave Winfield, Willie McCovey, Cito Gaston—and all my attention was on how I was going to get those guys out.

On Saturday I was in the outfield, and our pitching coach, Red Adams, came up to me and said, "You're not pitching tomorrow, you're pitching Monday night in Atlanta."

It was no big deal. But the word got around, and some of the Padres said to me, "Hey, man, they're saving you for 'the Hammer.'"

I didn't think of it that way. I knew Hank had hit the home run off Jack Billingham to tie the record and that he would be going for the record against me. But I didn't dwell on that. What I was concentrating on was having to change my focus. I'm thinking about pitching against the Padres, then all of a sudden I'm not pitching against the Padres, I'm pitching against the Braves, and it changes your whole perspective as a pitcher.

***

The record-breaking 715th home run came in Aaron's second at-bat, in the fourth inning off Downing, into the Braves' bullpen in left-center field. Henry Aaron, who had endured huge amounts of hate mail, including death threats and racial slurs from some who felt a black man was unworthy to break the record of the mighty Babe Ruth (Roger Maris, for different reasons, also was disparaged when he broke Ruth's single-season record with 61 homers in 1961), was now baseball's all-time home-run king.

Bowie Kuhn, who had witnessed Aaron's record-tying home run in Cincinnati, did not go to Atlanta for the Braves' home opener, a decision for which he would be criticized. He had been scheduled for a speaking engagement in Cleveland on that day and saw no reason to alter his plans.

***

BOWIE KUHN: The part that bothered me was that I was called anti-Aaron; I was called anti-black; I was called angry at him and the Braves, and that's why I didn't show up. That was baloney. I didn't feel any need to be there every day. He had tied the record when I was present, and I felt no obligation to follow him day to day until number 715 came along. Who could predict when that would be?

And I did have a commitment to speak in Cleveland, and in those days I was very worried about Cleveland. It's hard to believe it's the same Cleveland that's doing what it's doing today.

I think I made peace with Henry. Henry and I see each other every couple of years somewhere, and he's totally cordial. We've laughed over that. It obviously was not intended as a snub of Henry. The last thing in the world I'd ever do is snub Henry. I was a great admirer of Henry's. I still am.

AL DOWNING: I knew Hank was going for the record, and I knew I would have to pitch to him. I always had good luck against him, keeping him in the ballpark. He was a tough out for me, but his hits were mostly singles and doubles. I think he had hit only two home runs off me. By comparison, Willie Mays hit many more homers off me than Hank.

My thinking was that I didn't want to face Hank with anybody on base, and my approach to pitching to him was to try to keep the ball down and away, and if he tried to pull it, he might hit the ball to the right side or to the shortstop. The first time he came up, I walked him. The crowd booed.

The next time he came up, in the fourth inning, there was a man on base, so I was trying to get him to hit into a double play by throwing him fastballs down and away. The first pitch was a ball, low, and the crowd started booing. Then I was thinking I had to get the ball up. Joe Ferguson, my catcher, gave me the target low and away, and I threw the ball right at Ferguson's right knee. It was a little bit up, higher than I wanted it, and I didn't have the velocity I once had.

People who saw the pitch on television replays say it was right over the plate, but it wasn't. It was down and away, although not down far enough, and Hank just dived into the ball, which made it look like it was right over the plate. He still had pretty good bat speed, even at 40 years old, and he reached down and hit a line drive over the fence in left center. The place went crazy.

BUZZ CAPRA: I wound up pitching in that ballgame [Capra had been sold by the Mets to the Braves in March, one week before the start of the season]. But when Henry hit the homer, I was in the bullpen, which was just over the left-field fence, in front of the wall.

All us pitchers said everybody get their own little area, and we can't infringe on another guy's spot. So I was standing in my spot, Tommy House was in his spot, Jack Aker was in his spot. We were all out there, and you could feel the electricity. The place was packed; you had goose bumps. Here I was going to be part of baseball history, possibly that night or whenever. You knew he was going to do it before too long.

We were out there in the bullpen in our assigned spots, and people were getting really obnoxious. They were throwing things out of the stands, ice and beer, and dripping stuff down right where I was standing. So I said to House, "Let's switch places. I don't want to stand here; I want to stand over there. You can stand here if you want." And he said, "OK, no big deal." So he went over there and I was standing to his right, closer to the left-field line, and I'll be a son of a bitch, it wasn't three pitches later and here comes the ball right out toward him.

If you ever look at the film and you see a guy running—that's me. I'm running right behind him. I'm right behind him when he catches the ball. I could have just leaped over the top of his head maybe and caught it, but I didn't because we each had our designated spots. I was in that spot, but I switched with House. Tommy ran the ball in to Hank, and the game was stopped. Later, House got a television set out of it from Magnavox.

TOMMY JOHN: I was pitching two nights later, but he would not have hit it off me. I would have pitched to him, but Al challenged him with a pitch right down Broadway and Aaron hit it out. Hank would have hit my pitch or I would have walked him four times, because I would not have gone into the record book as the guy who gave up Hank Aaron's home run. Pride.

I struck Hank out for my 1,000th strikeout, a Sunday afternoon in Dodger Stadium. I would get him 3–1, and I'd take a little off on the sinker and throw it out there, and he'd look to pull the ball. He would call me every name in the book.

AL DOWNING: I wasn't devastated by Aaron's home run. The one I gave up to Ken Boyer [a grand slam in Game 4 of the 1964 World Series] was much more devastating. Aaron's came in the first week of the season and it was early in the game and it made the score 3–3, so it didn't have a great impact on our ballclub. The way I felt is that it was a great tribute to him. To me, you just learn to put those things behind you. Now it's a tie score and you just go from there.

I came out of the game—it was a long game, almost four hours, with rain delays and stopping the game for a ceremony after Aaron hit the homer— and our director of public relations, Red Patterson, said to me, "You don't have to hang around here." I was talking to George Plimpton, and he said he was headed back to New York. He offered me a ride back to the hotel, and I took it.

As it turned out, in retrospect, I wish I had stayed around for the post-game press conference. I got a lot of criticism from the press for leaving, but the way I figured it, it was not my moment, it was Hank's moment. Let him have it.

Sure, I threw the pitch, but what are you going to do, bring back every guy who ever threw a pitch that Hank hit for a home run? This was a big moment, and I thought being there would have been a negative thing. There would have been questions about the pitch. The guy hit 715 home runs, and some of them had to be good pitches. They weren't all hanging curveballs. I was mature, and I would deal with it.

People remember me for giving up the record home run. They ask me to sign pictures and other things that Hank also has signed. I've done a couple of card shows with Hank and a luncheon, but not a lot. A few years ago, he opened a restaurant, and he sent me some baseballs and asked me to sign them for him. He's always been a gracious guy. He's done some favors for me. I consider him a friend.

THE DOCTOR OF KINESIOLOGY

On July 3, in the first game of a doubleheader against the Reds, Dodgers reliever Mike Marshall saved Tommy John's 4–1 victory. With his appearance, Marshall had pitched in 13 consecutive games, a major league record.

Halfway through the season, Marshall was on pace to become the first pitcher in major league history to appear in 100 games in a season.

————————

TOMMY JOHN: When Mike came over from Montreal, he said, "I want to pitch every day. I pitch better when I throw the ball often." He convinced Walt Alston that he could throw every day. Mike wanted to pitch even if the game was lost, because he felt it kept him sharper when he had to come in and win a ballgame or save a ballgame. If he didn't pitch in a day or two, Mike would come out and throw batting practice. And he didn't just pitch to one batter or one inning. Sometimes he'd pitch two or three innings.

When I was coming back from an elbow injury, Mike gave me a series of exercises to do using a shot put, and I did them right up until the end of my career. And everybody laughed at Mike. Some years later, Dr. Frank Jobe came out with a set of shoulder exercises that are almost identical to the ones Mike did, and because Dr. Jobe is a respected and noted orthopedist, they said boy this is great. But Mike gave me the same exercises and I did them, and when I was with the Oakland A's, they tested about eight or ten pitchers in their organization. I was 42 years old at the time, and they concluded by their testing that I was the strongest pitcher shoulderwise, strengthwise, and in flexibility in their organization. And I attribute that to Mike Marshall's exercises.

————————

Michael Grant Marshall was born in Adrian, Michigan, and earned his bachelor's degree from Michigan State in physical education with a minor in mathematics. He then earned a master's degree in physical education from Michigan State and a doctorate, also from Michigan State, in the physiology of exercise, specializing in biomechanics (the study of human movement with the laws of physics) and motor skills acquisition.

He began his professional career as a shortstop, but a bad back and a bad bat forced him to try pitching. Using his knowledge of mathematics, physics, and physiology, Marshall taught himself how to throw a variety of pitches, and his unique training techniques enabled him to pitch frequently.

He reached the major leagues with the Detroit Tigers in 1967, pitched in 37 games, won 1 and saved 10, and had an earned run average of 1.98. He also quickly earned the reputation of a maverick, an eccentric, who eschewed wearing an undershirt even on the coldest days.

————————

The Boss Is Silenced

On April 5, the day before the Yankees were scheduled to open the new season against the Cleveland Indians at Shea Stadium, George M. Steinbrenner was indicted by a federal grand jury on 14 felony counts in connection with illegal campaign contributions by the American Shipbuilding Company to President Richard Nixon. In an effort to keep the Yankees out of the scandal, Steinbrenner voluntarily removed himself from the daily affairs of the team, pending further investigation. That investigation ultimately led to Steinbrenner's being suspended by Commissioner Kuhn for two years, commencing on November 27 of that year.

MIKE MARSHALL: During the off-season I came up with the screwball, and you'd think, after what I had done for the Tigers in 1967, if I showed up in spring training with another pitch, they'd be happy. They sent me to the minor leagues.

I went to Seattle in 1969. "Don't throw that screwball." In fact, whenever I would shake the catcher off and go to the screwball, he had rules that he had to turn and tell the bench that I was going to throw a screwball.

In 1970 I got sold to Houston, and they thought they were getting a guy who threw a sinker-slider and I came in throwing the screwball, so they sent me out. Two weeks, I'm gone. Jim Owens, the pitching coach, said, "Start the guy." "The Hat" [manager Harry Walker] said, "I don't want him." They tried to send me down to Triple A again, and I said, "I'm not going," so they traded me to Montreal.

The expansion Montreal Expos were in their second year, playing in old, cold, antiquated Jarry Park with a collection of castoffs and kids, managed by Gene Mauch. In Mauch, Marshall finally found a manager who understood him and welcomed him—and his screwball.

MIKE MARSHALL: I came to the Expos, and as far as they were concerned, I was a has-been shortstop and they weren't sure why I was there except that I wasn't going to pitch for Houston anymore. I was going to throw the screwball, and Mauch said, "I love it."

I said, "Great, we're going to get along." He was going to let me pitch, and pitch often. He attributed it to "Well, he played shortstop, that's why he can throw every day." Well, that's nonsense. It had nothing to do with it. It had to do with me training and the fact that hitters didn't hit my pitches. You don't pitch every day if they're hitting your pitches.

A lot of guys believe in throwing a lot, but they don't know why. To believe something you have to know why, otherwise you don't believe in it, you're guessing. I suppose that makes me cantankerous, but it does irritate me when people say, "This is what you should do," and then you say, "Why?" and they can't tell you. I believe in it because I know the facts.

I don't think any pitching coach can call himself a pitching coach if he can't name the 31 primary pitching muscles, tell me their origin and insertion and their action during the throwing motion. And they should be able to explain how they account for Newton's three laws of motion in the pitching motion, and most of them can't even spell Isaac Newton. Or they don't know Isaac Newton from Fig Newton.

You got some guys who say, "I can throw every day too." Yeah, but can you get major league hitters out? If you can't get them out, you're not going to pitch every day. I always think they shortchange me when they say, "I can throw every day too." Yeah, but can you get major league hitters out every day? Satchel Paige, great guy, bless him, I'm not saying a bad word about him, but he wasn't getting major league hitters out when he was barnstorming and pitching every day. Try to do it against major league hitters in game-winning and game-losing situations and see how easy it is. That changes things.

I was battling to do what I wanted to do, get my defense set and everything, and finally, in the last half of 1971, Gene started to understand what I was talking about. Gene isn't a man who listened to his players too much. He never had that reputation of "What's a player saying?" Gene was pretty dictatorial about things. But I finally got it through to him, what I was trying to do and how he could help me instead of making it tougher for me, and it started clicking.

———

In 1972 Marshall won 14 games and saved 18, had an earned run average of 1.78, and appeared in a league-high 65 games. In 1973 Marshall again won 14 games, led the National League with 31 saves and 92 appearances, pitched 179 innings, and was second in the Cy Young Award voting. Best of all, Gene Mauch had become a believer.

MIKE MARSHALL: How did I convince him? I said, "Gene, you got somebody else around here you think can go out and do it more often for you? Well, let's find out what the limits are. What do we have to lose? Run me out there. If you see me falling apart, then you're going to have to back off. But why keep sending these other guys out there because you think I might start falling apart? Wait till I do, and then run the other guys out there."

Well, I didn't fall apart, and it probably surprised me more than it did him. I didn't fall apart. I didn't wear out. I didn't get so tired that I couldn't produce. I didn't always have my best stuff, but I still could dance. And I still could wriggle my way out of situations, and with defensive alignment and understanding of the hitters and good catching from John Boccabella I got through that 1973 season pretty good.

Inexplicably, after his spectacular 1973 season, Marshall was traded to the Dodgers for a troubled and declining Willie Davis.

MIKE MARSHALL: It was not Gene Mauch. He knew I was going to do this and more in the future. There were others making the decisions for the Expos. What was their rationale? I didn't have enough interest to try to find out. They don't hire geniuses to run these clubs. These guys don't have a clue about baseball. They don't understand baseball at all.

I've never understood major league teams' rationale. How much research and development do they have? They don't have anybody around who knows anything. If George Steinbrenner ran his other businesses with the same logic that he runs his baseball program, he'd have been bankrupt a long time ago. Most of these guys are successful businessmen because they go out and get the best professional advice they can get, the best research and development in all their other businesses, and they get into baseball and they hire Joe Schmoe, who pitched once in Triple A ball, to run their programs. He didn't have a clue what he was doing, how's he going to teach anybody else? Don't ever get somebody who's properly trained to do this.

A Real Kroc

The day after Henry Aaron's record-breaking home run, the Padres opened their home season against the Houston Astros. Ray Kroc had been the Padres owner for all of two and a half months, had seen his team play a week's worth of games that, as we have come to understand of the new breed of owner, made him an expert on baseball.

In the eighth inning, with the Padres on their way to their fourth straight defeat, trailing Houston by a score of 9–2, Kroc grabbed the public address microphone and made an announcement to the crowd: "Ladies and gentlemen, I suffer with you . . . I've never seen such stupid baseball playing in my life." When Commissioner Kuhn heard of Kroc's remarks, he ordered the Padres owner to apologize, which Kroc did.

I went out there to Los Angeles, and I found Walter Alston to be Gene Mauch's equivalent on strategy of a baseball game—and Gene is number one in my book in intelligence in running a game—and superior to Mauch in interpersonal relationships. Gene did not know how to get the most out of his players. He used fear, and fear is the last thing you want a player to have on the field. If you're playing out of fear, you cannot succeed; you've already failed. You can't create, you can't motivate, you can't innovate, you can't come up with anything new, different, positive, or better out of fear. Gene never understood this.

I wasn't afraid of him, because I didn't care. I was out there trying an experiment. I was a lab study; that's what I was as far as I was concerned. I was a doctoral candidate doing this lab study. It was my summer job that I was doing this research with, that's all I considered major league baseball to be.

It was never life or death. I never believed in the life. I thought it was all phony-baloney bullshit, and it all is. It's all nonsense. It's all toys in the attic garbage. There was never any reality in it for me. It was all silliness, and I treated it like that. And that really made people mad. They didn't understand why. You mean you want me to act like I am really important because I throw a baseball? I know better.

I didn't care about winning. That's somebody else's value system on whether or not I succeeded. I don't allow people to tell me how I succeed or fail in life based on their measurements. So winning wasn't important.

Competition, facing the best in the world, that was fun, but that wasn't the motivating factor. The motivating factor for me was could I get better tomorrow than I was today? Could I do something, learn more, train better so that I would eventually reach the very best I could be given the tools that I had? And that was the only thing that motivated me.

Obligation to my teammates? I believe that was met by always working to get better. I don't mean that I would say, "OK, I'm just going to go out there and throw a cookie pitch up there, I don't care if I lose." In fact, I thought it gave me a better chance of winning, because the thought of defeat was not a hindrance. The only thing that excited me—was I selecting the correct pitch for this hitter in this situation, and how good could I throw that pitch? That's all that mattered to me. So I would sometimes be madder after a game that we won than after a game that we lost, and people sure didn't figure that out. They'd say, "What the devil is going on now?" And after I'd lose a game, I'd be in the shower and I'd come out whistling and happy and they'd look at me like I was crazy, because we just lost.

Well, if you do everything you can do and you lose, or it doesn't work, or the things in baseball are out of your control . . . all a pitcher can expect to do, I believe, is take the big swing away from the hitter, keep the swing to a single and try to get the ball on the ground, keep the ball in front of the outfielders and on the ground. If that's what you're trying to do and you have succeeded in doing that, you've done everything you can do. To think you can strike out major league hitters all the time is wrong, because a major league hitter sitting on any pitch, I don't care how good it is, I don't care how perfectly located it is, if a major league hitter thinks you're going to throw that pitch in that location, he will hit it hard, and there's nothing you can do to stop it. They are the greatest hitters in the world. So what you have to do is anticipate what they're anticipating and not give them what they're looking for, and that's what the real challenge is.

Have you ever stood on the side watching a pitcher throw in the bullpen and not known that he's changed from throwing a fastball to throwing a curveball? You're standing there watching the fastball. That's nice. Then he throws a curveball, and, geez, that was the greatest curveball I ever saw. And then you watch him throw three or four curveballs, and, aah, that's just a good curveball. The difference between the one you thought was the great one is that you were anticipating something else.

Money wasn't important. Still isn't. When I was with the Minnesota Twins, I had a three-year contract with a fourth-year option and I wanted deferred payments, but old Calvin Griffith said he didn't believe in it.

I said, "Calvin, I agree with you. I think deferred payments are ruining baseball, but I'll tell you what I'll do. You want to pay me X dollars for that first year, that's great, but I don't need all that money, Calvin. Let me loan half of it back to you, and you pay me prime interest on it."

And he said, "Good, I'll do that."

So I not only got deferred payments, I got prime interest on it—the buffoon.

That's baseball. It was fun. I was toying with these people. It's a shame.

But Walter Alston was solid. I have never worked with a man who was so completely in control of the situation all the time like Walter Alston was. He worked with a general manager [Al Campanis] who didn't know his butt from a hole in the ground, and he finally told the nation that he didn't. And I liked Al. I can understand the foibles of people. We're all not perfect. I'm not perfect by a long stretch. I don't even want to think of the thousand mistakes I made in my life, so I'm sure not going to raise hell with somebody else because they've made some, too. But he made Walter's job difficult.

Then the Pollyanna nonsense of the O'Malleys made Alston's job difficult. Getting rid of players because they didn't suit the Dodgers' family thing. Nonsense. Get rid of Dick Allen? Are you serious? Golly, gracious me. Because he didn't fit the Dodger family thing? He was awesome, and if anybody would ever have treated him with any respect instead of trying to control him . . .

I would love to manage a dozen Dick Allens. "Hey, Dick, what do you think we ought to do today to win this game? Here's the pitcher, here's the situation, what do you think, pal? You want to just go up and hit him hard? Let me know when it's over. I'm going to enjoy watching you do this." But they didn't treat him that way. They put rules, restrictions, nailed him in, pulled him in, and he just said the hell with you. Who wouldn't rebel? I understand we should be adults and try to get over the buffoons who try to control our lives, but he said he didn't want to bother with it.

I got over it, and I acted like I played the game as best as I could, as long as I could do what I wanted to do. I didn't believe it or buy into it. The Dodgers said I had to ride a bus down to San Diego. My family was going to go down to see the zoo and have some fun. I didn't ride a bus. I drove my family down. They got mad. You know what I said? "What if my family had been in an accident and been killed and I'd have been riding on the bus?" They said, "What if you'd have been killed?" They were only concerned about the team. Who cares about their team?

That's what's wrong with major league baseball. But in Walter Alston and pitching coach Red Adams, I found two footholds. Two reality-based people who didn't believe all that nonsense about Dodger Blue and all that hocus-pocus.

I think Alston is one of the great managers of all time, deadly serious, and he didn't put up with nonsense, but he gave you room to create. Not a spitfire, not showy, not a politician, and I don't think he gets his just due. He was a physical education major and he understood a little about kinesiology, so he asked me about it. We talked for a while, and he said, "I understand you up to here, but you're getting a little bit farther than what I'm able to understand. So I'll tell you what, you just tell me when you can't pitch. I'll use you no matter what." He was ahead of everybody else I've ever talked to.

It Takes a Thief

Cardinals speed merchant Lou Brock broke Maury Wills' single-season steal record with his 105th stolen base in a game against the Phillies on September 10, 1974. He was presented with the base by Hall of Famer and Negro Leagues star Cool Papa Bell.

Marshall appeared in a record 106 games in 1974 and pitched the staggering total (for a relief pitcher) of 208 innings. He won 15 games and saved 21 and was the National League Cy Young Award winner. Andy Messersmith won 20 games, Don Sutton 19, and the Dodgers got 100-plus RBI seasons from Jimmy Wynn and Steve Garvey. They won 102 games and beat out the Reds in the National League West by four games.

THE REDBIRDS

After a poor start, the Pirates turned their season around and won the National League East by one and a half games over the Cardinals, who came down to the wire and lost for the second straight year.

Caught!

Maverick A's owner Charles O. Finley had some strange ideas about changing the game of baseball. One of them involved hiring a world-class sprinter, Herb Washington, to be the A's designated runner. However, reading a pitcher's pickoff move isn't the same as anticipating the starting gun, and Washington was embarrassed when he was picked off first base by Dodgers reliever Mike Marshall in the ninth inning of Game 2 of the 1974 World Series. The Dodgers won the game, 3–2. In two seasons with the A's, Washington appeared in 105 games, yet never batted or played the field. He stole 29 bases and scored 29 runs in 1974, appeared in two playoff and three World Series games in 1974 without a steal or a score, and stole 2 bases and scored 4 runs in 1975 before Finley's experiment came to an end.

AL HRABOSKY: We were in Montreal, the next to last day of the season, and Mike Jorgensen hit a home run off Bob Gibson in the bottom of the eighth. We lost that game, and it knocked us a half game behind. We got rained out the last day of the season, and we had to listen to [Cardinals announcer] Jay Randolph giving the play-by-play description of the Cubs and Pirates in Pittsburgh.

We already lost the coin flip, so if the Cubs beat the Pirates on the last day of the season, then we would have had to stay over to play Montreal. If we beat Montreal, we would have finished in a tie; then we were going to fly to Pittsburgh for the one-game playoff.

The Cubs had a two-run lead after seven. A two-run lead going into the ninth inning and Bob Robertson, pinch-hitter, struck out. Rick Reuschel threw him a spitter. Steve Swisher dropped the third strike. Robertson was lumbering down to first base. Swisher threw the ball, it deflected off his shoulder down into the right-field corner. The tying run scored. Robertson got all the way to third. The next guy hit a swinging bunt. Bill Madlock failed to pick it up, and we lost the chance to go to the postseason sitting in the lobby of the Queen Elizabeth Hotel.

All through the seventies, the Cardinals were very competitive. We had some great players when you think of Lou Brock and Bob Gibson, Joe Torre, and Tim McCarver, Bob Forsch. We had fun, but it was a very balanced division where usually a few games over .500 would win it, but from the Cardinals' standpoint it was extremely frustrating.

The Pirates were no match for the Dodgers in the National League Championship Series. The Dodgers won the best-of-five series in four games, holding the Pirates to zero, two, and one runs in their three victories.

THREE IN A ROW

With Alvin Dark managing in place of Dick Williams, the Oakland A's romped to a five-game victory over the Texas Rangers in the American League West. In the AL East, the Orioles came from eight games behind on August 28 to beat the surprising Yankees by two games for their fifth division title in six years.

After the Orioles won Game 1 of the American League Championship Series, the Athletics got superior pitching from Catfish Hunter and Ken Holtzman to win three of the next four games and clinch their third straight pennant.

Controversy swirled around the Athletics on the eve of the World Series. Catfish Hunter, a 25-game winner and the American League's premier pitcher with 88 victories in the last four seasons, was threatening to declare himself a free agent, charging that Charlie Finley had breached his contract by a failure to meet the deadline and pay $50,000, half of Hunter's salary, to a life insurance fund. Mike Andrews filed a $2 million libel suit against Finley for their 1973 World Series incident. Pitchers Rollie Fingers and John "Blue Moon" Odom punched each other out in the Oakland clubhouse on the day before the first World Series game. It was typical of the brawling A's style. Earlier in the season, teammates Reggie Jackson and Billy North had engaged in a clubhouse brawl.

RAY FOSSE: We were in Detroit when Reggie and Billy got into the skirmish in the clubhouse, right in front of my locker. Vida Blue stepped in to get involved and try to break it up, but he was pitching that night and I said, "Hey, Vida, come on, get out." So I tried to break it up, and I ended up injuring my neck. I shattered the sixth and seventh vertebrae in my neck and ultimately had neural surgery and missed three months of the season.

I did come back, and we went on to play the Dodgers in the World Series. We were in Los Angeles the day before Game 1. We just beat the Orioles, and we were working out in Dodger Stadium.

I was lockering beside Rollie Fingers, and across the clubhouse was Blue Moon Odom. All of a sudden, they started arguing back and forth, and I said, "Wait a minute, guys," and I started shaking and I ran directly to the back of the clubhouse. I was still shaking, and I was thinking, "Here comes another fight."

Sure enough, one guy threw a shopping cart at the other one. One guy was bleeding, one guy was limping, and the equipment manager said, "I've been in this game for 30 years, and I've seen it all, right here."

But the irony of that whole thing, when the World Series was over, and I have the picture in my den, after Game 5, we were in the press conference in the big room in the Oakland Coliseum. I was up on the podium talking, and down below me Rollie Fingers and Blue Moon Odom were sitting there, arms around each other. And here five days before, they were fighting each other.

We kind of used it. We only had two writers following us, and they realized what we were doing. We'd kid each other, which is normal on all teams. But once we got into postseason, all these writers would come around and we were doing the same thing, but instead of just playing around, we were fighting. So we kind of created a lot of stuff. We said, the media expects us to be doing this, so we created it. However, that incident in Los Angeles was true. It wasn't making up stuff when you're throwing shopping carts at one another.

For me to play with the Cleveland Indians from 1969 through 1972 and struggle to try to win, then you go from that club to a club in spring train-

Ray Fosse hits a home run in Game 5 of the 1974 World Series to help the A's to their third consecutive championship. Rollie Fingers, however, was the star and MVP of the Series, winning Game 1 and saving Games 4 and 5.

ing, and I remember standing next to Dick Green in the outfield with 10 days to go in spring training and I said, "Greenie, I get the feeling it's just kind of this lackadaisical attitude here, nonchalant."

And he said, "We're ready to go. We're going to win the division. We're going to play somebody from the East, we're going to beat them. And somebody from the National League, we're going to play them, and we're going to win the World Series again."

I looked at him, and I said, "Are you crazy?"

And he said, "No, that's the Oakland A's."

Whether it's arrogance or confidence, but for me to come from a team where you're struggling not to lose a hundred games to a team that wins all the time . . . The thing that stands out for me about those Oakland teams was to play games 2–1, 3–2, 1–0. By the time we got to the postseason, I said,

"Heck, this is like our normal season." We were playing one-run games, great pitching, great bullpen, and we were used to it.

_____

The Athletics somehow managed to put their differences aside when the games began, perhaps rallying together against their disliked and frugal owner.

Pitching would dominate and determine baseball's first all-California World Series with four of the games ending in 3–2 scores. The A's won three of them and became the third team in baseball history (the others were the Yankees from 1936 to 1939 and from 1949 to 1952) to win three straight world championships.

On November 26, Catfish Hunter and Charlie Finley met in the New York offices of the American Arbitration Association for a hearing to determine the validity of Hunter's claim. Two weeks later, arbitrator Peter Seitz declared Hunter a free agent, setting a precedent that was destined to have far-reaching consequences in baseball.

After a short moratorium, commissioner Bowie Kuhn ruled that teams could contact and negotiate with Hunter, and they beat a path to the office of Cherry, Cherry & Flythe, Hunter's attorneys, in Ahoskie, North Carolina. Every major league team, represented by its owner, general manager, or manager, and in some cases even some players, made a pitch to sign Hunter.

On New Year's Eve, some four hours before the end of 1974, the Yankees held a hastily arranged press conference at their temporary offices near Shea Stadium to announce they had won the Catfish Hunter sweepstakes and signed him to a five-year contract for $3.75 million, which was three times the salary of any other major league player and almost half as much as George Steinbrenner had paid to buy the Yankees less than two years earlier.

Having served a little more than a month of his two-year suspension, George Steinbrenner nevertheless had started to make good on an earlier promise to bring better players to the Yankees—no matter the cost.

CHAPTER 6

1975

THE SIXTH INNING

BERNIE CARBO

He was 22 years old, a handsome young man with dark, curly hair and Castilian good looks, and he was a major leaguer, a member of the powerful Cincinnati Reds, the Big Red Machine.

The year was 1970, and Bernie Carbo had it all. Including drugs and alcohol.

BERNIE CARBO: Drugs were always available. I played 11 years in the big leagues, and there wasn't a day that I played without any drugs. Amphetamines, Dexedrine, Benzedrine, Darvon, Darvocet, codeine, sleeping pills, shots. I was addicted to drugs. Marijuana and cocaine.

I lived in hell my whole baseball career. I wasn't a Christian. I didn't know God. I was bipolar, manic-depressive. I wasn't taking medication, so there were a lot of things in my life that I didn't understand. My privacy was violated when I was young, which I kept in my subconscious mind. My mother committed suicide. My dad died, so all these things were going on.

I lived in the darkness. I lived with the drugs and alcohol. I lived with the bipolar manic depression.

I went into baseball loving the game, a 17-year-old kid, the number one draft pick of the Cincinnati Reds. By my third year I was already into alcohol. I was going to be released, and I credit Sparky Anderson with saving my career. He was managing in the minor leagues, and he said, "This kid can be a ballplayer." Sparky worked with me for a whole year in the minor leagues, and I had a great year. He went on to San Diego as a coach, and I went to Triple A. He became manager of the Reds in 1970, and he brought me to the big leagues.

SPARKY ANDERSON: I had Bernie in Asheville. I called him Bernardo. Bernie had a great arm. Oh, he could throw.

I had been managing in the Cardinals organization, and in 1967 I went over to the Reds organization and they asked me to go down to the Instructional League for two weeks to sit on the bench and observe. We were in Bradenton, and I noticed everybody made fun of Bernie, the players, everybody. When I went to spring training that year, I told them, "Let me have that boy."

So they sent him with me to Asheville, and I held a meeting with the players before we broke camp, because I watched in spring training. The same thing. They were making fun of him.

I said, "Let me tell you guys something right now. This young man here is not a village idiot. If I ever catch one of you making fun of this young man, one time, I promise you your ass will be out of here so fast you won't know what hit you. This young man can play baseball, and you better hope he plays good for you guys."

It seemed like, then, everything just changed for him. He played great for me in Asheville, and when I brought him to Cincinnati, he played great for me there. He shared left field with Hal McRae that first year [1970], and both of them were extremely productive. Both of them played very well.

All that other stuff, the drinking and the drugs, had to come after he left us. There never was any of that type of stuff, and I don't believe there was anything in Boston. It had to come later, and there had to be a disaster area there, somewhere.

In Cincinnati Carbo joined a team already loaded with outfielders—Bobby Tolan, Hal McRae, Ty Cline, and the irrepressible Pete Rose.

BERNIE CARBO: I liked Pete Rose. When I looked at him, he looked like my father. Big, strong, big arms and a husky body. When you watch him work out and sweat and take hundreds of ground balls and swing hundreds of swings . . . I would get tired just watching him. I admired Pete Rose for his hustle and his performance and what he accomplished.

God didn't give him a lot of ability. He didn't run fast, he didn't have a lot of power, he didn't throw well. If any ballplayer ever made himself great through his work ethic, his work habits, and in believing that he could do

The Beginning of the End

Three years after the Supreme Court upheld the decision in the Curt Flood case, the Major League Players Association was ready to move again. Invoking a little-known and rarely used rule in baseball's Basic Agreement, eight players declined to sign contracts for the 1975 season, which forced their teams to exercise the renewal option on their 1974 contracts. Seven of the nine players would sign their 1975 contracts during the course of the season. An eighth, Dave McNally, then a member of the Montreal Expos, would retire. That left Dodgers pitcher Andy Messersmith, who would play the entire season without signing a 1975 contract.

whatever he wanted to do in his life, it was Pete Rose. He made himself into an All-Star, and he hit more line drives than you can throw.

The first day I went to the big leagues, it was in San Diego, and Pete said to me on the bus, "Come on, kid, you're coming with me." We got off the bus and we went to Kelly's Steak House and he said, "Order anything you want." So I ordered a big steak with all the trimmings and dessert, everything. Had a great meal and then the bill came and he said, "Well, kid, welcome to the big leagues," and he handed me the bill. What are you going to say to Pete Rose?

I had about $30 or $40 on me, so the rest of the trip I ate in the clubhouse. I starved myself all day and couldn't wait until the game was over so I could eat.

In his rookie year, Carbo found himself playing in the World Series and in the middle of a controversial play. Game 1 against the Orioles in Cincinnati. Bottom of the sixth of a 3–3 game. With one out, Carbo walked and Tommy Helms' single to center sent him to third. Ty Cline was sent up to pinch hit for Woody Woodward against Jim Palmer.

BERNIE CARBO: Anything hit on the ground, I was going home, keep them from making the double play. A high chopper in front of the plate, and I take off for home. Umpire Ken Burkhart was going to call the ball fair or foul, and he was in my baseline. I couldn't see home plate. Either I was going to run around him or run him over. So I slowed down, and I was thinking, "What am I gonna do here?"

I decided to go around him. Elrod Hendricks grabbed the ball and tagged me with his glove. He had the ball in the other hand. I slid and I missed home plate, but when I stood up and Burkhart was calling me out, I was yelling and screaming. I was jumping on home plate. Sparky Anderson came out and got hold of me and said, "Bernie, it's going to cost you $5,000 if you get kicked out of the game." And I thought, "I'm making $10,000 and you're going to fine me $5,000 for getting kicked out of the game?"

Sports Illustrated used the picture of my slide into home plate for 10 years. Hendricks, Burkhart, and I each got 50 bucks.

Carbo was used mostly as a pinch-hitter in the 1970 World Series, which the Orioles won in five games. In the fifth game, with the Orioles leading 7–3 in the seventh, runners on first and second and one out, he was sent up to hit for Tony Cloninger against Mike Cuellar. He hit a comebacker that Cuellar turned into an inning-ending, rally-killing double play.

BERNIE CARBO: After the game, we came into the clubhouse. I was sitting next to Tony Perez, and I was in awe of everything and I said to him, "When's our next game, Tony?"

Tony looked at me, and he said, "What?"

"When's our next game?"

He said, "Not till spring training, Bernie. No, man, it's not till spring training, the first game of spring training is the next game, wassa matter with you?"

That's how much in awe I was.

Carbo was hitless in the 1970 World Series, but he had a magnificent rookie season for the Reds, a .310 batting average, 21 homers, and 63 RBIs in 125 games. He had the makings, and the promise, of a star.

But he never again had a season like his first one. A combination of his drug use and contract disputes eroded his skills. He held out in the spring of 1971, again in the spring of 1972, each time signing for the same salary as the previous year. The lack of spring training hurt. His average tumbled to .219 in 1971, and his home runs dwindled to five. On May 19, 1972, off to another slow start with the Reds, his drug use becoming more serious, Carbo was traded to the Cardinals for journeyman outfielder Joe Hague.

BERNIE CARBO: The St. Louis organization was great to me. I loved Red Schoendienst. I loved playing there. I got to play with Bob Gibson.

I was with the Reds, and one day we were playing against the Cardinals and Gibson was pitching. I liked to sneak up behind the catcher and see how a guy's ball was moving, what he was throwing. I was back by the backstop, and, all of a sudden, this pitch went over my head about 100 miles per hour. I hit the ground, and here comes Bob Gibson, and he said, "You won't be looking again, will you, kid?"

He was the best competitor and the meanest pitcher I ever saw. He was a tremendous athlete. When you played for the Cardinals and Bob Gibson was pitching, you would dig in and swing from your heels and you would know that if somebody drilled you, or threw at you, that when he went to the mound and a batter came up, he'd hit him.

I remember going into San Diego when Don Zimmer was the manager of the San Diego Padres and he put in the paper, "I'm tired of my pitchers getting ahead of hitters two strikes and no balls and throwing a pitch in there and getting the balls hit for home runs and not wasting pitches. I want my pitchers to knock guys down."

That night I was the third batter in the first inning, and I had two strikes on me and I got drilled. From that time on, every batter that Gibson had two strikes on and no balls on, he either hit him or he threw at him. And he threw hard.

I remember a game Gibson pitched against Tom Seaver. They didn't seem to get along very well with each other. They used to say things back and forth in the paper. They pitched against each other in New York, and I think Seaver beat Gibson 2–1, and there were more things going on in the paper. When they got to St. Louis, they matched up again, and each time Gibson and Seaver came to the plate, they tried to throw at the other guy. And every time Seaver went down, when Gibson came up, he went down.

We just folded our arms and watched. The umpires were told to stay out of it. The whole game, each time one or the other would come up, they went down. No one else in the lineup, just Seaver and Gibson.

Gibson would throw at you on first base. If you were leading off first base and he didn't like that, he'd hit you. He threw a lot at Joe Morgan. There were certain individuals he would throw at. There was an incident in a spring training game, and Red Schoendienst said to him, "Bob, you're done." And Bob said, "No, one more hitter." That one more hitter didn't play too much after that.

That's the way baseball was played in the seventies. It was an unwritten rule if someone hit a home run before you, you got knocked down. If you hit a home run, the next time up, you got knocked down. I was told as a rookie that each time I was hit, I was to run down to first base and try not to rub it. Then I was to run to second base and take the second baseman out of the game. It was part of the game back then, but it's changed a lot.

In St. Louis, Carbo's career had a little resurgence. In 1973 he batted .286 with eight homers and 40 RBIs in 308 at-bats. After the season he was traded with Rick Wise to the Boston Red Sox for Reggie Smith and pitcher Ken Tatum.

NO MORE MIRACLES

After winning the National League East in the "Miracle of 1973," beating the heavily favored Cincinnati Reds in the National League Championship Series and taking the powerful Oakland Athletics to seven games in the World Series, the New York Mets went through tough times in 1974, finishing fifth in their six-team division with a record of 71–91.

Tom Seaver, who had won 60 games in the previous three seasons, came down with a sciatic nerve problem, started only 32 games, and finished with a record of 11–11, the lowest win total in his eight-year career.

Already there were rumblings in New York, in newspapers and on radio talk shows, calling for manager Yogi Berra's job. The pressure may have made Berra a little testy in the spring of 1975.

BUD HARRELSON: We had a rare night game in spring training, and a girlfriend of my wife's came down to Florida for a visit. One day my wife said, "Let's go get a boat and go out for a ride." We lived on the Intracoastal Waterway, so we just went down the street and got a boat, and we were going to spend the afternoon on the boat.

We went tooling around in this boat, and it died. Me not being very mechanical, I said to my wife, "I'm going to pull the cover off the engine and turn it over." I wanted to see if I could see anything, because it just died.

I took the cover off and turned the engine over and stuff started flying out of it. Parts, smoke. All these parts going in the water, so then I got in the water, in the Intracoastal, and you know there are stingrays in there, you know there are probably alligators in there, and I was pulling this boat to shore. I didn't have a long way to go. But it was far enough.

I finally got it in, and I made a call back to the place and they come to get the boat. This took hours. I got back to my apartment and the telephone was ringing. It was Joe Torre [who had come to the Mets from the Cardinals in a trade during the previous off-season].

Joe said, "Pee Wee (Joe always called me Pee Wee), where are you? Yogi's pissed. You're not here."

You know me. I was never late. Give me the benefit of the doubt.

I said, "My boat broke down, I just got in. I'll be there as soon as I can."

I got there, and I didn't miss anything. They had just started exercising. I busted in there and Yogi came in, looked at me, walked by me, walked into his office, came back again, and said, "Next time, get a boat that works."

THE SECOND COLOR LINE IS FINALLY BROKEN

Frank Robinson was 11 years old when Jackie Robinson broke in with the Brooklyn Dodgers. He was winding down his Hall of Fame career when Jackie died. With three weeks to play in the 1974 season, the Angels traded Robinson to the Cleveland Indians, so he was in place when the Indians decided to replace manager Ken Aspromonte.

On the Indians coaching staff at the time was Larry Doby, a Cleveland idol and the first black man to play in the American League (and second in the major leagues). Doby had managerial ambitions, but the Indians bypassed him and on October 4, 1974, named Frank Robinson a player/manager.

BOWIE KUHN: I had promised Jackie Robinson I would work for the hiring of minorities in management positions, and I did. I created a committee. It was

On April 8, 1975, Frank Robinson, who also served as the team's DH and hit a home run in the April 8 game (above), became the game's first black manager, guiding the Cleveland Indians through the 1975 season. He won 186 games over two and a half seasons of managing the Indians.

a committee of three—Peter O'Malley, Bud Selig, and me. I worked very hard on that, and early on we targeted Ted Bonda [owner of the Cleveland Indians] as a guy who would listen to us.

Ted was a terrific guy who never got the credit he deserved in my book, because Cleveland continued to flounder while he was there, but Ted was wide open to this, and we worked on him and some others. But Ted particularly, and he finally said he'd go for it.

On April 8, 1975, 28 years after Jackie Robinson broke baseball's color line, two and a half years after Jackie Robinson's death, another Robinson, Frank, was making his debut as manager of the Cleveland Indians, the first black manager in baseball history.

A crowd of 56,715 showed up in cavernous, antiquated Municipal Stadium on a cold, raw, and misty day in Cleveland. Jackie Robinson's widow, Rachel, participated in pregame ceremonies and addressed the crowd: "I want to congratulate you all for honoring yourselves by being the first to take this historic step. I've wished since I was asked to do this that Jackie could be here, and I'm sure in many ways he is. I hope this is the beginning of a lot more black managers being moved into front-office and managerial positions and not just having their talents exploited on the field."

Rachel Robinson threw out the first ball, and the game was on, the Indians against the New York Yankees.

In his first lineup, player/manager Robinson was the Indians' designated hitter and batted himself second. In the bottom of the first, with one out, Robinson came to bat against George "Doc" Medich. On a 2–2 pitch, Robinson ripped a line drive into the left-field seats. It was his eighth home run on Opening Day, a major league record.

BOWIE KUHN: It was a great moment. I was sitting with Frank's wife. The crowd went crazy, and I admit I joined in and was cheering myself.

HAMMERIN' HANK RETURNS TO MILWAUKEE

Three days after his dramatic debut as player/manager, Robinson took his Indians to Milwaukee for another historic opener. On November 2, 1974, the Brewers had engineered a trade with the Atlanta Braves to bring baseball's home-run king, Henry Aaron, back to Milwaukee, the scene of his greatest triumphs.

He was 41, his best days obviously behind him, but Brewers owner Bud Selig figured it was a way for Aaron to take a kind of victory lap around the American League.

BUD SELIG: I had been reading that the Braves and Henry were having a problem getting together on a contract. So I called Bill Bartholomay and asked for permission to talk to Hank. He put me in touch with his attorney, and we worked out a deal.

Bringing Henry back to Milwaukee was a great thrill for me. He was so popular in Milwaukee, in the whole state of Wisconsin, in fact.

After going hitless in his first two games in Boston, Aaron returned to Milwaukee for the Brewers' opener against the Indians on April 11, officially called "Welcome Home Henry Day" at County Stadium. Despite a temperature of 37 degrees at game time, 48,160 fans attended, and the start of the game had to be held up 10 minutes to allow the crowd to find their seats.

Aaron got his first hit as a Brewer in the sixth inning, an infield single. Three weeks later, on May 1, he was 4 for 4 in a 17–3 rout of the Tigers, and he drove in two runs for a career total of 2,211, surpassing Babe Ruth's published record of 2,209. (On February 3, 1976, the Special Records Committee would revise Ruth's total to 2,204, meaning Aaron actually broke the record two weeks earlier, on April 18, 1975.)

Aaron would hit .234 for the season with 12 home runs, but he was such a presence in the clubhouse, such a positive influence on their younger players, the Brewers would coax Aaron to play one more season.

JOHNNY BRIGGS: How many guys get a chance to play with a guy like that? The young people seeing him for the first time are just awed by the way he goes about everything, not boasting or drawing attention to himself.

OILED AND READY

On May 21, the Cincinnati Reds stood at 20–20, five games behind the first-place Dodgers in the National League West. That day, the Reds bludgeoned the Mets, 11–4. They would go on to win 41 of 50 games and finish with a record of 108–54, 20 games ahead of the Dodgers.

No Reds pitcher would win more than 15 games, but the team presented an awesome batting order with four .300 hitters—Joe Morgan, Pete Rose, Ken Griffey, and George Foster. Tony Perez and Johnny Bench each knocked in more than 100 runs, and Bench, Perez, and Foster each hit 20 or more home runs.

One in a Million

Bob Watson of the Houston Astros scores baseball's 1 millionth run since the formation of the National League in 1876. He touches home plate in San Francisco's Candlestick Park ahead of teammate Milt May, who'd homered off John "the Count" Montefusco. Marc Hill is the Giants catcher.

GEORGE FOSTER: We didn't have any big winners, but our pitchers were consistent and our bullpen was good. And Sparky Anderson was great as far as when to take out a pitcher or leave a pitcher in. He had great timing. We could beat you in many ways, with the home run, with stolen bases, with our defense, and with pitching.

BREAKFAST OF CHAMPIONS

In the National League East, the Pittsburgh Pirates featured a balanced attack and cruised to victory over the Philadelphia Phillies by six and a half games. With only two .300 hitters (Manny Sanguillen, .328, and Dave Parker, .308) and only one player with more than 100 RBIs (Parker, 101), the Pirates nonetheless were a potent offensive force.

Willie Stargell, Richie Zisk, Rennie Stennett, Al Oliver, and Bill Robinson all batted .280 or better. On September 16, Renaldo Antonio Stennett Porte, a 24-year-old Panamanian second baseman already in his fifth major league season, made baseball history by collecting seven hits in seven at-bats in a nine-inning game against the Cubs in Chicago. No player in that century had been 7 for 7 in a nine-inning game, and only Baltimore catcher Wilbert Robinson, 83 years before Stennett, had ever done it, back in 1892.

Stennett slammed two hits in the first and the fifth innings on his way to the record. He had four singles, two doubles, and a triple and scored five runs in a 22–0 massacre of the Cubs.

—————

RENNIE STENNETT: I remember what I had for breakfast that day: two peppermint patties.

I didn't feel like eating, and I knew that Willie Stargell would always come down 10 minutes before the bus was scheduled to leave. He'd come into the restaurant where we were having breakfast, and he'd walk around to everybody's table. He'd come over and say, "Hey, top of the morning to you," and he'd take something off your plate. He'd take a slice of bread from this guy, a piece of sausage from that guy, and he'd stop at seven tables and he'd have his breakfast.

So this day I said he's not getting nothing from my plate. All I had was two peppermint patties, and he came down and he looked at me and I said, "What's up, man?"

He called me Lucius George. There was some guy he went to school with, and he said the guy looked just like me. He said, "Hey, Lucius, what's happenin', man? You eatin' this morning?"

I said, "No, man, not today."

Going to the ballpark, the bus went down Michigan Avenue near the lake and when you get there, there's a statue in the park of a guy on a horse and the horse is up in the air and the guys always yell, "Don't look at the horse's balls. If you look, you'll go 0 for 4." So everybody looks toward the beach, every time.

I got to the ballpark, and I wasn't supposed to play that day. I had twisted my ankle, and it was badly swollen. But I taped up the ankle and I played.

The first time up, I hit a ball between first baseman Andre Thornton and the bag, and in my mind that told me that day I was gonna do good because as a right-handed hitter, when I'm hitting the ball to the right side, I know I'm hitting good. That was a shot, and it triggered something. I felt all I had to do was make contact and I was going to get a hit.

We scored nine runs in the first and after I had four hits my first four times up, somebody said, "Hey, Rennie, you might get five hits today." But I just wanted to have a perfect day, because I was the leadoff man and that's my job, to get on base, it doesn't matter how. I was the type, I didn't worry about what I did before every time I went to bat. I felt that when I got up there to hit, I'm trying to do the same thing every time and I'm not thinking about what I did the last time.

After I had four hits, I told the trainer, Tony Bartirome, to tell the manager, Danny Murtaugh, to take me out because of my ankle. But Danny told Tony, "No, let him bat until he makes an out." After the game, Tony said if it wasn't for him, I wouldn't have had the record because the manager wanted to take me out and he talked him out of it.

After I had six hits, I came up to bat in the eighth inning for the seventh time and I hit a line drive to right center, and they said Champ Summers could have caught it, but he dove and he missed it and I ended up with a triple.

When I got to third, they sent Willie Randolph, who was with us then, to run for me. Then, in the ninth inning, we bat around again. We had Kenny Brett, George's brother, pitching for us at the time. Two outs in the ninth and Kenny was batting, a good-hitting pitcher. And Willie Randolph was in the on-deck circle. He was hitting in my spot. Brett hit a rocket, and they caught it. If that ball had dropped, Willie would have hit in my spot and I would have missed a chance to get eight hits.

I didn't know about any record. I just thought I had a perfect day at the plate. After the game, they asked me about Wilbert Robinson. Wilbert Robinson? I don't know anything about Wilbert Robinson.

With their fifth division title in six years, the Pirates met the Reds for the National League Championship. The Reds wiped out the Pirates in a three-game sweep and advanced to the World Series, the third time in six years the team dubbed "the Big Red Machine" by *Los Angeles Herald Examiner* sportswriter Bob Hunter had made it to the fall classic.

THE DYNAMIC DUO

Winners of three consecutive world championships, the Oakland Athletics seemed headed for a fourth straight title, despite the loss of Catfish Hunter, who won 23 games for the Yankees. Vida Blue won 22 games for Oakland, and Reggie Jackson, then established as the most feared power hitter in the American League, tied Milwaukee's George Scott for the league lead with 36 homers and knocked in 104 runs as the A's finished seven games ahead of the Kansas City Royals in the West.

But a new star, and a new threat to Oakland's supremacy, was rising in the East: the Boston Red Sox, fortified by a pair of sensational rookies, Jim Rice and Fred Lynn. On June 18 in Detroit, Lynn belted three home runs, a triple, and a single; knocked in 10 runs; and tied a major league record with 16 total bases in a game.

TIM McCARVER: I had been traded by the Cardinals to the Red Sox in the last month of the 1974 season, and I was with the Red Sox until June 1975, so I saw Lynn and Rice break in. I had impressions of both of them. Strong impressions.

Lynn had a stance that it looked like you could never get him out. I don't think I've ever seen a young hitter look as good as he did in the beginning of the 1975 season . . . and even at the end of 1974. You hear that tag a lot, "can't miss," but this guy was something else.

And the thing about Rice, he was so strong even at a young age, and you knew he was going to get stronger; he was hitting balls out with regularity in right-center field, over the bullpen, in batting practice.

So both of them impressed you for different reasons, Lynn with the great stroke and Jim because of his strength. Both very, very impressive guys.

The rookies Rice and Lynn augmented a veteran cast that included future Hall of Famers Carl Yastrzemski and Carlton Fisk, Rico Petrocelli, Rick Burleson, and a pitching staff that included Rick Wise, Luis Tiant, and Bill "the Spaceman" Lee. On the bench was the former Cincinnati Reds rookie sensation of 1970, Bernie Carbo, who was enjoying a resurgence in his career and would bat .257 with 15 homers and 50 RBIs in 319 at-bats.

BERNIE CARBO: The Boston Red Sox were my favorite team. I fell in love with baseball again. For the first time I felt a part of the uniform. Great town, great ballpark, Fenway Park, great organization. I loved Mr. Tom Yawkey. He

Boston's Fred Lynn was named Rookie of the Year in 1975, batting .331 and clouting 21 home runs.

showed me something I don't think you'll ever see in baseball again: an owner who lives and dreams and eats baseball and sleeps baseball. Mr. Yawkey was in the clubhouse with old work shoes on, cutoff T-shirt, spit-shining shoes of players and being a part of the team. He would close the ballpark from 11:00 to 1:00 and take his old cronies out there, and he would play pepper off the Green Monster. They'd throw, they'd play catch.

I hadn't been there long and I walked into the clubhouse one day, and I saw this old man and I figured he worked there, so I pulled out 10 bucks and I walked over to him, handed him the $10, and said, "I need a cheeseburger and some fries." He took the 10 bucks and I sat down in front of my locker, and here comes a clubhouse boy with my cheeseburger and fries, and he said, "Bernie, do you know who you gave that 10 bucks?"

I said, "No."

He said, "That's Mr. Yawkey. He owns the ballclub."

Mr. Yawkey loved us, not only as ballplayers but as people. He loved us as a family. We were his children, and he treated us as though we were his children. He called me Bernardo and loved me. He was there all the time, and that's the first owner I've ever seen in the clubhouse, the first owner I've ever met. That was the first time in my life I ever played for the uniform. I played to win for him. We played as a family. Our team was a family.

I was the first player to take Mr. Yawkey to arbitration. For $10,000. He offered me $40,000, and I wanted $50,000. I lost, and I came back and went to Mr. Yawkey, who was in the clubhouse, and I said to him, "Mr. Yawkey, I want to buy a house, but I don't have enough money."

He said, "How much do you need?"

I said, "I need $10,000 down, and I just don't have it."

Three days later the clubhouse man said, "Mr. Yawkey left an envelope for you in your locker." It was a check for $10,000. I lost to him in arbitration, but he gave it to me anyway, and it was never taken out of my check.

I always used to go to the ballpark early just to be around him, to listen to him. And when he died, I cried like a baby.

No one understood that Boston Red Sox team. I've been in clubhouses even in recent years and they're not the same. There was camaraderie. When you left the clubhouse, your belly hurt, your face hurt from laughing so much.

You had Luis Tiant and Carl Yastrzemski. Nobody knows this, but Carl Yastrzemski was probably one of the funniest major league superstars that I ever knew. Comical, funny, a prankster. Always playing tricks on Luis Tiant and Tiant going crazy. Looey would always walk around with his street shoes on and a big cigar in his mouth and no clothes. He'd go, "Hey, man, what you theenk about my choe, man? Hunred and fifty dollar. Look at that crap you wear, man. Thom McAn. Ten bucks. You no have no good choe. I have good choe, hunred and fifty. Whyna spend some of dat money?"

Defense was another of rookie Fred Lynn's calling cards. He made a spectacular catch in Game 2 of the 1975 World Series against the Reds.

We'd be laughing, and then, after the game, you'd hear Looey saying, "I keel you, I keel you, sumovabitch, I keel you." And we'd watch Looey and he'd get up and go into the back room and get a hammer and he'd pry the nails out of his new shoes. Yaz had nailed them in his locker.

We were all watching this, and Looey was yelling, "I keel you, you nail my choes. I can't believe it, I can't believe it you do this to me, man. You act like you my fren an you do this to me."

Then he got dressed and he put on his new shoes, and he said, "I no care; it no rainin'."

That 1975 team, I thought at that time, was the best team I ever played on. Better than the Big Red Machine.

———

The Red Sox were led by their sensational rookies Fred Lynn, who batted .331, second in the league to Rod Carew (.359), hit 21 homers, and knocked in

105 runs (third in the league), and Jim Rice, with a .309 average (fourth in the league), 22 homers, and 102 RBIs (tied for fifth in the league). And with the rookies' performance and Rick Wise, Luis Tiant, and Bill Lee combining for 54 wins, the Red Sox won the American League East by four and a half games and took on the mighty Oakland A's in the American League Championship Series.

BATTLING BILLY

When the Texas Rangers fired Billy Martin as manager, you could practically see the wheels turning in George Steinbrenner's head. Martin was the type of fiery competitor Steinbrenner liked, a fierce battler, a crowd favorite, a manager who would keep the pot boiling. Besides, he was an old Yankees hero.

"Battling Billy" Martin, as he came to be known, arrived with the Yankees from Oakland in the Pacific Coast League in 1950 and immediately became a favorite of Casey Stengel's. The Ol' Perfesser loved Martin's feistiness and his hard-nosed approach to the game. Martin would do anything to win, sometimes using tactics that stretched the limits of fair play and the rules.

Martin was particularly effective in big games. In 28 World Series games, he batted .333, 76 points above his career average in the regular season.

Eventually, Martin's questionable lifestyle and his frequent nocturnal forays caused the Yankees to trade him to Kansas City in 1957. The Yankees claimed he was a bad influence on their stars, Mickey Mantle and Whitey Ford.

"Mickey and Whitey both made the Hall of Fame, and I didn't," Martin said years later. "So how was I a bad influence on them? Maybe they were a bad influence on me."

Martin was heartbroken when he left the Yankees. In his mind and his heart, he would always be a New York Yankee.

After his playing days, Martin managed in the minor leagues, then became a coach with the last major league team of his playing career, the Minnesota Twins. In 1969 he succeeded Cal Ermer as Twins manager and led them to the American League West championship.

As a manager, Billy Martin was certain to do two things—improve the team he managed and quickly get into a feud with the front office and get fired.

In 1969 he took a team that finished seventh the previous season and won a division title, but he was fired after the season.

In 1971 he took over as manager of the Detroit Tigers, who had finished fourth in the American League East in 1970, and brought them home second in 1971, won the American League Eastern Division title in 1972, and was fired late in the 1973 season.

He went to Texas at the end of 1973 and in 1974 improved the Rangers from sixth place to second, then was fired a little more than halfway through the 1975 season.

Now Martin was being brought back to his beloved Yankees as number one, replacing Bill Virdon, who was named American League Manager of the Year in 1974 and who would forever be the answer to a trivia question: Who was the first manager fired by George Steinbrenner? (Ralph Houk, remember, had resigned after the 1973 season, Steinbrenner's first as owner.)

In recent years, it has become fashionable for trivia buffs to say that Bill Virdon was the only manager of the Yankees never to manage a game in Yankee Stadium. Although it is true that Virdon never managed a game in Yankee Stadium, since his entire career as Yankees manager came while the team was playing in Shea Stadium, he is not the only Yankees manager never to manage a game in Yankee Stadium. The New York Highlanders became the New York Yankees in 1913. That same year, they moved into the Polo Grounds as tenants of the New York Giants. Yankee Stadium didn't open until 1923. Therefore, Frank Chance, who managed the Yankees in 1913 and 1914, Roger Peckinpaugh, who managed them briefly in 1914, and William E. "Wild Bill" Donovan, who managed them from 1915 through 1917, were other Yankees managers who never managed a game in Yankee Stadium. Their next manager, Miller Huggins, did manage in Yankee Stadium.

On the surface, the demanding, competitive Steinbrenner and the fiery, combative Martin seemed made for each other, although their combined egos would prove to be a combustible combination, too big even for New York.

Four days after the triumphant return to New York of one old Yankees hero, the ax fell on another old Yankees hero. On August 6, with his team in third place just three games over .500, Yogi Berra was fired by the Mets and replaced by Roy McMillan.

REGGIE

The best-of-five ALCS was scheduled to start in Boston on Saturday, October 4. On Friday the two teams worked out in Fenway Park, first the visiting Athletics, then the home-team Red Sox.

With his workout concluded, Reggie Jackson took a seat in the stands down the left-field line and watched the Red Sox go through their paces. Soon, a group of about eight baseball writers, of which I was one, had drifted over to where Reggie sat, as Jackson no doubt knew we would, and began to talk with him.

Jackson was almost always affable with the press and usually accessible. He considered himself a thinking man's ballplayer, an intelligent man who boasted a 160 IQ, and he liked displaying his extensive vocabulary with these men of words. He would often question the writers, about their experiences, about players he had not seen but they had, about the game as it was before he came around.

He called most writers by name, and if he was unfamiliar with a writer, he would ask who he was and what paper he represented.

Not only was Jackson the key player for the three-time defending world champions, and therefore a prominent player in the upcoming series, but he was also becoming a news story for another reason. He had made it known that he no longer wanted to play in Oakland for Charles O. Finley and he would look to go elsewhere if he was able to obtain free agency status. Rumors were rampant that Jackson wanted to play in New York for the Yankees, who had the tradition he admired and an owner who had made it clear he was willing, and able, to pay top dollar for talent.

Someone asked Jackson how he felt about one day playing for the Yankees.

He paused for a moment and then, glancing up pointedly at those of us from New York newspapers, replied, "If I played in New York, they'd name a candy bar after me."

It was a revealing comment, carefully thought out and just as carefully delivered, and it was fraught with all sorts of innuendo. It spoke of his desire to play in New York. It served as a notice to Steinbrenner (who was certain to hear of Jackson's comment) that he wanted to be a Yankee. And it told of Jackson's knowledge of history, for legend had it that the Baby Ruth candy bar was named for the mighty Babe Ruth, and Reggie was implying that in New York he'd be as big as Babe Ruth, big enough to have a candy bar named after him.

It did not matter that the legend was incorrect, that the Baby Ruth candy bar was named for President Herbert Hoover's daughter, Ruth, not for the baseball player. As far as Reggie Jackson was concerned, he had made his point.

MATT MEROLA: That was typical Reggie. He said it, nobody prompted him, it was nothing that we had discussed before. It was spontaneous. It was a beautiful line, because it said so much in so little.

Reggie Jackson had a good series against the Bosox. He batted .417, and his home run in the first inning of Game 2 staked the A's to a 2–0 lead. But there was no stopping the Sox, who steamrolled the defending champions in a three-game sweep despite the absence of Jim Rice, who broke his wrist in the final week of the regular season.

Luis Tiant pitched a three-hitter in Game 1. Carl Yastrzemski and Rico Petrocelli homered in Game 2. And Yaz, moved from first base to left field in Rice's absence, made two defensive gems and had two hits in Game 3.

So complete was the Red Sox's dominance that they played the entire three games without a lineup change. Nine players, including the designated hitter, played every inning of every game, and the pitching was handled by five men. Having dethroned the Athletics, the Red Sox went in search of their first world championship in 57 years, opposed by the Big Red Machine.

THIS IS WHAT BASEBALL IS ALL ABOUT

To open the World Series in Fenway Park, the Reds called on their left-handed, 24-year-old flamethrower, Don Gullett, who had posted a 15–4 record during the regular season. The Red Sox counted on the ageless, cigar-chomping Cuban with the whirling dervish delivery, Luis Tiant, one of the game's great comeback stories. Tiant had been a 21-game winner with the Cleveland Indians in 1968, but an arm injury threatened his career. After winning only nine and losing twenty in 1969, the Indians traded him to Minnesota. His career was believed over when the Red Sox rescued him from the scrap heap and brought him to Boston in 1971.

After going 1–7 in 1971, Tiant won 75 games for the Red Sox over the next four seasons and was their ace.

On the mound, El Tiante was a sinister and foreboding figure, a fierce competitor who belied the fun-loving, cigar-chomping Cuban out of uniform who would strap on a pair of roller skates and tool around the corridors of the stadium on days when he wasn't pitching.

He had a large belly and a barrel chest, and he wore a drooping Fu Manchu mustache and peered at hitters with piercing, penetrating eyes, all of which added to his mystique and his intimidation of batters.

He was a man of many deliveries. He might throw overhand on one pitch, sidearm the next, and underhand the next. Before delivering the ball, he would pivot on his right leg, spin completely around until he faced second base, then wheel and throw, giving the hitter the impression that he was never sure exactly where his pitches were going.

Gullett and Tiant dueled for six innings of a scoreless game. Then, in the bottom of the seventh, Tiant led off with a single, igniting a rally that produced six runs for the Red Sox. Tiant went on to hold the mighty Machine to five hits for a 6–0 victory, and the Red Sox had the jump on the Reds.

The Red Sox, behind left-hander Bill Lee, took a 2–1 lead into the top of the ninth in Game 2. But Johnny Bench opened the inning with a double, chasing Lee in favor of Dick Drago. Drago retired Tony Perez and George Foster, and the Reds were down to their final out when Dave Concepcion beat out a hit to deep second, Bench scoring with the tying run. After Concepcion stole second, Ken Griffey came through with a double to left center and the Reds had evened the Series with a 3–2 victory.

Game 3 in Cincinnati's Riverfront Stadium featured a World Series–record six home runs, but a hotly disputed call on a bunt was the game's pivotal play. The Reds, on home runs by Bench, Concepcion, and Cesar Geronimo,

Johnny Bench homers in Game 5 to help put the Reds up three games to two.

led 5–1 after five innings when the Red Sox started their comeback. They scored one in the sixth and another in the seventh on a pinch-hit home run by Bernie Carbo. Dwight Evans' two-run homer in the top of the ninth tied it 5–5, and the game went into the tenth inning.

The Red Sox went down quickly in the top of the tenth, and Geronimo started the bottom of the inning with a single to right. Ed Armbrister was sent up as a pinch-hitter for Rawly Eastwick against Boston reliever Jim Willoughby with orders to sacrifice the winning run to second. Armbrister bunted in front of the plate. Red Sox catcher Carlton Fisk jumped out quickly from behind the plate to field the ball.

GEORGE FOSTER: Carlton thought he could get a double play. Instead of just going for the out at first, he wanted to make a spectacular play.

As he attempted to throw to second, Fisk was blocked by Armbrister, who stood at home plate instead of running to first. As a result, Fisk's throw to second flew into center field, sending Geronimo to third and Armbrister to second with none out. Fisk argued that Armbrister had interfered with him, but home-plate umpire Larry Barnett ruled no interference and the runners were allowed to remain on second and third.

SPARKY ANDERSON: The way I see it to this day, and I've seen it on film, when he bunted, the ball hit the ground and went, boom, straight up in the air. If you watch the film, Armbrister does bump Fisk, there's no question of that. But he bumps him while that ball is still up there.

When he cleared Fisk and the ball came down, there's nobody there. Fisk just took the ball and threw it behind. And if you watch the film, he never interfered with his throwing. The umpire was 100 percent correct. There was no interference at the time that he could get the ball.

Pete Rose was intentionally walked to load the bases with none out, and the Red Sox brought their infield and their outfield in. After Merv Rettenmund struck out looking, Joe Morgan lined a shot over the head of center fielder Fred Lynn to give the Reds a 6–5 victory and a two-games-to-one lead in the Series.

Game 3 of the 1975 World Series ended on a tenth-inning hit by the Reds' Joe Morgan. It was just the beginning of the Series' many twists and turns.

An epic moment in the history of baseball: Carlton Fisk's game-winning home run in the twelfth inning of Game 6 at Fenway Park.

The Red Sox again relied on Tiant in Game 4, and although he allowed two runs in the first and two more in the fourth and threw 163 pitches, Tiant went all the way for the win as the Sox once more came up with one big inning, five in the fourth for a 5–4 win. Again, Tiant had a big hit in the Red Sox's rally.

Game 5 belonged to Tony Perez, who had driven home 109 runs during the season but had been hitless in his first 15 at-bats in the World Series. He ended the drought with a solo homer in the fourth to tie the score, 1-1, then belted a three-run homer in the sixth. The Reds won, 6–2, and went back to Boston needing one win in two games to win their first world championship since 1940.

Friday, October 17, was designated a day off for travel, with Game 6 scheduled for Saturday, October 18. But a deluge soaked the Boston area, and the sixth game was postponed for three days. Finally, on Tuesday, October 21, the Reds and Red Sox met in what has been called the greatest baseball game ever played.

The three-day postponement enabled Red Sox manager Darrell Johnson to bring Luis Tiant back to pitch Game 6, and he held the Reds scoreless through the first four innings, protecting a 3–0 lead fashioned by Fred Lynn's three-run homer in the first off Gary Nolan.

The Reds tied it with three in the fifth, and they grabbed the lead with two in the seventh on singles by Griffey and Morgan and Foster's two-run double after two were out. Then they padded their lead to 6–3 in the eighth when Geronimo led off the inning with a home run that knocked Tiant out of the box. He left to a standing ovation from the Fenway Park crowd of 35,205.

The Red Sox were down to their last six outs when Fred Lynn opened the bottom of the eighth with a single and Rico Petrocelli followed with a walk. But Red Sox hopes sagged when Dwight Evans struck out and Rick Burleson lined to left.

With two on and two out, Darrell Johnson sent Bernie Carbo, who had hit a pinch-hit home run in Game 3, up to bat for relief pitcher Roger Moret.

BERNIE CARBO: Darrell Johnson told me to pinch hit, but he also told Juan Beniquez to get ready. When I went to the on-deck circle I knew I wasn't going to hit, because I'm a left-handed hitter and [Reds pitcher] Rawly Eastwick is a right-handed pitcher and [Reds manager] Sparky Anderson never, never manages against the book. It's left-hander against left-hander, right-hander against right-hander.

So when I went up there I had it in my mind that I was just waiting for Sparky to come out of the dugout, change the pitcher, and I'd go sit down because Juan Beniquez was going to hit. The umpire was saying, "Come on, come on, it's time for you to hit," because I was still in the on-deck circle. I got into the batter's box and I was digging in a little bit and I was still peeking into the Reds dugout, and still no Sparky. He was gonna let me hit.

Eastwick threw the first pitch, and I swung and missed it. The next pitch was a ball. The next pitch was a ball. I swung at another pitch, making it 2–2. I was still in awe to even be in this situation. I thought Sparky sure would have brought in a left-hander.

Then he threw me a slider and I took the worst swing in the history of baseball. I barely hit it out of Johnny Bench's glove. It was in Johnny's glove, that's how close it was. The umpire called it a ball and John was arguing it was a strike and I was thinking, "I just took the worst swing in the history of baseball," and I'm like, "This is unbelievable." Then the umpire changed his call and said it was a foul ball, and I stepped out of the box to get it together again.

I worked the count to 3–2, and on the next pitch, a fastball, I hit the ball, probably the best swing I've ever taken in my career. I was rounding first base and I was looking at the ball in center field. Geronimo turned his back. I was heading for second base, and I saw the ball land in the bleachers. Then I rounded second base and I was looking at Pete Rose and I was yelling at him, "Don't you wish you were this strong?"

And Pete was yelling back, "Isn't this fun? This is what the World Series is about. This is fun."

I came running into the dugout, excited as can be, jumping up and down, going crazy, and realizing the game was tied and the next thing I knew I was out in left field in place of Carl Yastrzemski, who moved to first base. It was the tenth inning, runner on second, two out, and Dan Driessen hit a ball down the left-field line. Because of the wind and the left-field wall, a ball hit high down the left-field line has a tendency to drift back toward fair

Pete Rose dives into third base after Joe Morgan's two-out single in the ninth inning of Game 7 put the Reds up 4–3.

territory, so I went over there, the ball came back, and I reached my glove back, and the ball went into my glove. I came running in, and I was sitting next to Yastrzemski in the dugout and I said, "Carl, I almost missed that ball." And he said, "Rick Miller, left field," meaning get me out of there and put Miller, an excellent defensive player, in my place.

———

To start the bottom of the tenth, Sparky Anderson, who was dubbed Captain Hook during the season because of his frequent pitching changes, went to his bullpen again and brought in Pat Darcy, the Reds' eighth pitcher of the game, a World Series record.

Darcy retired the Sox in order in the bottom of the tenth. Neither team scored in the eleventh. In the twelfth, Darrell Johnson brought in 19-game winner Rick Wise, the game's 12th pitcher, who allowed one-out singles to Perez and Foster but retired Concepcion on a fly to right and struck out Geronimo looking.

The game moved into the bottom of the twelfth with Carlton Fisk due to lead off for the Red Sox. It was past midnight, but surveys would show that an estimated 70 million viewers were watching on television when Fisk swung at Darcy's second pitch and sent a drive high and far toward the left-field corner.

Frozen in time, and in our mind's eye, is the picture of Fisk, bat in hand, standing at home plate, his body contorting as he tries, with body language, to keep the ball from going foul. All eyes are following the ball heading into the darkness, watching it hit the foul pole, then ricocheting back onto the field, as Fenway Park explodes in a crescendo of joyous shouts and screams and Carlton Fisk is jumping up and down as he takes off for first base to run out his dramatic, game-winning home run. Joe Morgan remained anchored at his position at second base, watching closely to make certain Fisk touched every base.

The Red Sox won, 7–6, in a four-hour-and-one-minute marathon. There would be a seventh game to decide the 1975 world championship.

———

GEORGE FOSTER: I was in left field, and I caught the ball off the foul pole. It was great for baseball as far as Carlton hitting that home run and Boston winning, but it was a situation where we knew there was going to be a tomorrow for us even if we lost that game. All the delays and the postponements, we just wanted to get it over with. It didn't matter overall who won that game, we wanted that game to end because it seemed like it took so long and it was going into the late hours of the night. There was no tomorrow for them if they lost, but there was a tomorrow for us.

We weren't worried that the emotion of them winning that game would carry over to the next game. We had such confidence that we knew that in the important game, when it's all on the line, we would respond. We felt it was like running a race. The guy who's catching up, it's going to take him more energy to try to stay up, and we felt it took a lot out of them to get to where they did get and we still had energy left to go to the finish line.

SPARKY ANDERSON: My players weren't worried, but I was. Baltimore really beat us up [in the 1970 World Series]. Oakland, I thought we should have won that Series [1972] and we lost it, four games to three. At that time, the Dallas Cowboys would get there and they couldn't win, and I said, "Oh my God, they're going to be saying the same thing about me. That I can't win the big ones." It felt like the whole world had come to an end when Fisk hit that home run. Then we were three games apiece. I knew we had Gullett the next day, but anything can happen in one game.

After the game, I was walking up that runway in Boston, going to right field where our bus was. Somebody put his arm around me, and he said, "Skip, that's the greatest game I ever played."

I looked, and it was Peter Edward Rose. I said, "Peter, how can you say that? You know something, I'm not going to sleep one minute tonight, and you're telling me it's the greatest game you ever played."

He said, "I tell you what, Skip. Relax, we're going to win it tomorrow."

That's a true story. But that's Pete. He's nuts. I went back to the hotel and I called home, and my wife said, "I hate to tell you, but we were pulling for Bernie Carbo."

My wife and my two boys knew Bernie in Asheville, and they just loved him. My boys were the batboys, and they loved Bernie. Bernie gave my oldest boy, Lee, a glove, and that was a big thing. My wife thought the world of Bernie because of the way he was to her two boys.

The Reds celebrate winning one of the greatest World Series ever. It was the Reds' first championship since 1940.

Now my wife tells me she was pulling for Bernie, and I said, "How can this be? My own family. Here I am, now I know I won't sleep tonight."

Emotion did carry over for the Red Sox, who reached Don Gullett for three runs in the third inning of the seventh game on a walk to Carbo, a single by Denny Doyle, an RBI single by Yastrzemski, an intentional walk to Fisk to load the bases, then consecutive walks with the bases loaded to Rico Petrocelli and Dwight Evans. With a chance to break the game open, Rick Burleson struck out.

After that one bad inning, the Reds' confidence and professionalism took over. Shut out for five innings by Bill Lee, the Reds scored two in the sixth on Tony Perez's two-run homer, his third home run of the Series. A key play in the inning was Doyle's wild throw to first on what would have been an inning-ending double play just before Perez was scheduled to bat.

The Reds tied it in the seventh on a two-out RBI single by Pete Rose, his 10th hit of the Series. Then, in the top of the ninth, Joe Morgan came through with a two-out bloop single to center to score Ken Griffey and put the Reds ahead 4–3. Sparky Anderson's bullpen held the Red Sox to just one hit over the last five innings, and the Reds were world champions.

CHAPTER 7

THE SEVENTH INNING

DAWN OF A NEW ERA

After the dramatic and exciting World Series of 1975, viewed by millions on national television and reaching such a climax with the incredible Game 6, "the greatest game ever played," baseball should have been on the upswing, basking in the glow of its spectacular showcase event. But the game has long had a penchant for shooting itself in the foot, and trouble brewed on the horizon as spring training, 1976, approached.

In February, major league owners announced they would not open their training camps until a new labor contract had been signed. A few weeks earlier, a federal judge had upheld arbitrator Peter Seitz's ruling that Andy Messersmith and Dave McNally should be declared free agents, having played the entire 1975 season without contracts.

With a chance to peddle himself on the open market, Messersmith had an outstanding season for the Los Angeles Dodgers, winning 19 games, with a 2.29 earned run average, and leading the National League with 40 starts, 19 complete games, 322 innings, and seven shutouts. McNally retired on June 8 with a record of 3–6 for the Montreal Expos.

The owners' lockout was seen as their way of protesting Seitz's decision.

MARVIN MILLER: Their lawyers had assured the owners that the courts were going to throw out the Messersmith arbitration decision and therefore the owners should not negotiate and change the reserve clause on the basis of that decision. That's what led to the lockout. They were appealing the December 1975 Messersmith decision. Here we are in negotiations—the agreement had expired, and it's a perfect time to negotiate—and they won't negotiate a change that is at all meaningful, because their lawyers are telling them to wait for the appeal.

Bowie Kuhn stepped into the fray and ordered the owners to open the training camps, and each of them complied within 48 hours of the commissioner's directive. But Kuhn could do nothing about the Andy Messersmith case except to request a one-week moratorium before teams could contact Messersmith. Again, all clubs complied.

The seeds for the Messersmith case, perhaps the most important advance for players in baseball history, were sown in the spring and summer of 1970, when the owners and players agreed to impartial arbitration for settling players' grievances.

MARVIN MILLER: That was the most important advance up to then for the players, because without that you don't really have an agreement. You have a contract that says you get paid on the first and fifteenth and if you don't get paid, you can declare yourself a free agent. So if you don't have arbitration and you don't get paid, how can you be a free agent?

You say, "Look, I'm a free agent, this is what it says," and the league president says, "Unh-unh, you're not a free agent until I say so."

You go to the commissioner. "Not a free agent."

That agreement was not worth the paper it was written on. You can strike, but are you going to strike in the middle of the season, disrupt the major leagues for one player? No. The impartial arbitration of grievances was coming of age, coming into maturity. You now had an enforceable contract. You now had a means of seeing that what you negotiated is what you negotiated.

Its importance cannot be overestimated, yet it was greeted by the press like a lead balloon. But it was the origin of everything that took place after that, including Messersmith, McNally, and free agency. Without it [impartial arbitration of grievances], free agency never would have happened.

To this day, the more thoughtful people in labor relations keep asking, "How did you ever negotiate it without a strike? How did they give this up?" I don't know all the answers to that. You have to remember that those negotiations in 1970 continued while the Flood case was being heard in court. What's the significance of that?

One of the defenses of major league baseball against changing the reserve clause had always been "We really don't have to be regulated by antitrust laws like other industries. We have our own regulations. We have a commissioner. Other industries don't have a czar who sees that everybody does things right." And the courts would buy that nonsense.

The commissioner is just another employee of the owners, but the Supreme Court bought that. "This is regulated. This is a czar, and they have their own internal regulation system. They really don't need regulation through antitrust laws." All through the years, you look at their briefs and this nonsense was sold and never questioned.

What was different about the spring and summer of 1970? The difference was that nobody on the players' side was going to let this go unchallenged. We were going into court as the moving party. We were going to say the commissioner is a stooge. The commissioner is recruited by the owners, he's hired by the owners, he's paid by the owners, what duties he has are given to him by the owners. When a majority of them don't like him, he's fired by the owners. He hasn't got a single chance of doing anything that the majority of the owners don't want him to do.

He doesn't have one penny invested in the game. You have to be a political moron to believe he controls the game—these multimillionaires who own all the franchises, who hire him, who pay him, who fire him—you have to be an intellectual moron to believe *he* controls *them*.

They knew what we were going to say in court, so they needed a new argument—"We're not covered by the antitrust laws because the Supreme Court says so *and* we have our own internal system of regulations, we have a strong union that represents the players, we have collective bargaining contracts. If disputes arise under the collective bargaining agreement, we have impartial outside arbitration deciding what the sides must do. Both the owners and the players choose the outside arbitrator. Both the owners and the players pay him, one half each. Both the owners and the players make decisions about firing him. We are a self-regulated industry, not because we have a commissioner but because we have a strong union and we have impartial arbitration."

While I can't prove that was the deciding factor in getting arbitration without a struggle, I firmly believe that was the reason. They first agreed on impartial arbitration of grievances so they could use that as an argument in court, and that's exactly what they did.

Having agreed to impartial arbitration of grievances in 1970, perhaps as a trade-off for keeping the reserve clause, the owners had no way of opposing Andy Messersmith's claim to free agency by virtue of his having played the entire season without a contract.

MARVIN MILLER: From way back, every player's contract had what was known as a renewal clause. Almost every contract in those days was for one year. At the end of the contract, there was a paragraph that said the player and the club agreed that, by the following March 1 after this contract expires, if the player and the club have been unable to agree on a salary for the forthcoming season, the club, by serving a written notice to the player within 10 days, shall have the right to renew the contract for one additional year for any amount no less than 80 percent of the previous year's salary.

When you reached March 1, the player no longer had any options. The club then made a decision. Do I want to continue this player? If I do, I give him a notice and this gives me the right to put any figure in here as long as it's at least 80 percent of his previous salary. And it gives me the right to renew it without his signature for an additional year.

The first time I looked at that I began asking players—and, eventually, casually, general managers, owners, and lawyers—"What do you think this means?"

They said, "Well, they can renew it."

I said, "Suppose you let them renew it for a year, and you don't sign a contract, and then the next year you don't reach an agreement by March 1. Aren't you a free agent?"

By dint of much questioning, I discovered that every time the clubs renewed a player that way, they wouldn't let him into camp and into a uniform until he signed a new contract, even though he was now under contract without his signature. And that perpetuated the renewal to the following year, and so on.

That cemented in my mind that their lawyers knew what I knew—if a player didn't sign, that one year was only one year—and they feared exactly what I knew. Therefore, "You can't come into camp unless you sign the contract." And this system went on unchallenged for years.

In testimony before the arbitrator in the Messersmith case, Bowie Kuhn, the commissioner of baseball, and Chub Feeney, the president of the National

Back to the Future

To celebrate the centennial of the National League, the retro 1876-style caps were used for certain games during the 1976 season. Here the caps are modeled by Bill Robinson, Danny Murtaugh, and George "Doc" Medich of the Pirates. The Pirates would be the only team to use the old-style caps beyond the 1976 season, and the caps became a trademark of the "We Are Family" Pirates of 1979.

League—under oath, as witnesses—said that if the arbitrator ruled for Messersmith, it would mean the end of one league—the poorer league, the American League—terminate it, and several of the less affluent teams in the National League would go bankrupt immediately, and they would be down to one league. That's testimony, under oath, from the commissioner of baseball and the National League president.

Prior to Messersmith, others had played without a contract, but in each case their differences were resolved before the period by which they could have claimed they were free agents. In 1972 Ted Simmons refused to sign and was renewed by the St. Louis Cardinals. He came to terms by the All-Star Game. Sparky Lyle played an entire season with the Yankees without a contract, then signed on the final day of the season. It wasn't until Messersmith played the entire 1974 season without a contract, and played the 1975 season under the renewal clause, but never signed a 1975 contract, that the reserve clause was tested.

The irony of the Messersmith situation was that he not only was asking for a raise in salary, but he also wanted the Dodgers to include a no-trade clause in his contract, indicating that free agency was not his goal. He was happy with the Dodgers and so much wanted to remain a Dodger that he asked them to assure him in writing that he would not be sent elsewhere.

Further irony in the Messersmith case came just before he filed his grievance. The Dodgers extended an offer to him for the exact amount he had requested and they had previously refused to pay. By then it was too late.

BOWIE KUHN: What the Messersmith case did was set up arbitration. The arbitration should never have worked, because the agreement clearly said matters relating to free agency were not within the ambit of the arbitration provision. The arbitrator determined that they were, and there was no basis for that.

Major League Baseball would have been foolish to agree to an arbitration decision where an arbitrator could have wiped out the reserve clause, and it didn't. But he decided that didn't mean what it said, and he had jurisdiction to hear that case.

Because of that decision by the arbitrator, it had enormous impact on the game. It changed the modern game, and not for the better.

THE RETURN OF BILL VEECK

Baseball welcomed two new high-profile owners in 1976. Actually, one new owner—television magnate, sportsman, bon vivant, unpredictable Ted Turner, who purchased the Atlanta Braves—and one returning to the fold, the irreverent, maverick, rebellious, superpromoter Bill Veeck, who had owned the late St. Louis Browns, the Cleveland Indians, and the Chicago White Sox and headed up a syndicate that bought the White Sox again.

Veeck's promotional stunts were legendary. In 1951, as owner of the Browns, Veeck found a 3'7" midget named Eddie Gaedel, signed him to an official contract, dressed him in a Browns uniform with No. $1/8$ on his back, and

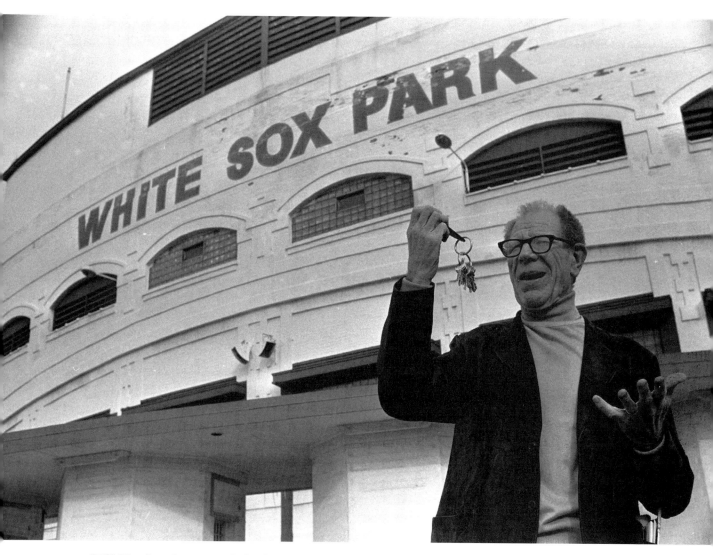

Bill Veeck, who owned the St. Louis Browns in the forties and ran them in a very unconventional way, bought the Chicago White Sox at the end of 1975.

sent him up to bat as a pinch-hitter against the Tigers with strict orders not to swing at a pitch.

Gaedel walked on four pitches from the Tigers' Bob Cain. Two days later, commissioner Happy Chandler ruled Gaedel's contract void and barred him from appearing in any more games.

In 1947 Veeck signed the first black player in the American League, Larry Doby, for the Cleveland Indians. In 1948 Veeck signed the legendary Negro Leagues pitching star Satchel Paige, reputed to be 42 years old, to a contract with the Indians.

To mark his return to Chicago, Veeck staged a stunt on Opening Day that would make headlines and be pictured in newspapers across the country. Drawing on the nation's bicentennial celebration, Veeck; his manager, Paul Richards; and his business manager, Rudie Schaffer, marched onto the field in Revolutionary War regalia—Richards with a flag, Schaffer with a drum, the peg-legged Veeck (who had lost his leg from wounds received during World War II in the South Pacific and been fitted with a wooden leg) as the wounded war hero with a fife.

On August 8, the White Sox dressed for a game in shorts, another Veeck innovation.

***

BUCKY DENT: Veeck was a guy who tried to make it fun for people going to a baseball game. He kind of overdid it a little bit, I thought, but he tried to bring that family atmosphere, do different things like making us wear shorts on Sunday and stuff like that.

He was kind of weird, but he was a guy who tried to market the game and get people to come out and have fun at the ballpark.

The players didn't resent it, except the times when it got overdone, when he had too much stuff going on. One night, when Goose Gossage was a starter and he was trying to warm up in the bullpen, he had to get off to the side because Veeck had a parade of cows and horses going through the bullpen. Stuff like that used to annoy you a little bit, but generally, he tried to create excitement at the park.

GOOSE GOSSAGE: Veeck was unbelievable. It was like a three-ring circus, and we were the third act to go on. I was the first pitcher to pitch in shorts; I was a starter that year.

***

Before the 1976 season had concluded, Veeck would bring 53-year-old Minnie Minoso out of a 12-year retirement so he could become one of only a handful to play major league baseball during four different decades. Minoso would

Baseball commissioner Bowie Kuhn, second from the right, served from 1969 to 1984, longer than any commissioner in baseball history. His successor, Bud Selig, is on the right.

get a hit against the Angels to become the oldest player in major league history to hit safely. (Veeck also brought Minoso back to the White Sox in 1980, enabling him to join pitcher Nick Altrock as the only players to appear in a major league box score in five different decades. Minoso, then 57, pinch hit twice but failed to hit safely.)

THE MESSERSMITH MESS

On March 31 the Yankees called a press conference at their spring training home of Fort Lauderdale and announced they had agreed with Andy Messersmith on a contract as a free agent. Twenty-four hours later there was a change. Messersmith claimed his agent, who had negotiated the deal with the Yankees, did so without his authority.

Bowie Kuhn held a hearing on the Messersmith matter and concluded that, although the Yankees had negotiated in good faith, the agent was acting without Messersmith's authority. Kuhn told George Steinbrenner he had no choice but to void the contract.

Four days after announcing Messersmith's signing, the Yankees withdrew their claim in a rambling, long-winded press release from their owner.

One week after the release of Steinbrenner's statement, Messersmith signed with the Atlanta Braves. Messersmith pitched for the Braves for two seasons with a combined record of 16–15. After the 1977 season, they sold him to, of all teams, the New York Yankees. He pitched six games for the Yankees in 1978, spent most of the season on the disabled list, posted a record of 0–3, and was released. In 1979 he returned to the Dodgers, with whom he was 2–4, then retired.

NOT FOR THE BIRDS

After leading the American League with 36 homers and driving in 104 runs for the Oakland Athletics in 1975, Reggie Jackson figured he was deserving of a healthy raise. He had made $137,500 in 1975 after losing in arbitration. Jackson's arbitration figure was $160,000; Finley offered $135,000, and when the arbitrator ruled in Finley's favor, Finley, perhaps guilt-ridden, voluntarily gave Jackson a $2,500 raise.

Instead of the big raise he was expecting in 1976, Jackson got a contract from Finley calling for $140,000, another $2,500 raise, which was not close to Jackson's expectations. His agent had proposed to Finley a three-year package totaling $525,000—$150,000 for 1976, $175,000 for 1977, $200,000 for 1978. Not only were the increases nominal even for those years, Finley would be assured of at least three more years of Jackson's services and his potent home-run bat.

But Finley played hardball, even with the knowledge that Jackson could refuse to sign a contract and become a free agent. Charlie O. held firm on his offer of $140,000. Reggie also held firm, but on March 1, Finley exercised his option and renewed Jackson's contract, adding insult to injury by reducing his salary by the legal limit of 20 percent, down to $112,000. Jackson had no choice but to go to spring training with the A's, but he did so confident something would be worked out. Something was.

Six days before the start of the 1976 season, Finley pulled off a blockbuster, six-player trade with the Baltimore Orioles. Jackson and Ken

Player Agents

The player's agent was another rapidly growing phenomenon in the decade of the seventies. Players had had agents, or business managers, back to the time of Babe Ruth, who employed a former sportswriter, Christy Walsh, as his business manager/agent.

But Walsh and others, such as Frank Scott (representing Mickey Mantle, Roger Maris, Whitey Ford, and Yogi Berra), were used to book commercial endorsements and appearances, not to negotiate contracts.

Before the emergence of the Players Association as a force in baseball, owners and general managers would not tolerate negotiating a contract with anyone but the player himself. As a result, players were forced to deal with a take-it-or-leave-it ultimatum and, for the most part, were grossly underpaid.

"If I ever took an agent in to George Weiss [the Yankees general manager and a notorious penny-pincher]," Mickey Mantle once commented, "he would have thrown both me and the agent out on our ear."

Years later, Joe DiMaggio, commenting on the obscene salaries being paid the modern player, was asked what he thought he would be worth in the current market.

"I'd walk into the owner's office," said the great Yankee Clipper, "stick out my hand, and say, 'Hiya, partner.'"

The first player's agent to gain national attention was Jerry Kapstein, who represented Catfish Hunter in his dealings with Oakland owner Charlie Finley and was instrumental in discovering the loophole in Hunter's contract that Finley breached, allowing Hunter to gain his freedom.

By the end of the seventies, most of the big-name stars in baseball had an agent who negotiated contracts. Today, every major leaguer and most minor leaguers are represented by an agent.

Holtzman (who had won 18 games in 1975, had been embroiled in his own contract dispute with Finley, and also had designs on free agency) were sent from Oakland to Baltimore along with a minor league pitcher. In return, the A's received Don Baylor, who, like Jackson, was on the verge of becoming a free agent; Mike Torrez, who had won 20 games for the Orioles in 1975; and a young pitching prospect named Paul Mitchell.

The Orioles hoped to tie Jackson up long-term, but his asking price of $1.2 million for five years was too rich for Baltimore's blood. It was agreed he would play the 1976 season for $190,000, then at the end of the season make a decision about his future.

EARL WEAVER: Reggie was good. The only problem with Reg was he held out. We had given up on signing Baylor, and Finley had given up on signing Reggie, so we made the trade. And when we made the trade, Reggie had the gun, and he went home and was enjoying himself at home. No spring training. I don't think he came in until the first week of May.

Reggie's agent was Gary Walker, and he wouldn't fly, so Orioles general manager Hank Peters had to keep flying out to Phoenix [where Walker had his office] to try to get Reggie. And I said, "Lookit, we're without a player. We're without Baylor, and now we're without Reggie; we gotta do something."

And Peters said, "Earl, he's way out of line. The figures are mind-boggling." "Mind-boggling," he kept saying. Well, what are mind-boggling figures? He wouldn't tell me.

He finally got Reggie to come in, and I still don't know what Reggie was asking or what we had to pay him to get him in. But we finally got him in. He had no spring training; he had nothing. And he was taking batting practice before the game; we were turning on the lights after the game so we could give him batting practice. We were rushing him as much as we possibly could. He had a terrible first half, but he told me, "I'll take this season over in the second half," and he did. He really came through strong.

John Mayberry had signed a $1 million contract with the Kansas City Royals, $200,000 per year for five years. I think we went to Reggie at that time, and I think Peters finally offered him the same deal. And Reggie said, "What's that little boy in Kansas City that just got that contract?" And that was the end of that.

That's when it all started. How did Kansas City know that you were going to have to do that? We had a guy by the name of Wayne Garland. Had to go out four times to win his 20th game, and I had to leave him in the third or fourth time. We had built a big lead, and I had to leave him in until it was about 10–6 and he got his five innings in. But we lost him anyway. That was the first big one we lost . . . no it isn't. We lost Bobby Grich the same year. Oh, my goodness.

I thought after the second half we'd try to keep Reggie there. He was happy, and I wanted him. Anybody'd want Reggie when he starts playing baseball. And a pretty good guy in the clubhouse. Except sometimes, it was like Jim Palmer, he wanted to say a little too much and do too much.

We started offering him money, but I think his designs were New York City anyway. The commercials. You know, he's smart. He probably made more money in endorsements than he did in salary. What I respect about Reggie, I think he got $400,000 a year for four or five years and never, as people were passing him up, he never asked to renegotiate.

Reggie's problem. Well, it wasn't a problem, it's just a funny thing. Dock Ellis was pitching, and he sailed one by Mark Belanger's head. And it was probably accidental, but he whistled one by Belanger's head. Belanger had to duck. Now Reggie got up and stood on the edge of the dugout and said, "Hey, you, you want to throw at somebody, throw at me." Oh, Reggie. And he did, he got him. Reggie went up there, and Ellis hit him right in the face and broke four or five bones in his face. And then we lost Reggie for another seven or ten days.

I don't remember where we finished or anything, but we'd have won if Reggie had been there all year.

PATRIOT IN THE OUTFIELD

On April 25 the Dodgers and Cubs met in an afternoon game at Dodger Stadium, Los Angeles. As he took his position, Cubs center fielder Rick Monday noticed that two people had climbed out of the stands onto the field. They were carrying an American flag, which they were about to set on fire in some protest. Acting quickly, Monday raced to the scene and snatched the flag away from the two men.

The following day, the Illinois state legislature, in a unanimous vote, designated May 4 as Rick Monday Day.

BIRD IS THE WORD

When Ralph Houk took over as manager, the Tigers were growing old, a team in decline. Hall of Famer Al Kaline retired after the 1974 season. Ed Brinkman was traded to San Diego. Jim Northrup was traded to Montreal. Bill Freehan, Willie Horton, and Mickey Stanley were all on the downsides of their careers. After the 1975 season, Mickey Lolich was traded to the Mets for Rusty Staub.

Houk was charged with rebuilding the Tigers with youth, but he had no way of anticipating such riches when he found a young right-handed pitcher in the spring of 1976. The young right-hander, just 21, was named Mark Fidrych. They called him "the Bird."

MARK FIDRYCH: I got the name from Jeff Hogan, who was my coach when I broke in with Bristol, Tennessee, in the Appalachian Rookie League. He said I reminded him of Big Bird from Sesame Street.

RALPH HOUK: My pitching coach, Fred Gladding, had seen him pitch in the minor leagues, and he said, "This kid just gets people out." He told me all about him, and, as you know, he was a very hyper young man, but Gladding told me, "Don't pay attention to all that stuff he does out there. This kid can pitch." And he could.

Among the things Fidrych did were smooth out the dirt on the mound with his hand, jump over the foul line on his way to and from the mound, and talk to the baseball.

RALPH HOUK: I don't think he really talked to the ball. He talked to himself. But as far as that went, that's great if they wanted to say he talked to the ball. Every time I used him that spring, he got hitters out. He had unbelievable control with a fastball that moved. Breaking stuff wasn't really that great, but the ball always moved. We finally decided, "Let's take him north." He had jumped the year before, I think, three leagues and ended the year in Triple A. I brought him along quite slow, and I picked places to pitch him.

MARK FIDRYCH: Ralph called me into his office and told me I was going north with the club. He said he didn't want me to go to Triple A for a month, that it would be better to go with the big club and just sit and observe. He said he wasn't going to throw me to the wolves right away. That was fine with me. I

Coming off only their second 100-loss season, the 1976 Tigers were in need of a lift and got it from an unlikely source— 21-year-old Mark Fidrych, who talked to the ball, won 19 games, led the league in ERA (2.34), and captivated the entire baseball world.

was just happy to be there, and surprised.

The older guys on the team were good to me. They took me under their wing. Joe Coleman was my roommate. Bill Freehan, Rusty Staub, John Hiller, Mickey Stanley. I was lucky to have them. They kept me under control.

We opened the season in Cleveland, and after the game, Coleman, Freehan, Stanley, Rusty, John Hiller, Dave Roberts, Jim Crawford, they came to me and said, "You're going out to eat with us tonight." We went to this restaurant, and they sat me at a table and talked to me. "This is what it's going to be like for you. This is what you're going to find in baseball. We feel you have the talent." They just talked to me and pumped me up and gave me advice. I really appreciated it. When the bill came, I put my hand in my pocket and they said, "No, save your money. This is on us." And they all split the check and wouldn't let me pay.

RUSTY STAUB: The first time I saw Mark Fidrych was in spring training. He was a pretty high-strung kid that I don't think anybody really thought was going to make the big leagues that year. He looked extremely good in spring training, and the one thing that stood out is that he always kept the ball down. And he seemed to have good control. It wasn't like he was as impressive as he got later on during the course of the year, but he was throwing the ball harder than people realized.

When spring training was over, he made the club, and when the season started, he was just a guy who was happy to make the ballclub.

The antics were real. The biggest thing about Fidrych is that all those things he did, he did all the time. That was him. He talked to the ball, he talked to the ground, he talked to the sky, I mean he talked to everything. He would fidget on the mound, and he'd go to the back of the mound and pick up mud and rub it on his hands.

Things like that were a little bit awkward for people who may have seen major league baseball and how professional it can be, but it was so real. It's almost like when people see some of the older films now and they see some of the antics of the older players, there was a thing of the past, a character of the past, like Damon Runyon used to write about in the city of New York. In Detroit, no one had ever seen anything like that. I don't think anybody had ever seen this anywhere.

The House That New York City Built

The nation was celebrating its bicentennial in 1976. The Yankees—with Billy Martin starting his first full season as manager and with new acquisitions Willie Randolph and Dock Ellis (obtained from Pittsburgh for Doc Medich), Mickey Rivers and Ed Figueroa (obtained from California for Bobby Bonds), and Oscar Gamble (obtained from Cleveland for Pat Dobson)—were celebrating the opening of remodeled Yankee Stadium. The cost was estimated at up to $100 million.

The most famous address in sports reopened on April 15. The seating capacity was scaled down from 65,010 18-inch-wide seats to 54,099 22-inch-wide seats and dimensions were reduced from 402 feet in left field, 457 in left center, 461 in center, 407 in right center, and 344 in right field to 387, 430, 419, 382, and 352, respectively, but the new model retained much of the old stadium look, including its familiar, intricate latticework facade now made of concrete and only in the outfield.

A crowd of 52,613 jammed the new stadium, its seats a bright, majestic blue, to watch the Yankees open their home schedule by clubbing the Minnesota Twins 11–4 with a four-run fourth and a six-run eighth for their fourth straight win after an Opening Day loss in Milwaukee. Already, pennant fever was beginning to swell in the Bronx, and the magic of Billy Martin had been witnessed in the second game of the season, five days before in Milwaukee.

With the Yankees leading 9–6, in the bottom of the ninth, the Brewers' Don Money connected for an apparent game-winning grand slam off Dave Pagan. Because of the raucous crowd noise, Pagan failed to hear Yankees first baseman Chris Chambliss call timeout. Martin protested to the umpires that time was called and Pagan's pitch should not have counted, and the umpires upheld the protest, nullified the home run, restored the three Brewers to the bases, and had Money bat again. He hit a sacrifice fly, and the Yankees held on for a 9–7 win. Billy Martin, who thought of everything, had struck again, to the delight of hopeful Yankees fans.

In the first month of the season, Fidrych pitched exclusively in relief, usually in games in which the outcome was not in doubt. It was Houk's way of breaking him in slowly, allowing him to get his feet on the ground, get a feel for pitching in the major leagues at age 21.

On May 15 he was pressed into emergency service as a starter. Joe Coleman, Fidrych's roommate, was scheduled to start against the Indians but was ill. Fidrych started in his place. Talking to the ball, getting on his hands and knees to pat down the dirt on the mound before each inning, he held the

Indians hitless through the first six. He would pitch a complete-game two-hitter and win, 2–1, which got his career off to a jump start.

Joe Coleman had befriended the Tigers rookie, Mark Fidrych, had accepted him as a roommate, had schooled him on major league life, and had tutored him on pitching. It is one of the cruel ironies of baseball that Fidrych would benefit from the misfortune of his friend and roommate. When Coleman got sick, Fidrych got his chance to make his first major league start and pitched so brilliantly that he got other starts. When he continued to pitch well, the Tigers needed to make room for him in their rotation, so they opened up a spot by selling Coleman to the Chicago Cubs.

It didn't take long for the baseball grapevine to spread the word of the flaky rookie pitcher with the Tigers.

EARL WEAVER: I was sitting in my office one night after a game, and Pat Santarone, our groundskeeper, came running in. He had the Detroit game on television, and he said, "I seen the damnedest thing I've ever seen. There's a pitcher that's talking to the ball." I said, "What are you talking about?" He said, "He gets down on the mound and he does everything and he talks to the ball."

Then they pitched him in Baltimore, and we never filled that park all the time in Memorial Stadium, but when the Tigers came in and they announced he was pitching, we had forty-five thousand in the place.

It was funny, but the guy won. He was a winner. The strange thing about it was the ballplayers didn't get mad. When you're winning and he keeps getting you out, a guy like Frank Robinson is going to say something nasty. The guy talks to the ball and does the dirt and then gets Frank out. Frank woulda went nuts, I think. But he [Fidrych] just entertained everybody.

RALPH HOUK: The thing that made him was the game he pitched against the Yankees in Tiger Stadium. The thing about Mark that people really didn't know was he was a lot more serious about it than they thought he was. Before the game, he would come in to talk to me in the manager's office and ask me, "Should I pitch this guy this way or that way?" and I said, "All you do is just pitch your game."

He never missed much. During a ballgame when he was pitching, he never said a word on the bench, but when he got on the mound, all the actions really made him what he was. He was an easy pitcher for our players to play behind, because he never wasted any pitches, and, as you know, any pitcher who gets the first ball over and gets ahead of the hitters, usually the fielders play better behind him because they're always ready; they think the ball is going to be hit.

I always figured, after knowing him, if he could get to the eighth inning, if we were ahead, we were going to win because he was a great finisher. I've never seen a young man who could finish as good as he could.

I think as it went on, Mark might have exaggerated a lot of the stuff he was doing. I'm not saying he did, but I know if I had been him, I would have, because, man, he was popular.

RUSTY STAUB: As the season progressed, he really pitched well. It was such a consistent job by him. Just hard slider, sinking fastball, hard slider, sinking fastball, and he just had location. On the mound, whatever the antics were, his concentration about where he wanted the ball to go was as good as anybody's I ever saw.

I played the three years that Ralph Houk finished up managing in Detroit, and I think Ralph left the game because . . . he always felt that people wanted to be the best that they could be and he always felt that people wanted to play as good as they could play . . . and I think he got a little frustrated with some of the people who had talent but didn't care enough to work hard. That wasn't Fidrych, though. Fidrych was always running somewhere. I think Ralph enjoyed it.

The biggest night came on a Monday night, the Game of the Week. The lowly Detroit Tigers against the massive New York Yankees. This was in the Yankees' heyday.

June 28, 1976. A national television audience saw "the Bird" for the first time and watched him shackle the Yankees, 5–1, in a complete game, with all the gyrations and antics, the patting of the dirt on the mound, the talking to the ball, the pumping of his right arm after a strikeout. They loved him. "The Bird" was a sensation and became the darling of baseball.

Fire Sale

Having lost Catfish Hunter to free agency and traded Reggie Jackson before he too left for free agency, A's owner Charles O. Finley thought it would be the prudent thing to sell off some of his high-priced stars before they too walked away and left him with nothing. He announced that he had sold Joe Rudi and Rollie Fingers to the Red Sox for $1 million each and Vida Blue to the Yankees for $1.5 million.

Commissioner Kuhn reacted immediately, holding up the sales until he had an opportunity to investigate. He feared that Finley's fire sale would upset the balance of power in the American League, that it would destroy the Oakland franchise and enrich the already wealthy New York and Boston clubs. In good faith, Kuhn felt he owed it to Athletics fans to prevent Finley from dismantling his team. At the same time, he agonized over the prospect of the richer teams stockpiling the game's best players.

In a conversation with Kuhn, Finley insisted that his intention was to take the $3.5 million and use it for player development. He planned, Finley said, to spend the money to sign young players and rebuild the Oakland club.

Kuhn was dubious, but he called for a hearing attended by, among others, Finley, George Steinbrenner, and Marvin Miller, who would represent the players' interests. Finley, never cordial to Miller ("He hated me," Miller said), objected to the presence of the executive director of the Players Association and demanded that Miller be removed from the room. Kuhn held firm, insisting that the players had a right to be represented.

In the course of the hearing, Miller made an impassioned plea that the sales be permitted to go through on the grounds that an owner had the right to sell his property. When Miller had completed his testimony, Finley got up and said, "Where have you been all my life?"

On June 18 Kuhn called a press conference to announce he was "disallowing the assignments" of Rudi and Fingers to the Red Sox and Blue to the Yankees. Kuhn wrote in his decision:

Shorn of much of its finest talent in exchange for cash, the Oakland club, which has been divisional champion for the last five years, has little chance to compete effectively in its division. Whether other players will be available to restore the club by using the cash involved is altogether speculative although Mr. Finley vigorously argues his ability to do so.

Public confidence in the integrity of club operations and in baseball would be greatly undermined should such assignments not be restrained. While I am of course aware that there have been sales of player contracts in the past, there has been no instance in my judgment which had the potential for harm to our game as do these assignments, particularly in the

What did Charlie Finley think of Kuhn's decision?

"He's the village idiot," the A's owner said.

RUSTY STAUB: It was a great night for the Detroit Tigers because we won the game. I was fortunate enough to have gotten a good pitch and hit a home run. Fidrych was brilliant. Just brilliant. It was like an overmatch. He just had games when he didn't make a mistake, he just got you out. And people started realizing he was throwing hard. All of a sudden, they started putting a gun on him, and he was throwing 93, 94, 92.

There were fifty thousand people there that night. The Bird had become something already. People started coming to the ballpark waving, doing this kind of bird thing. Guys started wearing all kinds of things. Every time he pitched in Detroit, there were fifty thousand people there.

It just so happened that he pitched on a Monday night and beat the Yankees and the people would not leave. I was the right fielder. They made the last out of the game. I was coming all the way in, and it was more than just what you would normally see in a ballpark. This is when the whole deal started with him coming out to take a bow.

I was one of the last ones to get off the field, and I just stood around and the crowd was yelling, "We want the Bird . . . We want the Bird . . ." I went down into the runway, and they just kept saying it and saying it and saying it. So I walked into the clubhouse and I went up to Fidrych, and he already had his uniform shirt off.

I said, "Mark, put your shirt back on." He said, "What are you talking about?" I said, "Put your shirt back on, you're coming with me." He said, "What are we doing?" I said, "I'll tell you when we get there." He and I were really close. I said, "Put your shirt on, get your hat, and follow me."

I walked him down the runway, and I said to him, "I want you to come to the end of this runway and listen." And there were fifty thousand people, and this was 15 minutes after the game, and they were yelling, "We want the Bird." I said, "You're going to go out of the dugout, stand up on the field," and he said, "I'm not going, I'm not doing that." I said, "You're not going? Then you're going to have to go through me to get to that clubhouse. You're going to have to go out there and do this."

He said, "You gotta come with me, you hit a home run." I said, "They're not saying, 'We want Rusty,' they're saying, 'We want the Bird,' and you're going to give them the Bird. You're going to go out there, and I just want you to do one thing. Just like you have a clock. I want you to just tip your hat six times, as if you went around the clock, and at the end, just raise your hands and acknowledge the crowd."

It was as electrifying for me to watch that happen to him . . . it was more electrifying than if it happened to me, because I appreciated something that was new and great in the game that I hadn't seen in a while. I saw Koufax. When Vida Blue came up, he was pretty exciting. But nothing like this guy. There was nobody like Fidrych. I can only tell you that when he did that, the fans went crazy.

Fidrych had taken baseball by storm. On July 3, he shut out the Orioles, 4–0, for his eighth straight victory. He was a sensation, baseball's biggest attraction in years.

MARK FIDRYCH: The things I did on the mound I always did. My dad told me about filling the holes on the mound, so if the ball was hit back to me I wouldn't get a bad hop, or if I stepped, I wouldn't land in a hole. When I was a kid, I used to talk a lot when I was pitching, like, "OK, throw a strike," the same as you see some hitters talk to themselves about keeping their head down, keeping their shoulder in, or keeping their eye on the ball.

When I got to the Tigers, my pitching coach, Fred Gladding, told me to keep doing what I was doing. He said if I changed my ways, I might not be there. Ralph Houk just let me be myself.

Everywhere I went, the other team tried to do something to distract me. In Cleveland they threw birdseed on the pitcher's mound. Another time, somebody threw me a ball that had writing all over it. In Minnesota, when I was going for my 13th win, they released 13 pigeons around home plate.

I didn't mind. It was part of the game. The way I looked at it, they were having their fun and I was having mine.

RALPH HOUK: We'd go on the road, and I'd have general managers calling me and saying, "You've got to pitch him here." I tried to make out the rotation the best I could so that he'd pitch in Detroit so our fans could see him, but he pitched every fifth day. But I'd get calls, he hasn't pitched here and he hasn't pitched there. And everywhere we went and he pitched, he'd pack the place.

Even though he didn't make his first start until the season was a month old, Fidrych won 19 games and lost 9, led the American League with an earned run average of 2.34 and in complete games with 24, and was named American League Rookie of the Year. His future looked unlimited, but the following spring he tore the cartilage in his left knee and underwent surgery. Later, he hurt his arm.

Fidrych pitched only four more seasons for the Tigers. In those four seasons, he won 10 and lost 10. He tried several comebacks, the last in 1983, when he pitched for Pawtucket in the International League. In midseason, with a record of 2–5 and an ERA of 9.68, Mark Fidrych retired. He was 28 years old.

HANK CALLS IT A CAREER

On July 20, 1976, Hank Aaron of the Milwaukee Brewers homered off Dick Drago of the California Angels in Milwaukee's 6–2 victory. It was Aaron's 10th home run of the season and the 755th of his career. He would not hit another home run for the remainder of the season, after which he would retire as baseball's all-time home-run champion.

As a tribute to the home-run king, the Brewers staged Salute to Hank Aaron Night on September 17. Mickey Mantle, Ernie Banks, Eddie Mathews, and Vic Raschi, who had served up Aaron's first major league home run, joined in the celebration in County Stadium. Brewers players brought along cameras and lined up to get Aaron's autograph.

Mantle called Aaron "the most underrated player in baseball," and after a two-minute standing ovation, Aaron addressed the crowd of 40,383 and said, "I hope my presence has helped teach some kids on this club what being in the majors is all about."

One of those kids was a rookie infielder, Jim Gantner.

JIM GANTNER: He wasn't the same player he had been. But it was still a thrill to play with him. He was my idol when I was a kid.

On October 3, in his final at-bat in the major leagues, Henry Aaron delivered an RBI single, finishing his career with 3,771 hits, then second on the all-time list, and 2,297 RBIs, the most in baseball history.

FREAK ACCIDENT

One second Dodgers catcher Steve Yeager was in the on-deck circle at San Diego's Jack Murphy Stadium, the next second he was near death.

REGGIE SMITH: Bill Russell was hitting seventh, and Yeager, who was hitting eighth, was on deck, in San Diego. And Russell swung at a pitch that was slightly inside. The bat broke, and part of the barrel of the bat came around and was headed for the dugout. Everybody yelled, "Look out," and Yeager looked up and the jagged end of the bat pierced his throat.

I was on the bench. Yeager never lost consciousness, and the only time I can recall any real concern, we were standing around Yeager, and Davey Lopes said, "Oh, my God," and that's when we became afraid, because you could see the hole in his throat.

TOMMY JOHN: I was on the bench and Bill Russell was hitting and Yeager was in the on-deck circle. He was looking up in the stands, waving to his girl-friend, or whatever, and he wasn't even watching. Russell took a swing and

Hank Aaron takes the last swing of his career, as a Brewer in Milwaukee, where he began his career 23 years earlier. He would end up with 755 home runs and 2,297 RBIs, both all-time records.

got jammed and broke his bat. We were on the bench on the third-base side, and we saw the barrel go flying in back of him and it hit Yeager.

Bill Buhler [Dodgers trainer] went running out, and when he saw Yeager, he motioned to the San Diego trainer, who came running out. The jagged end had pierced Yeager's throat. They left it in, holding it there because they didn't know if it had hit an artery or a vein or something that was causing severe bleeding and as long as it was in, it kept the bleeding plugged.

It took them 20 minutes to get an ambulance, because at that time, there were no ambulances at the stadium. They came in and they came out on the field, and as the emergency people lifted him up, they held that bat straight up in the air and hauled him on a stretcher and they didn't take the bat out until they got him to the hospital.

We didn't know if the guy was going to live or die. It missed a main artery by a quarter of an inch, and if it hit that artery, he would have died instantly. He went to the hospital, they stitched it up, and four or five days later, Steve came back and was catching. To protect the wound, Bill Buhler devised this attachment to the mask that hung down and protected Yeager's throat so that if he got hit there, it would keep the wound from breaking open. Catchers are still using that attachment today, so something good came out of an unfortunate accident.

THE SHAPE OF THINGS TO COME

As the 1976 season wound down to its conclusion, three of the four races were runaways. The fourth, in the American League West, was a three-way race among the defending champion Oakland A's, the Kansas City Royals, and the Minnesota Twins. The Yankees in the American League East, the Phillies in the National League East, and the Reds in the National League West were safely in front and on their way to division championships.

Kansas City and Philadelphia represented an upswing in the fortunes of two teams who were enjoying newfound success. The Royals, an expansion team, had never won anything. The Phillies had gone 26 years without winning.

Kansas City had first come into the American League in 1955 as the Kansas City Athletics, the franchise moving from Philadelphia, where its lineage dated back to the days of Connie Mack. After 13 inept seasons in

Kansas City the Athletics moved to Oakland, and Kansas City was without major league baseball until 1969, when the Royals and Seattle Pilots joined the American League as expansion teams.

Thanks to skillful drafting and trading, the Royals enjoyed moderate success, but it wasn't until Whitey Herzog, the former Mets farm director who had been fired in Texas in 1973, took over as manager midway through the 1975 season that the Royals began to rise as a power in the American League. They were led by a young hitting sensation named George Brett and a fearsome slugger named John Mayberry, as well as Hal McRae, Frank White, Amos Otis, Al Cowens, and a pitching staff headed by Dennis Leonard, Paul Splittorff, and Doug Bird.

The Phillies had been National League doormats through the late sixties and into the seventies, but a trade with the Cardinals prior to the 1972 season that brought left-hander Steve Carlton to Philadelphia was the start of the club's exit from the wilderness.

In his first season with the Phillies, Carlton won 27 games, had an ERA of 1.97, completed 30 games, struck out 310 batters, pitched eight shutouts, and won the National League Cy Young Award.

Inexplicably, Carlton slumped the next three seasons, when he had a combined record of 44–47.

TIM McCARVER: When I was released by the Red Sox in 1975, I ended up back in Philadelphia, and Carlton had three below-par years and the Phillies were in a quandary. They had no idea what was wrong with him.

I signed with the Phillies, and we had a meeting one night, and I'll never forget that meeting. Catcher Johnny Oates, catcher Bob Boone, pitching coach Ray Rippelmeyer, manager Danny Ozark, owner Ruly Carpenter, and me. And everybody had their say about what was wrong with Carlton. And everybody but me and Ray were convinced that he wasn't throwing his fastball enough.

I said, "Well, I'll probably be voted down here, but I played against Lefty and I played with him in St. Louis when he developed the slider, and, to me, he's not throwing the slider enough."

They all voted me down. Rippelmeyer kind of agreed with me, but not vociferously. But at the end of the meeting, Ray came up to me and said, "You know, I've said that. That he's not throwing the slider enough, and Boonie wants to keep setting hitters up with that fastball."

And I said, right then and there, "If I ever catch him, I'm calling for his slider, I guarantee you that," because I had a chance to hit against it and I've also heard right-handed hitters come into the dugout and make comments like, "Well, at least he didn't throw me the slider," even if they made an out.

When you hear comments like that from good right-handed hitters, they know that slider's devastating, too. So, sure enough, as fate would have it, I ended up catching him some in 1975, but a lot in 1976, and I called for his slider. I've kidded about it since. I said I walked around shaking hands with three fingers there for about four years.

Carlton won 20 games in 1976 and would win 77 games and another Cy Young Award in four seasons with McCarver as his personal catcher.

THE LAST LINK TO BROOKLYN

On September 29, after 23 consecutive one-year contracts and 2,040 victories, Walter Alston stepped down as manager of the Los Angeles Dodgers and was replaced by their third-base coach, Tommy Lasorda.

TOMMY JOHN: I thought Walt was through. I wasn't around him when he was young, but I didn't think he managed that sharply at that time. And Tommy was our third-base coach. He was vocal: "Let's go, let's go." I think Walt just got tired, and when he called it quits, I wasn't surprised. And I wasn't surprised when Tommy got hired, because all the guys they had on the ballclub played for Tommy in the minor leagues.

When Tommy got the job, he came up to me and he said, "We're going to win next year. We're going to come to spring training in top-notch shape, so let's get ready this winter."

BATTING RACE

All four division titles were settled long before the final day of the regular season, October 3, but both batting titles were up for grabs. In the American League, George Brett was neck and neck with his Kansas City Royals teammate Hal McRae for the batting crown. When Brett hit a blooper that dropped in front of Twins outfielder Steve Brye, it gave him the title with an average of .333 to McRae's .332. After the game, McRae, believing Brye's misplay to have been deliberate, charged the Twins with racism. McRae is black. Brett and Brye are white. Rod Carew of the Twins, who had won four consecutive American League batting titles, finished third at .331.

GEORGE BRETT: We were playing the Twins in Kansas City, and Lyman Bostock, myself, Carew, and Hal were separated by about two points in the batting race. It was so close, after our second or third at-bats, they had to carry it out five numbers to see who was ahead.

It came down to the last at-bat of the season between Hal and me. I had two hits, Rod had one, Hal had one or two, and Bostock had an oh-fer going, so he dropped out.

I hit a ball off Jim Hughes to short left field. Steve Brye was the left fielder. He came running in and kind of quit on it a little early. The ball bounced over his head, and I got an inside-the-park home run. After the game, Brye said he lost the ball temporarily in the sun, which happens on occasion. I don't know. I just hit it and ran.

Hal was up next, and he grounded out to the shortstop. Gene Mauch was the manager of the Minnesota Twins, and after Hal grounded out, I had won the batting title.

I really don't know, to be honest, what would have happened if we both would have made out, or if Hal got a hit. But Hal made an accusation. He pointed to Gene Mauch in the third-base dugout in Kansas City, who flipped him off, gave the old fist up in the air, and the next thing you know there was an argument and Hal was claiming that Steve Brye let the ball drop intentionally so I could win the batting title and the black guy wouldn't. That's my interpretation of it.

It took a lot of fun out of winning the batting title, and I felt really bad for Hal because he and I were such good friends. He taught me how to play the game of baseball once I got to the major league level, with that all-out style of his. It didn't affect our friendship at all, but I felt really sorry for him.

The Big "O"

When the 1976 Olympics in Montreal ended, the Expos got an unfinished Olympic Stadium as their new home ballpark. It was years before the roof, which could be opened or closed depending on the weather, was finished. While the huge stadium was, in some respects, an improvement over the bush-league Jarry Park, where the sun set directly in the hitters' eyes, it is a fairly inhospitable and sterile place to watch a baseball game, as the fans are very far away from the field. It is shown here in its big-league debut, on April 15, 1977. Note the construction crane visible above the center-field scoreboard.

We've been great friends for a long time, still are. I had a chance to play for Hal [when McRae managed the Royals], and I got along with him great. The curious thing is why Brye would want me to win the batting title instead of his own teammates, Carew and Bostock.

By winning the batting title, I broke a streak of four straight championships for Carew. Teed him off so much, the next year, he went out and hit .388.

In the National League, the Reds' Ken Griffey led Bill Madlock of the Cubs, .338 to .333, on the final day and chose to sit out the last game. But when word reached Griffey that Madlock had stroked four singles against the Expos and raised his average to .339, giving him a one-point lead, Griffey entered the Reds' game against the Braves but went hitless in two at-bats and finished at .336, three points behind Madlock.

The Reds, who won more than 100 games for the second straight season, made short work of the Phillies in the National League Championship Series, a three-game sweep with George Foster homering in the first and third games.

THE BRONX BOMBERS

The American League Championship Series was a five-game struggle between the Kansas City Royals and New York Yankees.

The Yankees won Game 1 in Kansas City as Catfish Hunter, always an excellent big-game pitcher, went all the way on a five-hitter in a 4–1 victory. But the Royals came back to win Game 2, 7–3, and the series returned to New York for the last three games.

Chris Chambliss gave a hint of what was to come with two hits, including a home run, and three RBIs to lead the Yankees to a 5–3 victory in the third game. But the Royals rebounded in the fourth game, knocked Hunter out in the fourth inning, and beat the Yankees, 7–4, to force a sudden-death Game 5.

The Yankees seemed on their way to an easy victory when they opened a 6–3 lead after seven innings, but in the top of the eighth, George Brett silenced the capacity crowd at Yankee Stadium with a dramatic three-run homer that tied the game. The Yanks failed to score in the bottom of the eighth, and reliever Dick Tidrow kept the Royals off the board in the top of the ninth.

Chambliss was the first batter due up for the Yankees in the bottom of the ninth against Mark Littell, who had come in in the seventh and held the Yankees in check.

CHRIS CHAMBLISS: There was a long delay before I got up to hit. People were throwing paper and stuff on the field, and the groundskeepers had to clear the field, so I had a long wait before I stepped up to the plate. It was cold and I was waiting, and it was kind of an anxious moment.

I hit the first pitch. It was a high, towering drive, and Al Cowens, the right fielder, went back like he had a bead on it, but right at the end he put his head against the wall and the ball went over. I didn't know it was going

The Yankees returned to postseason play in 1976 and beat the Kansas City Royals in the American League Championship Series on this dramatic Game 5 home run by Chris Chambliss in the bottom of the ninth.

out until it got out there. It wasn't one of those no-doubters, you know, when you hit it you know it's gone. This one just cleared the fence, but I knew it had a chance when I hit it.

Running around the bases, I remember touching first and second, and then somebody tripped me between second and short. I got up and people were trying to steal my helmet, so I took my helmet off and put it under my arm like a football. Third base was ridiculous. There were people all over the place, and the base had to have been stolen by then. I went around them and went close to the other team's dugout, then I just took a beeline to our dugout because home plate was also full of people.

There was a guy in front of our dugout, and I just walked right over him. I gave him a little shoulder block to get into that dugout.

Later, Chambliss came out with a police escort and made sure he touched third base and home. It was a great moment. Chambliss' home run put the Yankees in the World Series for the first time in 12 years.

GEORGE BRETT: That was our first time in the playoffs, and afterward, it was like, OK, now we had a good learning experience. The next time we're in this position, I think we'll do a lot better. I think that was the consensus of our team.

The first time you're in postseason play, it's a big thrill, win or lose. Obviously, you want to win, but if you do lose, it's not the end of the world. We had a great year, the best year the franchise has ever had. You've lost, but we had a young team that looked like it was going to be successful for a long time, and it was.

THE BIG RED MACHINE IS BACK

For all their excitement at seeing their team win another pennant, Yankees fans were disappointed with the World Series. The Cincinnati Reds were an unstoppable machine, and they rolled on in the Series, sweeping the Yankees in four games, the first team to go undefeated in Championship Series and World Series play.

Johnny Bench was the star of the Series and its Most Valuable Player with a .533 average, including two homers and five RBIs in the fourth game.

After the final game, Reds manager Sparky Anderson and Bench appeared in the press interview room.

"Don't embarrass nobody by comparing him to Johnny Bench," Anderson said.

In the back of the room, waiting for his turn to be interviewed by the nation's press, was Yankees catcher Thurman Munson, who had batted .529 for the Series, including singles in each of his last six at-bats. A proud and fiercely competitive man, Munson was hurt by Anderson's remark. He would never forget it or forgive Sparky Anderson for having said it.

———

SPARKY ANDERSON: I said, "Let's don't compare Johnny Bench to anyone." I never said that Munson couldn't catch or anything like that. My God, this guy could flat play, but I don't believe to this day that you can compare anybody to Johnny Bench. I was wired for the World Series film, and there's one time I'm going to the mound to talk to my pitcher after Munson just got a hit and you hear me say, "That guy can flat hit."

The thing about him on our scouting report from Ray Shore was "This guy can hit, let's don't worry about his hitting, let's keep him from going

The Reds swept the Yankees, with the help of this Johnny Bench home run in Game 4. Bench hit .533, collected two home runs, and was named the MVP of the Series.

deep. Let's keep him in right and center field." And that's what he did and he hit over .500, but he never hurt us, because we kept him there.

I wrote him a letter and sent it to Yankee Stadium, personal handwriting explaining what I meant. He claimed he never got it, and that's fine, I'm not going to get into a media thing with him. I feel bad that he said he never got my letter, although going to Yankee Stadium, some mail, let's face it, in the winter, you might not ever see your mail, and then it's all just put away and trashed. He probably never received it. But I wrote it.

As far as George Steinbrenner was concerned, half a loaf wasn't better than none. He had made good on his promise to bring the Yankees back into prominence, to bring the city of New York another pennant. But he would not be satisfied until he brought them another world championship.

CHAPTER 8

THE EIGHTH INNING

REGGIE

Winning a pennant for the first time in 12 years elated most Yankees fans, who had suffered through some lean years during the CBS regime—a losing record in five seasons, a tenth-place finish in 1966, ninth in 1967. But while most Yankees fans were satisfied, the team's owner, George Steinbrenner, was not. In fact, he was irate when his team was swept by the Reds in the 1976 World Series, and he was determined that things would change.

Free agency came along just in time for Steinbrenner. Money burned holes in his pockets; he couldn't wait to spend it, and free agency gave him the opportunity to go to his checkbook and improve his team in search of the elusive world championship. If ego was his motivation, at least Yankees fans would be the beneficiaries.

The first class of free agents matriculated on November 2, 1976. There were 24 eligibles, including some of the biggest names in the game. There was 25-year-old Don Gullett, a hard-throwing left-hander who was considered one of the best young pitchers in baseball. There was slugger Willie McCovey, outfielder Don Baylor, infielder Bobby Grich, and the heart of Oakland's three world championship teams—reliever Rollie Fingers, catcher Gene Tenace, outfielder Joe Rudi, and the redoubtable Reggie Jackson.

Steinbrenner viewed the merchandise like a kid with his nose pressed to the window of the neighborhood candy store, his check-writing hand twitching with excitement. Like the kid in the candy store, he wanted it all, but baseball rules prohibited him from signing more than two free agents.

Steinbrenner's first move was to sign Gullett to a six-year contract for $2 million, confident the left-hander would take his place as the ace of a staff that already included Catfish Hunter, Ed Figueroa, Dock Ellis, Sparky Lyle, and a skinny young left-hander from Louisiana named Ron Guidry.

But the primary object of Steinbrenner's affections was Jackson, over the objections of his manager, Billy Martin, who urged the boss to sign Rudi instead. Martin argued that Rudi was a better all-around player and more of a team player than Jackson, whom Martin said was "not a Yankee type."

Steinbrenner disregarded Martin's objections and sought out Thurman Munson, the Yankees captain and team leader, to get a feel for how the Yankees players would react to Reggie.

"Go get the big man," urged Munson. "He's the only guy in baseball who can carry a club for a month. The hell with what you hear. He hustles every minute on the field."

Once he set his sights on Jackson, Steinbrenner pushed hard. His pursuit was relentless. He is renowned for his impatience and for being an exacting employer, for harassing managers and replacing them at will, for berating employees and firing them for minor lapses.

But there is another side to George Steinbrenner, the side Reggie Jackson saw: charming and gracious, generous and persuasive. In his pursuit of Jackson, Steinbrenner wined him and dined him and paraded him around New York City, knowing cabdrivers and construction workers would help George do his recruiting for him.

"Hey, Reggie," they would shout, "are you coming to the Yankees? We love you, Reggie. We need you."

And as George knew it would, the attention appealed to Jackson's ample ego.

This was New York, and Steinbrenner sensed Jackson was a New York kind of guy. He took him to Fifth Avenue, past all the elegant shops and luxurious apartments, and to "21" for lunch, and Jackson succumbed.

"He hustled me like a broad," Jackson said. "George can sell sand to the Arabs."

GEORGE STEINBRENNER: I remember walking down the streets of New York with Reggie and people recognizing him and coming up to him and asking him if he was going to sign with the Yankees. "Come to New York," they kept saying to him, and I think that had an influence on him. I remember we were

Springtime in Toronto

Spring training in 1977 started with two new American League expansion teams, one in Seattle (back in the major leagues after a seven-year absence and scheduled to play its home games in a structure called the Kingdome) and one in Toronto (a city steeped in years of tradition with a franchise in the International League).

Here, Canada's second expansion team, the Toronto Blue Jays, are greeted by their Exhibition Stadium nemesis before their first game ever on April 7, 1977—snow. White Sox second baseman Jack Brohamer, glad he's not wearing shorts, uses a couple of bats for ski poles and shin guards for skis. The game was played—despite the snow and freezing temperature—in front of 44,649 fans, and the Jays won 9–5.

walking past the Carlyle Hotel and Reggie turned to me and said, "We're embarking on an adventure together." He certainly was right about that.

While Jackson was succumbing, Billy Martin was steaming. He read about the pursuit of Jackson in the papers, about lunch at "21," and he felt betrayed.

"George was taking Reggie to the '21' Club for lunch all the time, and I was sitting across the river in my hotel room in New Jersey all winter and George didn't even take me to lunch once."

FRAN HEALY: I can remember being in Yankee Stadium, in the clubhouse. It was in the winter, and I was in the sauna. It was just me and Billy. Jackson had just signed, and I didn't know Reggie, except as an opposing player. And Billy said to me, "I'll show him who's boss." And I thought, "I wonder why."

On November 29, 1976, in the Americana Hotel, the Yankees held a press conference to announce they had signed Reggie Jackson, about whom his former Oakland teammate Darold Knowles had once said, "There isn't enough mustard in the world to cover that hot dog." Terms of the contract were not announced, but it was later learned Jackson would earn $3 million for five years, an exorbitant price at the time. It would prove to be a bargain.

Thurman Munson attended the press conference. Billy Martin did not. Reggie Jackson reported to the Yankees' camp in Fort Lauderdale to play for a manager who didn't like him and didn't want him and with players who didn't trust him and resented him.

Ordinarily, a manager would warmly welcome a new player on his first day, especially one who came with the established credentials that Reggie Jackson brought to Fort Lauderdale. But Martin's reaction to Jackson was practically to ignore him, a cold war that set up a barrier between manager and player. Jackson's teammates were only slightly less hostile. They seemed to speak to him only when he spoke to them first, causing Jackson to feel ostracized. To exacerbate the situation, Martin had told the writers early in spring training that Chris Chambliss, a more consistent hitter but hardly the home-run threat Reggie was, would be his cleanup hitter and that Jackson would bat fifth or sixth in the batting order.

It was a curious bit of strategy, to say the least. Chambliss' best season for RBIs and home runs was the previous one, when he knocked in 96 runs and belted 17 homers. Jackson had hit more home runs in his previous two seasons than Chambliss had hit in his six-year career.

AND IN THIS CORNER . . . LENNY RANDLE!

While the cold war continued between manager Billy Martin and Reggie Jackson in Fort Lauderdale, in the Texas Rangers' training camp, hostilities flared openly between manager Frank Lucchesi and infielder Lenny Randle. Randle, a six-year veteran, was angry that he was being benched in spring training to make room for rookie Bump Wills, son of base-stealing champion Maury Wills.

BUMP WILLS: In fairness to all parties, to Lenny Randle and Frank Lucchesi, that was my rookie year, and I truly believe they wanted me to have that job. But they didn't just hand it to me. Maybe they weren't sure and they wanted me to work for it. Whatever. They brought Lenny and me into the office, and they said, "We're going to give you guys equal playing time, and we're going to make our decision before Opening Day on who wins the job."

It just happened that I was getting a little more playing time. They already had Lenny Randle, they knew what Lenny could do. But they needed to see me, so I ended up getting more playing time, and my understanding was that Lenny was getting a lot of pressure from outside, from friends and family. "You're getting dogged by the organization; Frank's not being honest with you. They're not giving you enough playing time."

Lenny's a very easygoing, likable person, but I believe these people on the outside worked his head. That's what was so unusual about the situation, two likable people, but the pressures and the stress of the whole situation caught up to Lenny. We were in Orlando, taking batting practice. Ironically, Lenny was in the lineup that night. Lenny was standing at the cage and Frank was at the cage, and Lenny said, "Frank, I want to talk to you."

"Let's wait till after BP, I'll be glad to talk to you," Frank said.

Lenny said, "Let's do it now, I want to talk to you now," and Frank just turned away and said, "I'll be glad to talk to you . . ." and then—boom—here comes the hammer. Lenny hit him a couple of times in the face, knocked him down, straddled his body, hit him three or four kidney punches. Lenny's a black belt in karate, and I could tell by the blows that he was doing some pretty good damage. Ken Henderson approached Lenny to get him off Frank, and Lenny went into a karate stance. I think by that time Lenny had snapped. He went into his stance and said, "Don't touch me." Then he grabbed his glove and went out to stretch in the outfield.

Rangers general manager Danny O'Brien was at the park, upstairs somewhere. They got in touch with him and they got Lenny off the field, and we didn't see him after that. Frank was taken to the hospital.

Lenny Randle never played another game for the Texas Rangers. Less than a month later, he was traded to the New York Mets. He drifted from the Mets to the Yankees, to the Cubs, to the Mariners, and ended up playing in the Italian Baseball League, where he was enormously popular.

Wills got the starting second-base job for the Rangers, played in 152 games as a rookie, and batted .287 with nine home runs, 62 RBIs, and 28 stolen bases. He had the distinction of hitting back-to-back inside-the-park home runs with Toby Harrah against the Yankees, a major league first. He played five seasons with the Rangers and one with the Cubs, ending with a career average of .266 and 196 stolen bases.

Through the first 62 games of the 1977 season, the Texas Rangers, under Lucchesi, won 31 and lost 31. On June 22 Lucchesi was fired and replaced by Eddie Stanky, who had last managed the Chicago White Sox in 1968. When the Rangers called, Stanky was coaching at the University of South Alabama.

Stanky took over the team in Minnesota and won his first game. That night, in his Minneapolis hotel room, the 60-year-old Stanky began to have second thoughts. He looked at the four walls of his hotel room, contemplated many nights like this in his future, and decided that was not what he wanted. After one game, he resigned. He was replaced by coach Connie Ryan, who ran the team until Billy Hunter arrived to take over.

SOLID UP THE MIDDLE

With Reggie Jackson and Don Gullett added to a pennant-winning team, the Yankees, "the best team money could buy," were in good shape to make a strong defense of their American League pennant. But there was one piece of the puzzle still missing.

Throughout their long history of championships, the Yankees always had a top-notch shortstop, from Roger Peckinpaugh in the teens and early twenties, to Mark Koenig with the Murderers' Row Yankees of Ruth and Gehrig in the midtwenties, to Frankie Crosetti in the thirties, to Phil Rizzuto in the forties and fifties, to Gil McDougald and Tony Kubek in the midfifties and early sixties.

It was no coincidence that after Kubek retired, the Yankees failed to win a pennant until 1976, and even then it was with a shortstop platoon. Fred

The Straw That Stirs the Drink

The Yankees opened the 1977 season on April 7 in front of 43,785 fans at Yankee Stadium with a 3–0 victory over the Milwaukee Brewers. Catfish Hunter pitched seven innings but was forced to leave the game when he took a line drive on his right instep off the bat of Von Joshua.

In his first game as a Yankee, Reggie Jackson played right field and batted fifth. He singled twice and scored two runs, but the big bat belonged to another, less expensive newcomer, Jimmy Wynn, "the Toy Cannon," who homered over the center-field fence in the second, a 440-foot blast.

After winning their opener, the Yankees proceeded to lose eight of their next nine games and slip into last place. A series of minor skirmishes in the early going provided only a small taste of the kind of season it was going to be in the Bronx.

Sparky Lyle and Ed Figueroa were fined $100 each for sleeping through one of George Steinbrenner's clubhouse lectures; Lyle and Mickey Rivers were fined $500 each for missing an exhibition game in Syracuse; Billy Martin got miffed at Reggie Jackson and sat him down for a couple of games, even refusing to use him as a pinch-hitter in extra innings, after Jackson told the press he had a sore elbow; and Graig Nettles, who had walked out of camp in spring training because he was unhappy with his contract, refused to attend the team's welcome-home banquet.

"If they want someone to hit home runs and play third base, they have me," said the always sardonic Nettles. "But if they want somebody to attend banquets, they can get Georgie Jessel."

Possibly to ease the tension with the team at 2–8, Billy Martin had Reggie Jackson pick the Yankees lineup out of a hat for a game in late April. With the makeshift batting order, the Yankees won and were jump-started on a six-game winning streak. By mid-May, they had moved into first place and settled into relative calm.

Then the magazine article hit the fan.

On May 23 *Sport* magazine hit the newsstands with a story about Reggie Jackson. The interview had been conducted in spring training, over a couple of beers in a Fort Lauderdale watering hole. Feeling content and at peace, Jackson was apparently loose-tongued with the writer from *Sport*. But he was unprepared for what appeared in the article.

Later, Reggie would say that certain comments were taken out of context. Exactly what was said is known only to Reggie Jackson and the writer. But this, in part, is what was written and widely circulated: "I'm the straw that stirs the drink. Munson thinks he can be the straw that stirs the drink, but he can only stir it bad."

The article was a torpedo in the turbulent sea that was the Yankees clubhouse. Thurman Munson was stung by the words. His teammates, who respected their captain and viewed him as the heart and soul of the team, rallied around him. His manager, Billy Martin, sided with him. And Jackson, whose relations with his new teammates and his manager were already strained, became more of an outcast. If Jackson hit a home run, Munson, often batting in front of him, would not shake his hand.

Stanley played in 110 games at the position, Jim Mason in 93, clearly an unsatisfactory arrangement considering the position's importance.

Russell Earl "Bucky" Dent, 25 years old, had been the White Sox's starting shortstop for three seasons. Not flashy, Dent was solid and steady, the kind of shortstop about whom Tommy John would say, "With Bucky at short, an out is an out." And he was durable. In three years, he had missed only 16 games. He was the ideal shortstop to fit in alongside third baseman Graig Nettles and second baseman Willie Randolph.

BUCKY DENT: I was at a Bulls basketball game at the end of 1974. I had never been to a basketball game before. I was sitting behind the Bulls' bench and there was a gentleman sitting in front of me, and the guy I was with said, "Do you know who that guy is right there?" I said, "No," and he said, "That's George Steinbrenner. He owns the New York Yankees. Would you like to meet him?" I said, "Yeah, I'd love to meet him."

So my friend tapped him on the shoulder and said, "Mr. Steinbrenner, this is Bucky Dent from the White Sox," and George said, "Aw, I know you. I've been trying to get you." And I said, "Ohhh, I'd love to play for the Yankees," because that was my favorite team.

In 1975 the White Sox had done a study on mind control, and Morley Safer of *60 Minutes* came down to spring training in Sarasota to do a story about it, and that's when I met Joe Illigasch, who worked for CBS and had come to Florida with Morley Safer. Joe and I stayed in touch after he went back to New York and became the best of friends. The next spring, Joe called me up and said, "Bucky, do you know there are big rumors about you coming to New York?" I said, "Really, wow." He said, "Yeah, the rumors have started."

I went through all of 1976 playing for Bill Veeck, who had bought the White Sox. In the winter of 1976, Joe said, "The rumors are really heating up now," because the Yankees got beat by Cincinnati in the World Series and they needed a shortstop. And Joe was calling me up almost every day to tell me what they were saying in the New York papers.

I went to spring training and I was not playing much, so I knew something was going on. Birdie Tebbetts [scouting for the Yankees] was following us, and he came up to me and said, "Are you hurt?" I said, "No, no, Birdie, I'm fine. I'm just not playing."

Joe called me and said, "George and Gabe Paul are meeting tonight at the Columbia Restaurant in Tampa. You're supposed to be traded tonight. Stay home." So I stayed home, but nothing happened.

I just went about my business, and Opening Day we were getting ready to go to Toronto to open against the Blue Jays in their first game in the American League, in their old stadium. I was packing my car and the phone rang. I went in and picked up the phone, and I heard this crowd noise in the background and this voice said, "Bucky, this is George Steinbrenner from the New York Yankees." I said, "Who?" He said, "George." I said, "Get out of here," but I heard the crowd and I knew it was serious. He said, "No, this is George Steinbrenner. I have a deal that will bring you to New York if you'll sign a contract."

Nick Buoniconti [the former Boston Patriots and Miami Dolphins linebacker] was doing my work at the time, and I told George to call him. Then Nick called me back and said, "It's all done," and I wound up going to New York.

The thing that bothered me more than anything else was that I didn't have a chance to meet any of those guys until I got traded over there. Then I went into the Yankees' clubhouse, and the first thing Billy Martin said to me was, "Hey, kid, get a haircut." I said, "OK."

It was the kind of thing where I knew I could play and I knew that they had just come out of the World Series and I was going to a team that was going to win, and it was really exciting for me. I didn't think about there being pressure on me because they had lost the World Series and now they brought me over and I was supposed to help them win it all. I never even thought about that. Maybe I was too stupid back then.

I just wanted to be a part of the Yankees and win. I just wanted to play well. The first month or two, it took me a little while to settle in and to get to know the different personalities on that club. Thurman's sarcastic way of saying things, Nettles' sarcastic way, Reggie, Catfish. It was kind of like, hey, I just came from a last-place team, the White Sox, and now I'm coming over here with these guys, all these different personalities, and I just tried to mind my own business and go along.

When I look back on those years, the moment I remember most is my first World Series game, standing in the dugout, Bob Sheppard [the Yankees public address announcer] getting ready to announce my name. How much that stays in your memory. You're standing there and you're waiting for him to call your name. You get goose bumps.

CAPTAIN OUTRAGEOUS

The new baseball owners didn't take long to become experts in the game. The day of the behind-the-scenes owner who left the running of the ballclub to the general manager was long past. The typical new owner was a hands-on, involved participant in the daily operation of his team.

Ted Turner had owned the Atlanta Braves for one year. He figured that was enough time for him to know all there was to know about baseball and to know how to solve whatever problems his team might have.

The Braves got off to a horrendous start in 1977. On the morning of May 11, they were deep into a 16-game losing streak when Turner decided to take hands-on involvement one step further than any owner had since his predecessors Judge Emil Fuchs of the Boston Braves in 1929 and Connie Mack of the Philadelphia Athletics in 1950.

BUZZ CAPRA: We had lost 13 or 14 straight games. Nothing was going right. We couldn't get a pitcher through the first inning. We were in Pittsburgh, and a few of us went out to the park early. I was sitting at my locker, and here he came. It's Ted. He's got the hat pulled down and he's got the uniform on and he's got his pants all the way up to his knees and he's got the stirrups backward, with the high end in the front.

He just went into somebody's locker and grabbed a uniform, and he had Cito Gaston's shoes on. What are you gonna say to the guy—"Give me my shoes back"? He coulda said, "You're outta here." He could have disposed of any of us anytime he wanted to, that's how bad we were doing. You never knew what Ted Turner was going to do, because he was a Jekyll and Hyde kind of guy. You never knew what was on his mind.

I was at my locker, and I grabbed a towel and stuffed it in my mouth to keep from laughing hysterically—he looked so ridiculous. And he had a cigar in his mouth.

Then he said, "Dave Bristol [the Braves manager] has been under a lot of pressure, so we told him to take the weekend off, go fishing or something. Just get away from it. I'm going to take over the team."

Until 1977, when brash media magnate Ted Turner managed the Braves for one game, no owner had also managed his club since Connie Mack owned and managed the Philadelphia Athletics for six decades.

We were all in disbelief. We never had a clue. I was leaning back on my chair, and I almost went clear back in my locker and fell on my ass. I couldn't look at him; I had to look away because it was the funniest sight you'd ever want to see, him in a baseball uniform. Let alone now he's going to manage.

Later on I found out that Dave Bristol was hiding in Pittsburgh. Darrel Chaney told me that he was walking through the lobby of the hotel and he saw Bristol, who was trying to avoid being seen. He was hiding behind pillars so he could get out of there without seeing anybody. He was afraid he was going to see a bunch of reporters. He told Chaney, "Ted sent me fishing for the weekend," and then Bristol sneaked out of town.

Actually, Turner didn't manage the team, although he sat on the bench in full uniform. One of our coaches, Vern Benson, made all the moves.

Turner didn't have the answers. The Braves lost another, 2–1, to the Pirates, and that was the end of his managing career.

BOWIE KUHN: I conferred with National League president Chub Feeney, and we decided we would not allow such a farce. I don't know if there was any rule against an owner managing his team, but I never really thought of rules when I thought of Ted. It just wasn't right. It was embarrassing, and that's good enough for me. Conduct not in the best interests of the game. Chub ordered him out of the dugout the next day.

But for one day, Ted Turner was officially the manager of the Atlanta Braves. It's right there in *The Baseball Encyclopedia*, under the manager register:

TED TURNER
Turner, Robert Edward
B. Nov. 19, 1938, Cincinnati, Ohio

			G	W	L	PCT	Standing
1977	ATL	N	1	0	1	.000	6

THE TWO TOMMYS

True to his word, rookie manager Tommy Lasorda whipped his Los Angeles Dodgers into top shape in spring training.

Walter Alston (left) retired after the 1976 season, giving way to Tommy Lasorda.
Alston won 2,040 games in 23 years for the Dodgers.

TOMMY JOHN: We had a good spring. Tommy won ballgames. He did things down there that I had never seen done before. He played the regulars one day, all game, then gave them the next day off and played all the minor guys. Then, the next day, the regulars would start again and play seven innings and then get the next day off. The regulars played a lot so that they'd get their three, four at-bats, rather than get just two at-bats.

When we left spring training, the players were ready, the pitchers were ready, and we started off 1977 like a house afire. Boom. We started off something like 25–5.

Tommy came up to me—the only other manager who ever said this to me was Eddie Stanky—and gave me a hug and said, "You pitched a helluva game, I appreciate that. Thanks."

Nineteen seventy-six was my comeback year. [Editor's note: In 1974 the noted orthopedic surgeon Dr. Frank Jobe took a tendon from Tommy John's forearm, made an ulnar collateral ligament, and put it in the pitcher's elbow. The surgery was revolutionary at the time, but it saved John's career and gave him what he referred to as a "bionic arm." Because of John's success, the procedure has been employed numerous times in pitchers' elbows and is referred to as Tommy John Surgery.]

I started out 1977 2–3, and I had an earned run average close to double digits. Maybe even into it. I pitched a game in Atlanta. I pitched four innings. We scored 13, 14 runs, and I gave up five home runs in the first four innings.

It got so bad I called [home-plate umpire] Ed Runge out to the mound and I said, "Throw me out of the game. I'm going to start cursing you. Throw me out of the game." And he said, "If I have to stay on here with this mess, you're staying out here, too. You can call me any name you want."

Tommy took me out of the game, and I was upset and he said, "I want to see you after the game." And I thought, "Ohh, something's wrong. I did something. I teed him off."

After the game, I was dressed. We were flying back to San Diego. We had a four-game series in San Diego. Tommy called me into his office. "Shut the door," he said. "You're not throwing good. You're upset, aren't you?"

I said, "Tommy, I want to throw good, because I want to do good for you." I like Tommy.

He pulled out a schedule and said, "We're at the first of May. This is Sunday. Your next start, Monday, Tuesday, Wednesday, Thursday, you're starting Friday against the Pirates in Dodger Stadium. Your next start, Saturday, Sunday, Monday, Tuesday, you're starting Wednesday at Dodger Stadium against St. Louis. Thursday's off. Friday, Saturday, Sunday, Monday, Tuesday's your next start on the road, here."

He went through the entire season, marked off my starts. He said, "These are your starts whether you're 2–25 or you win all the rest of your games. These are your starts. Because if we're going to win this, we're going to win it because you're going to pitch well and help us win."

He said, "Line up your golf games, get everything ready, because these are the games you're starting and the only thing that's going to change it is rain. We're going to go to San Diego, and I don't even want you to come to the ballpark for the game. Come out, do your running, go home. Spend time with your family. Get the hell away from the ballpark."

It would have been very easy for him to come in and say, "What are you doing . . . you're this and that . . ." That would have only compounded the thing. All he did was pat me on the back, hug me, and say, "Hey, I believe in you." I walked out of there, and I said, "OK, let's go have fun."

We flew to San Diego. I had my wife come down. I worked out early in the morning. I went to the ballpark, I did all my running, we drove back home, spent the day with our family. The next day, I drove down in the morning, did my workout early in the afternoon, drove back home. I did that for four straight days. I wound up 20–7 that year.

Tommy was great like that. I always said I would give Tommy the shirt off my back. It wouldn't fit him, but I would give it to him.

THE END OF AN ERA—THE FRANCHISE IS TRADED

Tom Seaver joined the Mets in 1967, won 16 games, and was named National League Rookie of the Year. Two years later, he led the league with 25 victories, had pitched 18 complete games (including five shutouts), had an earned run average of 2.21, and was the key player in the Mets' miracle drive to the world championship. He was named National League Cy Young Award winner for that year.

The Mets traded Tom Seaver to the Reds in the middle of the 1977 season, and Seaver made his first start for Cincinnati (above) on June 18 of that year.

Going into the 1977 season, Seaver was the acknowledged leader of the Mets, their star attraction, the greatest player in the franchise's 15-year history. In his 10 seasons with the Mets, he had won 182 games and lost only 107; four times he had won 20 games or more; five times he led the league in strikeouts; three times he was named winner of the Cy Young Award; he had pitched 39 shutouts; he had struck out 19 batters in a game (against San Diego on April 22, 1970); and he held the major league record of consecutive seasons with 200 or more strikeouts (nine). M. Donald Grant, the Mets chairman of the board, called Seaver "the Franchise."

As the 1977 season was nearing the halfway mark, Seaver and the Mets were engaged in discussions about a new contract, but a rift occurred between the pitcher and Grant, who thought that Seaver's demands for a $250,000 salary were greedy. Grant also resented Seaver's activities with the players union.

Seaver was a players union activist, an outspoken advocate for players' rights, which caused him to fall out of favor with Grant.

On June 15, 1977, the Mets shocked the baseball world, and broke the hearts of thousands of their most loyal fans, by announcing the trade of Tom Seaver, "the Franchise," to the Cincinnati Reds for four young players: pitcher Pat Zachry, infielder Doug Flynn, and outfielders Steve Henderson and Dan Norman. The trade was announced during a game between the Mets and Braves in Atlanta.

JACK LANG: Seaver pitched his last game for the Mets in Houston on a Sunday, and we flew to Atlanta that night. And I went to him in the hotel lobby and I said, "Instead of asking for an increase in salary, why don't you get them to extend your contract? Then you'll be guaranteed that you'll stay here a few more years."

We talked about it, and the next morning he called Lorinda de Roulet [daughter of the late Joan Payson, then the principal owner of the Mets]. That morning, I was having breakfast at the Atlanta Marriott and Seaver came in and joined me, and he told me he had worked it out with Mrs. de Roulet and he was going to accept an extension.

In the *New York Daily News,* Dick Young and I had been writing opposing stories on the Seaver situation. Young was taking Grant's side, and I was taking Seaver's side. On the back page, they would run our columns side by side; they called it "The Battle Page."

Now, after I had breakfast with Seaver, he went to his room, and I went to my room and called my office to tell them what I was writing that day. And I asked the editor, "What is Young writing today?" They read me Young's column, and it was all about how Nancy Seaver was jealous of Ruth Ryan because the Angels had just given Nolan Ryan a longtime contract and a big raise in pay and that Nancy Seaver was jealous because Tom didn't get the same kind of deal.

Later, we were sitting around the pool, several writers, and Seaver came down and sat down with us, and he said to me, "Well, what did Young write today?" So I said, "He wrote that Nancy is jealous of Ruth." And he said, "What?" and with that, he bolted from his chair saying, "That's it! That's it!" and hurried to his room.

The Mets were having a board of directors meeting. Somehow, Seaver found out what hotel the meeting was at and called the hotel. He got Mets VP Arthur Richman on the phone and told him, "Tell Mrs. de Roulet the whole deal is off. I don't want any part of it anymore. That's it."

All because Dick Young had written this column that Nancy Seaver was jealous of Ruth Ryan. And before the day was over, they made the deal.

TOM SEAVER: This was something that had festered for a long time. Sooner or later, it became inevitable. You just knew what was going to happen. I trusted the guy [Grant] I was working for, and from that standpoint, I was very naïve to think that he would have respected what I had done for him and his organization. That was probably the most distasteful part of it all.

I wanted to get out of there. I just did not want to work for that individual anymore. The whole organization was chaotic. There was no direction, there was no strength, there was no Gil Hodges in the organization.

I voiced my opinion of what was going on, and they didn't like it one bit. Grant called me a communist. That was a plantation mentality that was going on there.

It was in spring training when I said what I felt. We were playing the Pirates, and Willie Stargell came over and he said, "They're putting the big N on you, aren't they?" I said, "What?" He said, "Your guy's putting the big N on you." I said, "What are you talking about?" He said, "He's putting the big

The 30-Homer Club

In the National League West, the Dodgers, under rookie manager Tommy Lasorda, finished 10 games ahead of the Cincinnati Reds. When Dusty Baker hit his 30th home run in his final at-bat of the season, he gave the Dodgers four players with at least 30 homers—Steve Garvey, 33; Reggie Smith, 32; Ron Cey and Baker, 30—the first team ever to have four 30-homer hitters in one season.

nigger on you." Stargell's telling me this. I missed it twice, and I finally realized that's exactly what was happening, and I said, "Yeah. From that standpoint, yes, the plantation mentality." Stargell was exactly right.

But it was time to get out. It fell right in place what they did. The scenario followed right in sequence. Did you expect them at that point to all of a sudden do something that was positive?

BUD HARRELSON: I cried. When I heard about the trade, I cried. I didn't leave the game in Atlanta, but I came back into the dugout and everyone was waiting because it was the trading deadline and people thought it was going to happen. He went, and Dave Kingman went [to San Diego for Bobby Valentine and Paul Siebert]. Dave found out on the flight to Atlanta, but Tom found out during the game. They got rid of him. They didn't want the press to talk to him.

Every inning we kept saying, "Have you heard, have you heard?" and then one inning, he wasn't there. He had gone back to the clubhouse to change. In Atlanta the clubhouses weren't that close, so I raced up to the clubhouse between innings. I was crying. He said, "I can't believe it. I can't believe they really did it."

Tom was somber. I was hurt. To me, my best friend was leaving. The game has changed because that's expected now, but with a new organization, with all these kids who came up together, the Seavers, Koosmans, to see it dismantled . . . it started being dismantled big time in 1977.

I think it was making a statement. We were all gone after that.

It was inevitable that Harrelson would have to bat against his friend Seaver, and it happened a few weeks later when the Reds came to New York.

BUD HARRELSON: The first game was a night game. He didn't pitch, and after the game we went to Lum's Chinese Restaurant near Shea Stadium. He was pitching the next day, and I said to him, "So, roomie, how are you going to pitch me tomorrow?" He said, "I just don't want to hit you."

When I came to bat, I stood right up on top of the plate and he threw me the first pitch. Outside. Strike one. Farther outside. Strike two. Farther outside. Strike three. I mean, I was standing on the plate, but I guess the umpire and the catcher were moving and he kept throwing outside and he struck me out.

The next day, I said to the umpire, "He's good, but he's not that good. You can't give him those strikes."

I said to Tom, "There's no way those were strikes," and he said, "Hey, he gave me the first one. I just wanted to find out how much I could get."

He struck me out twice, and I got a hit. He hung a curveball, and I hit it right through the middle. Why he threw me a curveball is beyond me, but he threw me a curveball, I guess out of necessity, and I got a hit. I'm 2–5 against him in my career, three strikeouts and two base hits.

I faced him when I went to the Phillies in 1978. I didn't play much with the Phillies, so I figured I wasn't going to see him much. If he was pitching, I wasn't playing. But I got in one game. I had set it up with Phillies manager Danny Ozark. I said, "Danny, have you ever squeezed 3–2?" He said, "I would never squeeze 3–2." I said, "Well, you could squeeze with me." He said, "I wouldn't do it with Larry Bowa." I said, "You can squeeze with me 3–2."

I don't know how much longer after I said that to him, Seaver was pitching, I was batting, and the count was 3–2, a runner on third base with one out. I looked down for the sign, and I got the squeeze. Seaver? I said to myself, "Not with *him*."

He threw a slider, believe it or not, 3–2, this little, dinky slider down and in. He knew I was not going to take anything close now, and he was going to give me a ball I couldn't lift in the air. And I bunted it right down the first-base line fair. He was going after the ball, and he was cursing me all the way to the ball because he never anticipated the bunt. Not because of me. He didn't think Ozark would do it. And he let me know it, "You so-and-so, blankety-blank," and he tagged me hard.

A TEAM IN THE DARK

Perhaps even the gods were displeased with the trade of Tom Seaver. Two days short of a month after the trade, with the Mets playing the Cubs at Shea Stadium and Lenny Randle at bat, a power failure hit New York City, the big 1977 blackout, throwing the stadium into total darkness.

***

BOB MANDT: I was in the ticket office where we have no windows and all the lights went out, and my first thought was we were being robbed. I didn't know what was going on outside. I didn't know there was a citywide blackout at the time. I yelled to somebody, "Lock the vault." Actually, that was ridiculous, because the vault was electric.

Craig Swan and Buddy Harrelson led some of the players' cars onto the field, and, in the cars' headlights, they did a pantomime of a ballgame, fielding, throwing the ball from the shortstop to the second baseman to the first baseman, to entertain the fans.

We had no incidents, and in those days we really didn't have the kind of emergency lighting that we have today. That game pointed out the need for more things to be on emergency.

We balanced the receipts that night. We had people counting the tickets by candlelight. The next day was called off, even though it was a day game and possibly you could get by without lights. But it was a health issue. The toilets operate on an electric ejector system and we would not have toilets working, so they called the game even though it was a beautiful, sunny day.

About six years later, my secretary said, "There's a man outside and he's got an old ticket, a full ticket, and he wants a refund or another game." I had her send him in. This elderly gentleman came in, and he had a full ticket for the day after the blackout game. The game that was called off. And it was a senior citizen's ticket for 50 cents.

He said, "I found this in my drawer. I was supposed to go to a game in 1977, and they called the game off. They had a problem at Shea Stadium. I've been holding it all these years. Is it worth anything?"

I said, "My friend, you're going to sit in a box seat today."

THE BRONX ZOO

Once he accepted his lot—outcast among his teammates, whipping post for the owner, scorned by the manager—Reggie Jackson seemed to adjust to life as a Yankee. He began to move about more comfortably in the clubhouse, initiating conversations with other players, becoming a part of the baseball players' customary needling and put-down humor on buses and planes, even making a concerted effort to engage his estranged teammate, Munson, in small talk.

Slowly, Reggie was winning over his teammates by showing an ability to take the needling, especially from center fielder Mickey Rivers, a free spirit with no hidden agenda who was impossible to dislike or take seriously. Exchanges between Rivers and Jackson—with Rivers doing most of the giving, Jackson most of the taking—were hilarious diversions on long bus rides.

Mickey Rivers: Reginald Martinez Jackson. You got a white man's first name, a Spanish man's second name, and a black man's last name. You all f***ed up.

Reggie Jackson: I must be crazy. I've got an IQ of 160 and I'm arguing with a man who can't even read or write.

Mickey Rivers: Well, you better stop readin' and stop writin' and start hittin'.

———

BUCKY DENT: The Reggies, Nettleses, Thurmans, Sparky Lyles. Those were character guys who understood how to have fun but knew how to get serious about what they had to do on the field. That Yankees team was special. They had a way of getting on you in a constructive way. They would embarrass you to where you didn't want to make a mistake.

Thurman. It's hard to describe Thurman, because he could get away with saying things that most people couldn't, because that's his personality. He used to irritate me all the time, because he knew I hated to get pinch hit for, and he started this thing where he would whistle at me when I was in the on-deck circle. And he'd start laughing, because he knew Billy was going to pinch hit for me.

So what happened was, I never left the on-deck circle. Every time they'd whistle at me, I'd just stand there. I'd look back to make sure Billy was going to let me hit before I went up. Thurman used to whistle at me from the dugout, and pretty soon everybody was whistling at me. It became a big thing, because they knew it bothered me.

Reggie. I liked Reggie. I always got along with him. The one thing I noticed about Reggie, in my first spring training with the Yankees, he worked as hard as anybody I've ever been around. He worked and he wanted to win and he went in hard at second base.

And those bus rides. They were unbelievable. Mickey Rivers was one of the funniest guys I ever met, but he was a fierce competitor. He could play.

And Lou Piniella. The way he used to get on Catfish. I'll never forget the bus ride in 1977. We were going to Boston, and Piniella was all over Catfish. He said, "You pitching tomorrow, Cat?" Catfish goes, "Yeah, I'm pitching tomorrow." And Piniella said, "They're going to have to wear hard hats over in Copley Square, because they're going to hit some bombs off you." The next game, Catfish was pitching, and four of the first five guys hit home runs off him. They set some kind of a record. They hit something like 19 home runs for the weekend.

We went to Detroit, and Jason Thompson hit one off Dick Tidrow on the roof. Then we went to Comiskey Park, and Richie Zisk hit one on the roof. That year, the ball was flying out, and Piniella told Catfish, "The next time you pitch, I'm going to stand out in left field with a crab net."

Those bus rides were incredible.

Lou Piniella to Catfish Hunter: "I know how George can get back some of that money he gave you. He's going to sell hard hats to the fans who sit in the right-field stands when you pitch."

Graig Nettles: "The best thing about playing for the Yankees is you get to see Reggie Jackson play every day. The worst thing about playing for the Yankees is you get to see Reggie Jackson play every day."

Carlos May to Mickey Rivers during a discussion on which player had the higher IQ: "You don't even know how to spell *IQ*."

By mid-June, controversy was the order of the day with the Yankees, causing someone to refer to Yankee Stadium as the Bronx Zoo and Nettles, with his acerbic wit, to crack, "When I was a kid, I wanted to do two things: play major league baseball and be in the circus. I'm lucky. I got to do them both."

Distractions came almost daily. George and Billy, George and Reggie, Reggie and Billy. But they were not alone. It seemed to be an epidemic, a daily soap opera that spread throughout the entire team like a fire out of control.

For instance, Sparky Lyle, irate at being removed from a game, barged into the clubhouse, changed into his street clothes, and left the park before the end of the game, causing Steinbrenner to demand that Martin fine the relief pitcher. Martin refused, setting off another Billy-versus-George confrontation.

The big explosion came on Saturday afternoon, June 18, in Boston. Full-scale war broke out in Fenway Park. All the tension, all the turmoil, all the frustration, all the festering hostility erupted in an ugly scene in the visitors' dugout, in full view of some 35,000 fans and a national television audience.

It came in the middle of what would be a three-game sweep by the Red Sox, which added to the frustration and the rising tempers. Jackson was slow retrieving a ball hit into the right-field corner by Jim Rice. Jackson said it was caution. Martin said it was indifference.

Suddenly, Paul Blair was on his way out to right field, sent there by Martin to replace a perplexed, astonished, and embarrassed Reggie.

When Blair reached right field, Jackson said, "You here for me?"

Blair nodded.

"What the hell's going on?" Reggie asked.

"You've got to ask Billy that," Blair said.

Jackson trotted in from right field to the Yankees' dugout and ducked into the far corner. Martin was at the opposite end, closest to home plate, but he headed toward the end of the dugout where Jackson was. There were words between them, and then Martin, red-faced, the veins bulging in his neck, was attempting to get at Jackson and being restrained in a bear hug by coach Yogi Berra.

FRAN HEALY: I was in the bullpen and Reggie was leaning over the railing, and we were talking, probably about nothing significant. I thought Reggie had lost his confidence in the outfield at the time. You knew he didn't want the ball hit to him.

The ball had fallen in that he really had a shot at catching. Then he was talking to me, and I saw Paul Blair running out and I said what I was thinking: "Uh-oh." He said, "What?" I said, "I think Billy wants you."

He turned around, and he left. He went in. The next thing you know, they had their thing in the dugout. Later, I was in the clubhouse and Reggie was going to stay there. They were going to have a tussle. So I said to him, "Why don't you just go back to the hotel?"

I was covering the Yankees for the *New York Daily News* at the time of the incident in Boston and had the opportunity to discuss the events of that day several times with the late Billy Martin. Each time, he stood by his version of what happened that day. The following is his version.

BILLY MARTIN: I didn't like the way Reggie went after the ball. I thought he dogged it, and I just can't have that sort of thing on my team. I had told my players at the beginning of the season if they embarrassed me on the field, I was going to embarrass them. I knew the other 24 players were looking to see how I was going to handle this, with Reggie being a superstar and having the big contract. I thought if I did what had to be done, that would bring George down on me. But if I let it pass, I would lose the other 24 players.

I knew what I had to do. I told Paul Blair to go out to right field and tell Reggie he was being replaced. I meant to teach him a lesson.

When he came into the dugout, Reggie challenged me. He kept telling me he didn't like being shown up, and I replied, "If you show me up, I'll show you up." Then he swore at me, and that did it—we almost came to blows. Elston Howard and Yogi Berra had to pull us apart.

Perhaps it's all in the eye of the beholder. Reggie Jackson's version at the time, and repeated often in later years, naturally differed considerably from Martin's.

REGGIE JACKSON: I'm sure Billy thought I didn't hustle after the ball. He was wrong. Hustle had nothing to do with it. It wasn't the greatest play I ever made in the outfield, but I was giving it 100 percent, even if it didn't look that way to Billy.

When I got to the top step of the dugout, I could see there was a fury about Billy, and it was all directed at me. He screamed over to me, "What the [bleep] do you think you're doing out there?"

I said, "What do you mean? What are you talking about?"

He started down the dugout toward me. "You know what the [bleep] I'm talking about. You want to show me up by loafing on me? Fine. Then I'm going to show you up. Anyone who doesn't hustle doesn't play for me."

"I wasn't loafing, Billy," I said. "But I'm sure that doesn't matter to you. Nothing I could ever do would please you. You never wanted me on this team in the first place. You don't want me now. Why don't you just admit it?"

"I ought to kick your ass" was the next thing I heard.

And then I'd had enough. "Who do you think you're talking to, old man?" I snapped.

"What?" Billy yelled. "Who are you calling an old man?"

He came for me. Elston and Yogi grabbed him. Jimmy Wynn grabbed me from behind. I was livid, but I wasn't going to fight him in the dugout. I walked past everybody into the tunnel and headed for the clubhouse. I could still hear Billy screaming from behind me.

PHIL PEPE: Later that night, two other reporters—Steve Jacobson of *Newsday* and Paul Montgomery of *The New York Times*—and I went to Jackson's room. Mike Torrez, who had started for the Yankees that afternoon, was there to console his friend. Jackson seemed near a breakdown. First he was calm, then he grew increasingly passionate. He was stripped to the waist, medals and chains around his neck, dangling at his chest. Perspiration glistened on his bare chest, and soon tears began to stream down his face.

He was on his knees, as if in prayer, delivering a sermon like an evangelist, pouring out anger, frustration, and anguish along with his perspiration and tears, wondering why he was being persecuted, why he was so misunderstood, unappreciated, and unwanted. The sweat and the tears were a pool on the floor at his knees.

"It makes me cry the way they treat me on this team," he said. "I'm a big, black man with an IQ of 160, making $700,000 a year, and they treat me like dirt. They've never had anyone like me on their team before."

Among the national television audience watching the Yankees–Red Sox game from Fenway Park on June 18 was Yankees owner George Steinbrenner, who was appalled at the ugly scene in the dugout. His first impulse was to fire his manager on the spot, but team president Gabe Paul intervened and, serving as fence mender, brought Billy Martin and Reggie Jackson together for a form of baseball *détente*.

A few days later, Steinbrenner held a press conference and outlined those things by which a manager should be judged. They would come to be known as George's "Seven Commandments."

1. Does he win?
2. Does he work hard enough?
3. Is he emotionally equipped to lead men?
4. Is he organized?
5. Does he understand human nature?
6. Is he prepared for each game?
7. Is he honorable?

It was decided by those writers attending the press conference that Billy Martin passed Steinbrenner's test, 4–3.

On the night of June 24, six days after the incident in the dugout in Boston, six days after completing a three-game sweep of the Yankees, the Red Sox arrived at Yankee Stadium for a three-game series leading the Yankees by five games.

Three home runs had given the Red Sox a 5–3 lead going into the bottom of the ninth, with their ace reliever, Bill Campbell, pitching. With two outs and nobody on, Willie Randolph hit a drive to left field that Carl Yastrzemski got a glove on but couldn't hold, and Randolph raced to third with a triple. Veteran Roy White followed with a tremendous, dramatic, game-tying home run into the upper deck in right field. Then, in the eleventh inning, Reggie Jackson singled in the winning run. The Yankees went on to sweep the three games.

On August 2 the Yankees crushed the Angels in Anaheim, 9–3, and stood a game and a half behind the Red Sox and Orioles. The Yankees were on a roll, gaining ground on the leaders. But once again, serenity was shattered.

Thurman Munson, still miffed at being slighted by Reggie Jackson in the *Sport* magazine article, still making noises about a trade to the Cleveland Indians so that he could play closer to home, was growing a beard. He had not shaved in five days, and the stubble was beginning to lengthen, in defiance of a team (i.e., George Steinbrenner) rule against facial hair.

When reporters asked him about the growth, Munson replied simply, "I like beards."

Was he making a statement, asking for a confrontation with Steinbrenner?

"I'm not asking for anything."

What about the rule against beards?

"Isn't that against the Constitution? Isn't that against the employment act or something? I'm worried about my hitting, not my beard. I'll blame it on the writers. Writers have beards. I think it looks good. Did you notice how short my hair is? Some guys have long hair. I got a haircut yesterday. I'm trying to keep up with the team code—short hair, team man, team player.

"Billy doesn't mind the beard. If Billy doesn't mind, that probably means George does mind."

Five days later, at the behest of his manager, who asked the catcher to "do it for me, as a friend" to avoid another confrontation with Steinbrenner, Munson shaved.

Peace came to the Yankees, at least temporarily, on August 10, when Billy Martin swallowed his pride and installed Reggie Jackson in the cleanup spot. He would remain there for the rest of the season, hitting 13 home runs and driving in 49 runs in the final 53 games.

Thirteen days later, with Mickey Rivers getting five hits and Mike Torrez recording his seventh straight complete-game victory, the Yankees moved into first place.

With four games remaining in the regular season, the Yankees needed one win, or a Boston defeat, to clinch their second straight American League East title. But they lost to Cleveland, then lost the following night to Detroit, while the Red Sox won both their games. With two games left, the Yankees' magic number was still one.

On the next-to-last day of the season, they fell behind the Tigers, 4–1, in the third inning, while up in Boston the Red Sox were ahead of the Orioles. It began to rain on Yankee Stadium, interrupting their game, so the Yankees players went to the clubhouse lounge to watch the Red Sox–Orioles game on television.

While the rain fell steadily in New York, the Yankees watched the Orioles take the lead over the Red Sox. Then they watched Jim Rice pop to Elliott Maddox for the final out. The Yankees were division champions.

For the second straight year, the Kansas City Royals won the American League West, setting up a rematch of their dramatic and thrilling 1976 Championship Series with the Yankees.

A MAN NAMED SCHMIDT

In the National League, the Phillies finished five games ahead of the Pirates in the Eastern Division. Steve Carlton, relying more on his awesome slider and with Tim McCarver as his personal catcher, won 23 games and his second Cy Young Award. Mike Schmidt, now the premier power hitter in the league, slugged 38 home runs for the third consecutive season (George Foster's 52-homer explosion kept Schmidt from winning a fourth straight home-run title) and drove in 101 runs.

TIM McCARVER: I called Mike Schmidt's first major league home run against Balor Moore in 1972. I was catching for Montreal at the time. When Mike was younger, I thought he had too many holes as a hitter. I thought he was an outstanding athlete, but I had no idea he had Hall of Fame credentials. I missed him. I just felt like with his stroke, he had too many holes.

I knew Mike was awfully strong, but I just felt that at the plate he swung through too many pitches. He hit .196 his first year. He hit some home runs, but I had no idea he would turn out to be the player that he did.

When I played with him in 1976, I knew his greatness. In April we were trailing 13–2 in Chicago, and Schmitty ended up hitting four home runs in that game. The first two off Rick Reuschel, the fourth one off Paul Reuschel

[Schmidt also had a single and eight RBIs, and the Phillies won the game, 18–16], and I realized that year that this guy is some kind of talent. But I didn't realize it until 1976.

GOING FOR 50

George Foster's 52 homers made him only the 10th man in baseball history to hit 50 home runs in a season—the other nine were Babe Ruth (four times), Jimmie Foxx (twice), Mickey Mantle (twice), Ralph Kiner (twice), Willie Mays (twice), and Roger Maris, Hank Greenberg, Hack Wilson, and Johnny Mize (once each).

But the true measure of Foster's accomplishment is in the list of players who never hit 50 home runs in a season—Hank Aaron, Frank Robinson, Harmon Killebrew, Mike Schmidt, Ted Williams, Willie McCovey, Eddie Mathews, Ernie Banks, Mel Ott, Lou Gehrig, Joe DiMaggio, and Reggie Jackson.

––––––––––

GEORGE FOSTER: When I had 49 home runs, all I could think about was what if I ended the season with only 49. Then I started to put undue pressure on myself, feeling I didn't want to get this far and end up with 49, even though 49 is a good number. Hitting 50 is like the difference between hitting .300 or .299. Getting that extra point puts you in a separate category.

My first time at bat after 49, I was really swinging for the home run and I didn't get a home run in that at-bat. The second time at bat, I had gotten some advice from Reds hitting instructor Ted Kluszewski. He said, "Whatever you did to get to 49, that's going to help you get beyond 49." So I took a nice, easy swing, got a good pitch to hit, and hit a line drive to left field for my 50th.

I didn't know how many guys had hit 50 home runs. I knew Willie Mays had done it, and, being my idol, I wanted to emulate what he had done. That's what made me feel good about hitting 50 home runs. It was something that an individual I had idolized had done.

In those days, you didn't get a lot of information about who did what before. Not like today when all that information is at your fingertips. Reporters make you aware of what's going on. I ended up with 388 total

The Big Red Machine added even more horsepower in the midseventies with the addition of George Foster, who hit 52 home runs in 1977. No one hit 50 home runs in a season again until Detroit's Cecil Fielder in 1990.

bases [only 21 times in baseball history had a player had 400 total bases in a season], but I didn't know that until the last eight or nine games. It probably wouldn't have made a big difference if I had known, but it does give you that extra incentive to go out and achieve certain things.

I needed three hits for 200 and one RBI for 150 and I would have been the fourth man in major league history [Babe Ruth, Jimmie Foxx, and Hack Wilson were the first three] to hit 50 homers, hit .300, get 200 hits, and drive in 150 runs in a season.

THE RAIN IN SPAIN . . .

The Dodgers, who hit a league-high 191 home runs during the regular season, hit only three in the playoffs, two of them by Dusty Baker. After losing the first game at home, the Dodgers got a complete game from Don Sutton and won Game 2, came from behind to win Game 3, and got a complete game from Tommy John, who outdueled Steve Carlton in Philly in Game 4—the game that never should have been played—to clinch the pennant.

TOMMY JOHN: When I pitched, I used to like to walk a lot. Sally [Tommy's wife] and I went down to Wanamaker's in Philadelphia and went all through and just walked around and I got back to the hotel and I took a nap. I told Sally, "Make reservations at Bookbinders, because this game's going to get washed out." That's how hard it was raining.

I walked over to the stadium, and the guys in the clubhouse were watching a football game, Alabama against Southern Cal, or some big game like that. So I lay down on the trainer's table and took a nap. I got up and they said, "The game's getting ready to start." I said, "What?" They said, "They're getting ready to start the game."

So I got myself ready. I got my arm loose and I got my uniform on, and I went down to the umpire's room and I said, "Are we really going to try to start it?" They said, "We're going to try to start it on time because of television. We've got a window of opportunity, maybe an hour or so, and we're going to try to get as many innings in as we can."

I started the game; it was a light rain. I told Dodgers pitching coach Red Adams, "You know, Red, this is the absolute worst kind of turf for a sinkerball pitcher to pitch on." I'd pitched on wet turf before, and the balls just really skid. It started to rain harder as the game went on, and it never stopped raining the whole game. But they had the infield covered all day, and, amazingly, the ball never got wet until Bob Boone hit a ground ball to Bill Russell in the ninth inning. When they threw the ball back to me, it was wet and I threw it out of play and I got another ball back from [umpire] Bruce Froemming. I struck out Bake McBride to end the game.

TIM McCARVER: What made that game so important was our loss the day before. We had a two-run lead with nobody on in the ninth inning and two outs. And we lost the game.

After the World Series, my wife and I were in New York and we went to Toots Shor's for dinner, and Chub Feeney was there and he came over and was all apologetic.

He said, "You know, some people said it was television that made us do that, but it wasn't."

I didn't even ask for an excuse, and he was apologizing to someone who didn't ask for the apology. Methinks he doth protest too much. I'm sure he felt self-conscious because we lost the game. The game should never have been played, and I'm not saying that because we lost. It's 20 years ago, and who cares now?

REMATCH

For the second straight year, the American League Championship Series between the Yankees and Royals was high drama in five acts. The Royals hit three home runs and won the first game in Yankee Stadium. But the Yankees tied the series by winning the second game, 6–2, on a three-hitter by Ron Guidry, the skinny little left-hander from Lafayette, Louisiana, who had not won a major league game before this season but came out of the bullpen to become a starter and win 16 games, including five shutouts.

Bad blood coursed between the two teams as they moved to Kansas City for the final three games. The Yankees were upset by Hal McRae's vicious takeout of second baseman Willie Randolph, the middleman on a double play.

GEORGE BRETT: We had a pretty good rivalry going, and there was some real overaggressive play. Hal McRae knocking Willie Randolph out in breaking up a double play, then laying on him and telling the guy from third base to score. It was real aggressive, almost to the point of dirty.

I remember Lou Piniella sliding into third base in Yankee Stadium on a play where I didn't even have the ball. I was standing about three feet away from the bag, and he came in and slid and tried to kick me with his spikes. That's the way the series was.

I was leading off an inning, and I hit a triple in my first at-bat and slid into third and kind of came up and threw a forearm and fell backward a little. As I fell backward, Nettles kind of stepped back and kicked me in the face. I got up and tried to throw punches. The funny thing about that is Graig and I were such good friends. Still are to this day.

Thurman Munson was one of the first guys down there on the pile right in front of the third-base dugout, and he just lay right on top of me and wouldn't let anybody hit me because we were so close to their dugout. I was on the bottom of the pile, and Thurman protected me.

The Royals took Game 3 at home, 6–2, and were one win away from their first pennant.

In Game 4 the Yankees opened a 4–0 lead in the third. The Royals came back with two in the bottom of the third, and the Yankees increased their lead to 5–2 in the fourth. When the Royals rallied in the bottom of the fourth and closed to 5–4, Billy Martin made a daring, if desperate, move. He brought in his "closer," Sparky Lyle, who had pitched two and one-third innings the previous day.

Lyle was brilliant. He held the Royals scoreless over the final five and one-third innings, and the Yankees forced a Game 5 with a 6–4 victory.

———

GRAIG NETTLES: Sparky saved us all season. He had an amazing year, but to do that in the playoffs and to pitch almost six innings was unbelievable.

———

Lyle said he would be available for Game 5.

"The most I can pitch is five or six innings," he said. "I'm serious. I can pitch five or six innings. I get better as I go along. My slider is better when my arm is tired."

*The Yankees returned to the World Series for a second straight year and won
Game 1 on this Willie Randolph run in the twelfth inning against the Dodgers.*

Before the start of the series, Reggie Jackson had predicted, "We'll win because we're a team of great character." Now, in Game 5, Jackson would need all the character he could muster, for when he arrived at the ballpark, Jackson noted that his name was not in the starting lineup.

With left-hander Paul Splittorff scheduled to pitch for the Royals, Martin decided to replace Jackson in right field with Paul Blair. It was a more subtle replacement than the one that afternoon in Boston four months earlier, but to Jackson it was just as humiliating, just as much of a slight and an embarrassment. And it was deliberate. "Billy slapping me down one more time," Jackson would say later.

Martin's rationale was that Jackson was 1 for 14 in the series, and Splittorff was a tough left-hander, the kind who gave Jackson trouble. But this was Reggie Jackson, a clutch player who always came up big in big games.

REGGIE JACKSON: I was surprised, shocked, hurt. You've got to be down. The season was on the line, and I was on the bench. Your pride's hurt. But I didn't want to be a problem. Not then. The writers came around looking for me to make a scene, but I wasn't going to do it. What I told them was "The man says I'm not playing, I'm not playing. He shouldn't be concerned about Reggie Jackson. He should manage the game."

Martin took his gamble, once again putting his job on the line, and Jackson took his seat on the bench. He was still there, and Splittorff was still on the mound, when the Yankees batted in the top of the eighth, trailing 3–1.

Willie Randolph led off the inning for the Yankees with a single, prompting Royals manager Whitey Herzog to lift Splittorff for right-hander Doug Bird to face Thurman Munson. Munson fanned, but Lou Piniella came through with a single. Two on, one out, and Cliff Johnson, the DH, scheduled up. Martin looked down the bench and said, "Reggie, hit for Cliff."

Jackson wanted a home run to put the Yankees ahead, but his time for dramatic home runs had not yet come. He settled for a single, scoring Randolph, and it was 3–2, which is how it stood going into the top of the ninth.

Paul Blair got a big hit to lead off the ninth. Roy White walked. Mickey Rivers singled in the tying run before Willie Randolph hit a sacrifice fly to put the Yankees ahead. Rivers scored an insurance run on Brett's error. The Yankees scored three in the top of the ninth, and Sparky Lyle, pitching for the third straight day, held the Royals scoreless in the bottom of the ninth. He had pitched nine innings in three days, allowed one run, and won two games.

There was champagne being sprayed all over the Yankees' clubhouse. Martin had a bottle of the bubbly in his hand when he spotted owner George Steinbrenner, sneaked up behind him, and emptied its contents on the boss's head.

"That's for trying to fire me," said Martin.

"What do you mean trying?" said Steinbrenner.

For the second straight year, the Yankees were headed for the World Series. Reggie Jackson? He was headed for destiny.

MR. OCTOBER

Reggie Jackson was back in the cleanup spot and in right field in Billy Martin's lineup for the opening game of the World Series in Yankee Stadium. Jackson batted four times. With two outs in the bottom of the first, after the Dodgers had reached Don Gullett for two runs in the top of the inning, Jackson blooped a single to center, sending Thurman Munson to third. He scored on Chris Chambliss's single, cutting the Dodgers' lead to 2–1.

Jackson popped to third in the fourth, was hit by a pitch in the sixth, and walked in the eighth, when the Yankees took a 3–2 lead.

The Dodgers tied it in the ninth, sending the game into extra innings, the Yankees winning with a run in the bottom of the twelfth. Ironically, the game-winning hit was a single by Paul Blair, once again sent in to replace Jackson in right field after the Yankees had taken the lead in the eighth.

Jackson was hitless in four at-bats in Game 2, with two strikeouts, a fly out, and a double play. The Dodgers flashed their home-run power with blasts by Ron Cey, Steve Yeager, and Reggie Smith off Catfish Hunter and by Steve Garvey off Sparky Lyle. The Yankees were stopped by Burt Hooton on a 6–1 five-hitter to square the Series at one game apiece as the teams headed for Los Angeles for the middle three games.

In Game 3 Jackson singled and walked in four plate appearances and drove in his first run of the Series in a three-run Yankees first.

The Dodgers tied it in the bottom of the third on a three-run homer by Dusty Baker off Mike Torrez.

MIKE TORREZ: I was really upset because I hung a slider. When I came back to the bench, I told Billy, "They're not going to get another run the rest of the game." I was really upset, because I knew I was throwing good. They did not get any runs the rest of the game. I shut them down.

While Torrez was shutting the Dodgers down, the Yankees pecked away for single runs off Tommy John in the fourth and fifth and took Game 3, 5–3, for a two-games-to-one lead in the Series.

Game 4 was marked by the end of Jackson's homer drought. He connected in the sixth for the final run in the Yankees' 4–2 win behind Ron Guidry's masterful complete-game four-hitter, which left the Yankees one win away from their first world championship since 1962.

There was hardly anything remarkable about Game 5 and nothing particularly noteworthy about back-to-back solo homers by Thurman Munson and Reggie Jackson in the eighth. They served only as window dressing as the Dodgers were on their way to a 10–4 rout that would return the World Series to Yankee Stadium. With two chances to clinch in their ballpark, the Yankees were filled with confidence, and so was Jackson. If nothing else, his home runs in each of the previous two games convinced him that he had regained his long-ball stroke.

MIKE TORREZ: Ed Figueroa was supposed to start the sixth game, but during the fifth game Eddie went in to trainer Gene Monahan and said that his right index finger was bothering him. So during the game, Monahan went and told Billy that Figueroa told him his finger was bothering him. I was supposed to pitch the seventh game if there was one, but once Billy heard that Figueroa had a little tenderness in his pitching finger, Billy changed his mind.

We were in the clubhouse, getting showered and dressed, getting ready to catch the plane back to New York, and Billy called me into his office and closed the door.

Steve Garvey, with 33 home runs, was one of four men who hit at least 30 home runs for the 1977 Dodgers. The others were Reggie Smith (32), Ron Cey (30), and Dusty Baker (30).

"How do you feel?" he said.

I said, "I feel good, why?"

He said, "You want to pitch Game 6?"

I said, "Hell, yeah, I'm ready to pitch anytime, you know me, Billy."

He said, "OK, you got the ball."

I said, "I thought Figueroa was pitching."

He said, "Aw, he gave Gene Monahan some kind of excuse that he had a little tenderness in his pitching finger. That's all I had to hear. I know you want the ball; you'll give me the effort I'm looking for. You got the ball. Don't say anything; I'll mention it to Figueroa."

Some way or another, Eddie got wind of it. Coming back on the plane, he asked me, "Hey, Mike, are you pitching the sixth game?" And I didn't know what to say, because I didn't know if Billy had told him. I said, "Well, yeah . . ."

He was upset. He really made a big deal of it. That's when he said he was going to quit; he didn't want to go to the stadium. He was pissed because Billy didn't give him the ball.

It was cool and clear in New York on the night of October 18, 1977, with a capacity crowd of 56,407 at Yankee Stadium in a festive mood as they anticipated the clincher. They remained undaunted when the Dodgers pushed two runs across in the first inning off Mike Torrez, pitching with three days' rest, and the Yankees were set down in order in the bottom of the first by Burt Hooton.

Leading off the bottom of the second, Jackson walked on four pitches, and Chambliss followed with a line drive into the right-center-field bleachers to tie the score at 2–2. The "other" Reggie, the Dodgers' Smith, put his team ahead with a solo homer in the top of the third, but Munson led off the bottom of the fourth with a single and Reggie Jackson stepped to the plate.

REGGIE JACKSON: I knew the scouting report the Dodgers had on me was to pitch me inside. So I decided to make a minor adjustment and back off the plate about six inches. The first time up, Hooton walked me on four pitches. This time, he threw me the first pitch inside and I hit it on a line into the right-field seats.

One of the greatest feats in World Series history: Reggie Jackson's three home runs on pitches off three different pitchers in Game 6 of the 1977 World Series. They helped the Yankees to an 8–4 win and the championship.

As he circled the bases, the television camera focused on his face and Jackson looked into the camera and mouthed, "Hi, Mom" twice. Then he ducked into the jubilant Yankees dugout, and the first one to greet him was Billy Martin, who patted the slugger on the cheek.

The blow put the Yankees ahead 4–3. They added another run on Chambliss' double, a ground ball, and a sacrifice fly by Lou Piniella. In the bottom of the fifth, Mickey Rivers singled, but Willie Randolph and Thurman Munson were retired and Jackson batted with a runner on first, two out, against reliever Elias Sosa.

REGGIE JACKSON: I'm saying to myself he [Sosa] hasn't had time to talk to Hooton. I was just praying he would throw me another pitch inside, and he did. When I hit it, I hooked it, and I wasn't sure it was going to go out until it did.

The Yankees led 7–3. They were on the verge of winning the World Series. But Reggie Jackson still was not finished. He was the leadoff hitter in the bottom of the eighth against knuckleballer Charlie Hough.

REGGIE JACKSON: When they brought in Hough, I said, "Man, I got eight or nine homers off Wilbur Wood, Eddie Fisher, and Hoyt Wilhelm [all knuckleballers]. They can't be bringing this guy in. The first pitch he threw me was like room service. I mean, the ball looked like a beach ball.

Jackson swung at Hough's first pitch and drove it deep into the night, deep into the seats in right-center field. Going back to his last at-bat in Game 5, Jackson had hit home runs in four consecutive official at-bats, home runs on four consecutive swings off four different pitchers. His three home runs in one game tied the World Series record set by Babe Ruth in 1926 and repeated in 1928. He had set a record with five home runs in a World Series.

He would be dubbed, by Thurman Munson of all people, "Mr. October."

As Jackson flew around the bases, the crowd chanted, "Reg-gie . . . Reg-gie . . . Reg-gie . . ."

Rounding third base and heading for home, Jackson blew kisses at the press level of the stadium, in the direction of the owner's box. He reached the dugout, and waiting for him there, ready to throw his arms around Jackson and embrace him, was Billy Martin.

CHRIS CHAMBLISS: The home run I hit in the second inning to tie the game was my only World Series home run. It was a big moment for me, but it happened to be the game Reggie hit three. I hit my only World Series home run, and nobody remembers it.

MIKE TORREZ: What Reggie did was great, because I was pitching that game and I needed all the runs I could get. I pitched a complete game, and I caught the last out of the World Series. Lee Lacy tried to bunt. Graig Nettles was

Jackson is mobbed by delirious Yankees fans after the final out of the 1977 World Series.

Billy Martin, who replaced Bill Virdon halfway through the 1975 season and managed the Yankees to pennants in 1976 and 1977, celebrates with World Series MVP Reggie Jackson after the Yankees' 1977 championship, the franchise's first since 1962.

playing back, so Lacy tried to bunt and he popped it up, and I caught the last out of the 1977 World Series.

REGGIE SMITH: The frustration of that Series was that I actually believed, and still believe to this day, that we had a better ballclub. On those days, they played better baseball and they won the World Series, and you can never take that away from them. But if you went down the line, man for man, we had a better ballclub.

I hit three home runs in that Series, but nobody remembers. He [Reggie Jackson] hit three in one game, and it will forever be remembered. It was a performance that will never be forgotten by anyone who had a chance to see it. Three different pitches, three swings, and three home runs.

When they started chanting "Reggie . . . Reggie . . . Reggie . . ." I never thought they were talking about me. In New York, I knew who they were talking about.

More than two hours after the final out, after the cheering had subsided in celebration of the Yankees' world championship, after the obligatory champagne had been splashed and sprayed and most of the reporters and cameras and many of the players had left the clubhouse, Reggie Jackson was still basking in the glow of his remarkable performance. It was as if he didn't want to go home, didn't want this night to end. He just wanted to stay in the ballpark and savor the moment.

He was still dressed in his uniform as he walked into the manager's office and plopped himself on a couch.

"I hit three home runs tonight," he said. "Do you realize that? Three home runs."

"Yeah," Martin said. "And you broke my record [for extra-base hits in a World Series], and that tees me off."

With that, both men, who had battled so often during the season, began to laugh.

"Billy Martin," Jackson said. "I love the man. I love Billy Martin. The man did a hell of a job this year. There's nobody I'd rather play for."

"Next year," Martin said, "is going to be super."

"Weak is the man who cannot accept adversity," Jackson said. "Next year, we're going to be tougher, aren't we, Skip?"

"You bet we will," Martin said. "We'll win it again next year."

"Yes we will," Jackson agreed. "We'll win because we have a manager who's feisty, and I'm feisty, and we're going to be tougher next year. I'll go to the wall for him and he'll go to the wall for me, and if anybody clashes with us, they're in trouble."

CHAPTER 9

1978

THE NINTH INNING

BILLY AND SPARKY

Billy Martin arrived in spring training the happiest he had been in years. He had brought his beloved Yankees their first world championship since 1962. He was idolized by thousands of grateful Yankees fans, a hero in the greatest city in the world. He had patched up his differences with Reggie Jackson. And his relationship was the best it had been with his boss, George Steinbrenner, who recognized Martin's managerial genius and the fans' adoration of his manager.

Martin was confident the Yankees would repeat as world champions. He had a veteran, battle-tested, talented team that remained intact. What's more, Steinbrenner had gone into his pockets again and signed free agent pitchers Goose Gossage, for $2.8 million for six years, and Rawly Eastwick, for $1.1 million for five years.

Gossage was the big prize of baseball's free agent class of 1977. He had won 11 games and saved 26 for the Pirates and had an earned run average of 1.62 and 151 strikeouts in 133 innings. At 6'3" and more than 200 pounds, he could throw up to 98 miles per hour and was the most intimidating pitcher in the major leagues.

But Sparky Lyle knew that the signing of Gossage would alter his role.

—————

SPARKY LYLE: I was driving cross-country from Arizona, and I heard about it on the radio. All I said at the time when they acquired Goose was why don't they trade me then? I knew both of us weren't going to work all year and I was going to be the guy left out.

For one thing, I knew I wouldn't be as good a pitcher being in fewer games. The more I pitched, the better I got. That's what hurt me.

Goose Lays an Egg

The Yankees opened defense of their world championship in Texas on April 8 and lost, 2–1, when Goose Gossage, in his Yankees debut, gave up a home run to Richie Zisk in the bottom of the ninth.

They won the next day, then proceeded to lose three straight, in Texas and Milwaukee, Gossage losing again to the Brewers, before returning to Yankee Stadium for the home opener.

The Yankees continued to struggle through the early part of the season, and so did Goose Gossage. In Toronto he fielded a ground ball and threw it into right field for an error, allowing the winning run to score. The Yankees had played eleven games and lost six of them, three of the losses charged to their $3 million, free agent relief pitcher.

BUCKY DENT: It was cold that day in Toronto. It was about 45 degrees, but with the windchill factor, it felt like below zero. It was freezing, and Gossage threw the ball away and we lost. Graig Nettles came off the field from third base, and he walked by Gossage and said, "Thata way to take one for the team, Goose." Then the next day we came home and Billy came to the mound to make a pitching change, and he called for Goose. Mickey Rivers got in the bullpen car, and he was yelling, "No, no, don't bring him in."

GOOSE GOSSAGE: I'd come to the mound and Thurman Munson would greet me at the mound with Billy Martin, and he'd look at me with that silly grin of his and say, "Well, how are you going to lose this one?" I'd say, "I don't know, get your ass back there and we'll find out."

GOOSE GOSSAGE: There never was a problem with Sparky, not at all. I came over there, and I told him when I came over, "Man, I can't wait to work with you." I thought we'd be the best left-handed–right-handed combination ever. That's how I had it envisioned.

It just didn't work out that way. They gave me his job on a silver platter. The Cy Young Award winner the year before. That's when Graig Nettles came up with the line, "From Cy Young to *sayonara*."

Billy Martin tried to sell Lyle on the idea that the hard-throwing, right-handed Gossage would complement the slider-specialist, left-handed Lyle and give the Yankees an unbeatable one-two punch out of the bullpen. There was no reason, Martin said, why the two couldn't coexist. He planned to alternate them as closers or use one of the two as a setup man for the other.

Outwardly, Lyle went along with the plan. Inwardly, he knew it wouldn't work. Ego is one of a relief pitcher's necessary assets, and it seemed certain one of the two egos would be bruised, probably Lyle's. He had been the Yankees closer since coming over from the Red Sox in 1972. In six seasons he had won 48 games, all in relief, and saved 132 games for the Yankees.

He was one of the most fun-loving Yankees, popular with his teammates and renowned for his clubhouse pranks, such as sitting nude on birthday cakes.

One day in 1976, after the final game of a series in Chicago, the Yankees were on the bus that would take them to O'Hare Airport, waiting for manager Billy Martin to board. Suddenly, a young woman in her twenties, attractive and trim, climbed aboard the bus and asked the Yankees for autographs.

"You don't have any paper," one player said. "Where do you want us to sign?"

"Right here," she said, as she pulled down her jeans and revealed her bare derriere. Several Yankees gladly obliged. When Lyle was asked if he gave the young woman his autograph, he replied, "Yeah, I signed 'Albert Walter Sparky Lyle Junior.'"

Another time, on his way to spring training, he stopped off to see a doctor friend and had the doctor fit him with a complete body cast just so he could see manager Bill Virdon's reaction.

Lyle was coming off his best season—a record of 13–5, an earned run average of 2.17, 26 saves, and a league-high 72 games, which earned him the American League Cy Young Award, the first American League reliever to win the coveted trophy. And he had been brilliant in the postseason with two wins and an 0.96 ERA in 9.1 innings in the American League Championship Series and another win in the World Series.

TIGER CUBS

In four seasons under manager Ralph Houk, the Detroit Tigers had finished sixth, sixth, fifth, and fourth. Improvement had been slight, but Houk had implemented the team's youth movement with players like Mark Fidrych, Tom Veryzer, Ron LeFlore, Jason Thompson, and Ben Oglivie.

With the start of the 1978 season, Houk was making a bold move, turning over his shortstop–second base combination to a pair of rookies, 20-year-old Alan Trammell from Garden Grove, California, at short and 21-year-old Lou Whitaker, from Brooklyn, New York, at second.

RALPH HOUK: Trammell was a shortstop and Whitaker was a third baseman, and Jim Campbell had told me all about them. He said, "We got two great-looking prospects."

I first saw them in the winter Rookie League, and you could just see the ability. I didn't think Trammell was going to be that great a hitter, but he had great hands and fast feet.

I remember him in spring training. He came with a pair of baseball shoes that must have been four sizes too big for him, with yellow shoestrings. Campbell saw that and went out and bought him a new pair of shoes, and, if I'm not mistaken, Jim even bought Trammell and Whitaker some clothes.

Trammell could field. He carried the glove close to the ground, and you could see he did all the things you're supposed to do naturally. And a good kid on top of it, a hard worker.

Whitaker had the great arm from third base, and he was fast. Jim and I decided to see what would happen if we put him at second, and it worked out real good. They roomed together and everything that first year.

A black and a white rooming together, while not unprecedented, was rare, even in the seventies. It wasn't long, however, that the practice of roommates on trips would become obsolete in baseball.

Times were changing, and the time-honored baseball traditions of players rooming together and lobby-sitting were being phased out. Players preferred private rooms. Some had it stipulated in their contracts that they get a single on the road. Now the Basic Agreement calls for all players to get single rooms, unless they prefer a roommate.

Lobby-sitting began to fade out with the advent of television. In bygone days, sitting around in the lobby and talking baseball was a way of passing the time and fighting boredom. Now players pass the time by remaining in their rooms, watching television, soap operas rating as their favorite programming.

Another reason for the end of lobby-sitting is that many hotels that the players stay in no longer have lobbies.

***

RALPH HOUK: I remember Whitaker making an error in Toronto, and he was so down, it was like he would never play again. They were just kids. Trammell helped out a lot with that. Whitaker made an error that cost us a game, and I went to their room to console him.

***

In his first season Whitaker batted .285, with three home runs and 58 RBIs, and was named American League Rookie of the Year. Trammell batted .268, with two home runs and 34 RBIs. They played together as a shortstop–second base tandem for a record 17 seasons and helped the Tigers win the World Series in 1984.

When his career ended, Trammell had a lifetime average of .285, had stolen more than 200 bases, and reached a personal high of 28 homers, 105 RBIs, and a .343 average in 1987. Whitaker joined Hall of Famers Joe Morgan and Ryne Sandberg as the only second basemen in history with 2,000 games, 2,000 hits, and 200 home runs.

THEY REALLY DID NAME A CANDY BAR AFTER HIM . . .

The prediction Reggie Jackson made before the first game of the 1975 American League Championship Series ("If I played in New York, they'd name a candy bar after me") came true on April 13, 1978. The Reggie Bar was introduced on Opening Day in Yankee Stadium. As a promotional tool, all fans entering the stadium that day were given a free Reggie Bar. It had nuts and caramel covered with chocolate, and it was round and flat, approximately the circumference of a baseball. Perfect for throwing. Attendance was 44,667. By the third inning, most of the Reggie Bars, it seemed, had been hurled onto the field.

***

MATT MEROLA: To be honest, I didn't get the idea when Reggie said that line, "If I played in New York, they'd name a candy bar after me." It wasn't until he signed with the Yankees and the headlines in the newspapers were "The Candy Man Comes to New York."

Welcome to the Club

On June 30, in the first game of a doubleheader against the Braves, Willie McCovey of the Giants connected off Jamie Easterly for the 500th home run of his career, thereby becoming only the 12th player in baseball history to hit 500 home runs in his career. McCovey added his name to a list that reads like a Who's Who of Baseball—Babe Ruth, Henry Aaron, Willie Mays, Harmon Killebrew, Mickey Mantle, Jimmie Foxx, Ted Williams, Eddie Mathews, Frank Robinson, Ernie Banks, and Mel Ott, each one a member of the Hall of Fame.

I said, "I've got to do something with this." I took all the headlines, and I went to every candy company with my idea. It wasn't until one of the last calls, to Standard Brands in Chicago, that this thing came to be. And the reason was—everything is timing and luck—they also made the Baby Ruth bar. They really were in the candy business. They also happened to be a sponsor of the Yankees, on radio or television.

When I talked to Ron Cappadoccia of Standard Brands in Chicago, he flipped out. He said, "I'm coming to New York to meet you." He didn't say, "Come to Chicago," he said, "I'm coming to New York." And that's how it started. We had meetings with Reggie. When Reggie hit the three home runs [in the 1977 World Series], that solidified everything. The name of the bar was going to be Reggie.

It was their idea to shape the bar like a baseball. They wanted to put a card inside for collectors. I didn't particularly like that. I wanted it to be in a bar shape. A candy bar is a candy bar. They did make it in a regular candy-bar shape for vending machines. One of the complaints from people was that when you bit into the patty, the nuts would come loose because it was a little more difficult to handle than a bar.

We had a lot of meetings with Standard Brands, and Reggie sat in on most of them. Reggie said what he wanted to see in a candy bar was good chocolate, nuts, and caramel. And that's what they put in it.

Typical of Reggie Jackson, the showman, on the day his candy bar debuted, he came to bat in the first inning with two runners on base and belted a three-run homer off Wilbur Wood. The Yankees won, 4–2.

Reggie Jackson and his famous Reggie Bar.

MATT MEROLA: When he hit the home run, they started throwing the candy bars on the field. They threw them all over the field. The publicity was tremendous for the bar. Everybody was so happy, except, of course, the Yankees and the cleanup crew.

PALMER AND WEAVER

Jim Palmer of the Baltimore Orioles was off to another brilliant start. He had led the American League in wins in each of the previous three seasons. Since 1970 he had won 20 games or more in seven out of eight seasons, missing only in 1974 when he was out with an injury for more than half a season and finished with a 7–12 record. Three times he had been voted Cy Young Award winner in the American League, in 1973, 1975, and 1976.

On June 10 Palmer beat the Oakland A's, 1–0. It was his third 1–0 victory in 18 days.

Many considered Palmer the best pitcher in the American League. He was the ace of the Orioles staff, Earl Weaver's most dependable pitcher—and one of his biggest headaches. Palmer was a thinking man's pitcher. He had a mind of his own and the courage to speak his mind. He often disagreed with Weaver on pitching philosophy, game strategy, the weather, anything, and Palmer was not one to keep his opinions to himself. Hall of Fame manager and star pitcher fought openly and constantly. Their arguments were the stuff of legend.

BROOKS ROBINSON: Weaver thought he knew more about pitching than Palmer, and Palmer thought he knew more about managing than Weaver. But they did give me a lot of laughs. They could be hollering at one another and the next day they were out playing golf.

I saw Palmer come into the clubhouse one day, and his locker was right near Weaver's office, and Jim just cleaned out his locker and moved down to the other end so he couldn't see Weaver.

Every time Weaver [5'8"] would go to the mound, he'd try to get on top of the mound so he could be eye to eye with Palmer [6'3"], but it was mutual respect. Both those guys wanted to win, and that was the thing that kept them at each other all the time.

One day I heard Palmer tell Weaver, "I don't think I can make it out there this inning," and Weaver said, "Hey, I don't have anybody in the bullpen. You're better than anyone I've got there. You're going out."

The first ball Palmer threw, Sal Bando hit a home run, and Palmer was standing on the mound, his hands on his hips, and he was yelling to Weaver in the dugout, "See, I told you I didn't have anything."

It was just a matter of different personalities. Dave McNally would never say anything. I don't care what Weaver said to him, Mac would just sit there stone-faced. Good, bad, or whatever, he'd never say a word while he was pitching. Palmer was always offering little explanations.

EARL WEAVER: It was great. A million arguments. It was fun. It was nasty at times, but it was fun. If I wanted to take him out, he wanted to stay in. If I wanted to leave him in, he wanted to come out.

He didn't like the manager to have the final word. He was hardheaded. He'd say the same thing about me. I made him throw a slider in Kansas City one time. I called the pitch and he didn't want to throw it and Rick Dempsey kept putting it down. He finally threw it and whacked the hitter right on the knee, real hard.

He was a terrific competitor, and I had less trouble with him than a lot of your kids. He was a big campaigner for me to get into the Hall of Fame. He wrote a lot of letters.

GATOR

In the middle of May, the Red Sox got hot and took over first place in the American League East. On June 17 Boston held a seven-game lead over the second-place Yankees. The main reason the Yankees were as close as they were was the pitching of Ron Guidry, the skinny left-hander his teammates called "Gator" and the media referred to as "Louisiana Lightning," who had stepped up and become the ace of the Yankees staff. He won his first 10 decisions of the season, and now he was going for win number 11 against the California Angels at Yankee Stadium.

Guidry was on his game. His fastball seemed to have a little extra hop, and his slider was biting down and in viciously on right-handed hitters. He was practically unhittable as he mowed down the Angels batters. The crowd of 33,482 got into it more and more as Guidry piled up the strikeouts. Whenever he got two strikes on a hitter, the crowd rose in unison and began a rhythmic applause in anticipation of strike three.

BUCKY DENT: I wasn't playing that game, I was hurt, but I was on the bench and I had a good look at the Angels batters. They were going up there just trying to foul the ball off. He was so overpowering that they were just trying to put the ball in play, because he was throwing the ball right by them. Wow! He was something.

The Angels managed only four hits as Guidry beat them, 4–0, striking out 18, a Yankees record and an American League record for a left-hander at the time.

Guidry would go on to have a storybook season. He would win 13 straight games before losing to the Brewers on July 7. He would win 25 games and lose only 3 (all three defeats to pitchers named Mike—Caldwell of the Brewers, Flanagan of the Orioles, Willis of the Blue Jays). He would lead the league in wins, winning percentage (.893), earned run average (1.74), and shutouts (nine) and finish second to Nolan Ryan in strikeouts (260 to 248).

THE END OF BILLY I

By July 17 the Yankees had slipped into fourth place, 13 games behind the runaway Red Sox, when the relative calm in Yankeeland was shattered in a game against the Royals at Yankee Stadium.

The score was tied 7–7, and the pitcher was left-hander Al "the Mad Hungarian" Hrabosky.

AL HRABOSKY: It was the tenth inning and Munson got a base hit off me leading off and Reggie was told to bunt. The first pitch, I threw up and in to him and took five steps at him and kind of challenged his manhood. I kind of said, "Swing the bat." Obviously, the whole time, with his abilities and swinging in Yankee Stadium, I want him to bunt because I'm tough to bunt on.

So it was ball one. The next pitch he bunted at the ball and missed it, so it was 1–1. Then they took the sign off, but he tried to bunt the next pitch and missed. Then Howser, the third-base coach, came down and told him, "Hey, we took the bunt off." Basically, Reggie said, "You guys wanted me to bunt the first pitch, I'm bunting all the way through."

Then he tried to bunt and popped to the catcher, and Billy was absolutely livid. So I always took credit for that, getting him a $50,000 fine. The whole time, I'm standing there thrilled to death, him trying to bunt against me, because I'm respectful for the type of hitter he is. He can take a checked swing and hit it out of Yankee Stadium. So I thought that was good.

When he returned to the dugout, Jackson was told by coach Gene Michael that Martin wanted him to go in and take a shower.

FRAN HEALY: I was broadcasting, but I knew the signs. I saw them take the bunt off, and I knew what was going to happen. When he bunted and popped out, I remember Reggie walking toward the dugout, and when he took his glasses off, he'da fought Tyson. He was mad. And "Stick" [Gene Michael] went down and told him to go inside, and Reggie said, "Tell him [Martin] to tell me."

Jackson didn't need to be told what was coming next. He knew. And if he had the slightest doubt, the sounds from the manager's office after the game, which the Yankees lost, 9–7, in 11 innings, told him. Screaming, cursing, objects crashing against the wall, glass breaking. In his rage, Martin tore a radio out of the wall.

Almost overlooked in the latest Reggie-Billy incident was the defiance of Sparky Lyle. Called in to pitch in the fourth, Lyle worked the fourth and fifth innings, then said, "I'm no long reliever. I'm going home."

Which he did. And which Reggie Jackson also did. Early the next morning, Jackson, unconcerned about the consequences and certain he knew what those consequences would be, boarded a plane for his home in Oakland, California.

It didn't take long for the other shoe to drop. Through his attorney, Jackson was informed he was being suspended for five days without pay. He was scheduled to rejoin the team in Chicago on July 23.

Time passed slowly for Reggie Jackson as he waited out his suspension, then flew to Chicago, as ordered, on July 23. Perhaps coincidentally, the Yankees had won all four games in his absence and had moved up a notch to third place, still behind the Red Sox, now by 11 games.

Jackson's return was not a triumphant one. He and Martin didn't speak, and when Reggie checked the lineup card, he saw his name was missing. He sat and watched the Yankees win their fifth straight game without him, 3–1, behind Ed Figueroa, and chip another game off the Red Sox's lead. Then Reggie, and the rest of the Yankees, boarded the bus that would take them to O'Hare Airport for the flight to Kansas City.

When they arrived at the airport, the Yankees learned that their flight would be delayed. Billy Martin passed the time in the airport bar. Leaving the bar, Martin encountered two of the writers traveling with the team who wanted to talk to him about the situation, about Reggie Jackson, about George Steinbrenner. His tongue no doubt loosened by drink, his anger rising because Jackson had offered no apology to the manager or his teammates, Martin let loose a tirade, lumping Jackson and Steinbrenner together in his rage.

"One's a born liar and the other's convicted," he said.

The liar, obviously, was Jackson. The convicted was a reference to Steinbrenner's 1974 felony conviction for making illegal contributions to Richard Nixon's reelection campaign.

It didn't take long for Martin's remarks to be relayed to George Steinbrenner or for Steinbrenner to act on them.

Shortly before noon the following day, reporters were summoned to a salon in the Yankees' Kansas City hotel. An obviously distraught Billy Martin showed up looking as if he hadn't slept all night, and he hadn't. He was wearing sunglasses, and his voice was husky and choked with emotion as he told the gathering he was resigning, stepping down as manager of the Yankees.

Martin talked about Yankee pride and said he would not answer any questions because he was a Yankee and "Yankees don't talk or throw rocks." Then he began to sob, and when it was clear he could not continue, his friend and former teammate Phil Rizzuto, the longtime "voice of the Yankees," put his arm around Martin's shoulders and gently led him away from the press conference.

Second Again

On June 30, White Sox owner Bill Veeck fired manager Bob Lemon and replaced him with Larry Doby, making Doby the second black man to manage a major league team. Lemon would not be out of work long.

Thirty-one years before, barely three months after Jackie Robinson broke baseball's color barrier with the Brooklyn Dodgers, Doby broke in with Veeck's Cleveland Indians. Doby had a distinguished 13-year career with the Indians, White Sox, and Tigers, a lifetime .283 average, 253 home runs, and 969 runs batted in. As the first black man in the American League, the second in the major leagues, Doby suffered all the same indignities, threats, and insults as Robinson, but never received the recognition that Robinson did.

Who remembers the second man to walk on the moon?

Coach Dick Howser would run the team that night in a 5–2 loss to the Royals, and then Bob Lemon would arrive the next day to take over as manager.

THE BEGINNING OF BILLY II

Saturday, July 29, was the annual Old Timers' Day at Yankee Stadium, a gala event that takes place each year when old heroes return and Yankees fans get to recall the team's glorious past. A crowd of 48,711 turned out for the ceremonies and the game against the Minnesota Twins.

The master of ceremonies, Yankees broadcaster Frank Messer, handled the day's festivities, introducing the dignitaries in attendance. When he introduced team president Al Rosen, whom the fans considered one of the villains of the piece in the Martin resignation, there were boos and chants of "Billy . . . Billy . . . Billy" and "We want Billy."

Messer completed the traditional introduction of the great Yankees stars of the past, Joe DiMaggio, Mickey Mantle, Whitey Ford. They were lined up along the first-base line when Messer turned the crowd over to public address announcer Bob Sheppard "for two very special announcements."

"Ladies and gentlemen, your attention, please," Sheppard began in his familiar stentorian voice. "The Yankees announce today that Bob Lemon agreed to a contract to continue as manager of the Yankees through the 1978 and 1979 seasons . . . ”

The boos grew louder, and signs saying, “Billy Will Always Be No. 1” and “Bring Back Billy” appeared in the crowd.

“. . . your attention to the rest of this announcement,” Sheppard implored. “In 1980 Bob Lemon will become the general manager of the Yankees . . .” More boos.

“Your attention, please,” Sheppard pleaded. “Your attention, please . . . and the Yankees would like to announce at this time . . . introduce and announce at the same moment, that the manager for the 1980 season and hopefully for many years after that will be No. 1, Billy Martin.”

The crowd went wild as Martin, who had been slipped into the stadium and secreted in a private dressing room, trotted onto the field in his familiar Yankees pinstripes with the No. 1 on his back.

For more than seven minutes, the crowd cheered and shouted, showering Martin with their applause, their love, and their affection. On the Yankees’ bench, most players sat in stunned silence.

“I nearly fell off the bench,” said Jim Spencer.

“Unbelievable,” said Joe DiMaggio.

SPARKY LYLE: I don’t think it really shocked me or Nettles or Tidrow or Thurman. Billy had been hanging around for a while and we always knew when Billy starts hanging around the ballpark, he’s coming back. All of a sudden, he popped up one day. I don’t know what he was there for. Billy never went anywhere or did anything if it wasn’t for his benefit, and I don’t mean that in a bad way. When I did find out, I said I figured something’s up. That was my reaction.

I was just as happy to see him back. He looked healthy, and I enjoyed playing for him. I used to like the way he took a bed check. He’d look in the room and say, “Yeah, the bed’s here.”

Martin’s dramatic return was all the carefully crafted work of George Steinbrenner. Later, he would say that he had watched Martin’s “resignation” speech and been moved by Martin’s remarks and his obvious contrition. He began thinking about it then, Steinbrenner said, and he realized Martin needed the Yankees and the Yankees needed Martin.

The Yankees were only 10 games over .500 and 10¹/₂ games behind the Red Sox when Yankees owner George Steinbrenner fired manager Billy Martin and replaced him with Bob Lemon (above), who led New York to a 48–20 record the rest of the way.

Sparky Lyle had been a dominant back-end relief pitcher for the Yankees before the term closer was used. But he was traded to the Texas Rangers after the 1978 season, the team with which he made his debut, on April 11, 1979.

More likely, Steinbrenner had been swayed by the thousands of telephone calls to Yankee Stadium from fans who wanted Billy back, by the possibility that those fans would stay away from Yankee Stadium if Billy was not there. He saw a chance to win over those fans and paint himself as the great and noble abolitionist by forgiving Martin and bringing him back.

THE HIT MAN

On May 5 Pete Rose of the Cincinnati Reds singled off Steve Rogers of the Montreal Expos to become the 13th player in baseball history to get 3,000 hits.

On June 13 Rose was held hitless in a 1–0 loss to the Cubs. He was in the worst slump of his life, 5 for 44, which had plummeted his batting average to .267, 44 points below his 1977 average. He would not go hitless again until August.

After going hitless, baseball's hit machine went on a tear. He hit safely in every game for the rest of June. By the middle of July, he had joined a handful of hitters who had batted safely in 30 consecutive games and was taking dead aim at Tommy Holmes' modern National League record of 37 straight games, which he set in 1945 when he was with the Boston Braves.

TOM SEAVER: Throughout the streak, Pete never changed. He loved it. One of the things that impressed me was that it never got into the clubhouse, and whether that's a credit to Pete or a credit to the PR department of the Cincinnati Reds, I don't know. As he kept getting closer to the record, there would be these press conferences afterward, but it never changed what was going on among the players.

His experience, he didn't bring that imposition into the clubhouse. The clubhouse was still the same for the guys. And there wasn't any abnormal disruption in the clubhouse because of what was going on.

There was one distinct level with the Reds, not individual maybe, but a group of players who stood above the rest. That was one of the best groups of guys ever assembled to play the game of baseball—Rose, Morgan, Bench, Perez, Foster, Griffey.

Pete was not a noisy guy in the clubhouse. He was relatively quiet. There wasn't anybody in the game who worked any harder, both on offense and defense. He and Rusty Staub and Joe Torre, those are three guys if I were to mention the hardest workers at their job, those three. Pete played three positions and made the All-Star team at all three, because he worked at it.

We played a doubleheader at Riverfront Stadium, and Pete went 0 for 9. A Sunday doubleheader. Terrible day. You get to work early and you leave late, and I was going to the elevator to go to my car and I heard somebody taking batting practice. I looked out on the field, and it was Pete. He was back on the field taking batting practice. He was one of the hardest workers and most dedicated I ever met.

SPARKY ANDERSON: During the streak, Pete was the same as he always is, very talkative, very confident. Like the guys used to say, "Nothing bothers this guy." That's what he was.

I wish he could have a school for young players starting out about what you're supposed to truly give this game. Then I think we would have a lot of guys who would understand, like that saying, "To know him is to love him," to know this game, you have to love this game. And if you don't love this game, you will never give it what it deserves.

I once told him, "You know, you get credit for things you shouldn't get credit for. First of all, you get credit because you bust your tail every day. You shouldn't get credit for that." He said, "I know it." I said, "That's the way everybody is supposed to do it."

Here's a guy that if you had to grade him out, average runner at best, below-average arm, below-average fielder at any particular position. Yet he's one of the most magnificent players I ever saw. Now if young people would just understand, you don't have to have grades. You have to have a big piece of you that loves this game. That's all.

On July 24, at Shea Stadium, Rose collected a pair of hits and tied Holmes' record. The following day, the Mets beat the Reds, but Rose had three more hits, broke Holmes' record, and took off after Willie Keeler's all-time National League record of 44 consecutive games set in 1897, when foul balls did not

Pete Rose tied Willie Keeler's National League consecutive-game hit streak of 44. But on August 1, 1978, it came to end against the Braves with this strikeout.

count as strikes. Rose tied Keeler on July 31 with a single off Phil Niekro, but the next day his streak was stopped by Larry McWilliams and Gene Garber of the Atlanta Braves.

GEORGE FOSTER: Pete showed his consistency and how he always had his game face on. You never saw him take any bad swings or swing at any bad pitches. He knew exactly what he wanted to do, and he never got any cheap hits, always sharp hits. During the streak, it seemed he got at least two or three hits every game.

It was exciting seeing that happen, but reporters were everywhere, so you had to try to get a locker that wasn't close to Pete so you could get in and dress and undress. But it was exciting to be involved with that.

THE BOSTON MASSACRE

Turning into August, with Bob Lemon at the helm, the Yankees' turbulent ship found a steady course. They began to win consistently. On September 1, the Yankees had narrowed the Red Sox's lead to six and a half games.

BOB STANLEY: We had gone to the West Coast and swept the West Coast. That was the All-Star break, and we were 14 games ahead of the Yankees. Then Burleson got hurt and Lynn got hurt and we went home and lost every game to the West Coast teams, and I remember Yaz saying, "We're going to blow this." Rick Burleson and Fred Lynn were very important to our club. Especially Burleson.

The Yankees were taking dead aim at a four-game series in Boston on September 7, 8, 9, and 10. It would be their chance to make a run at the Red Sox in a head-to-head confrontation. While the Yankees continued to win, the Red Sox suddenly began to give ground. On September 2, 3, and 4, the Yankees won two from Seattle and one from Detroit, lost the second game of a doubleheader to the Tigers, but cut the Red Sox's lead to five games. They beat the Tigers again on September 5 and 6 and went to Boston exactly where they wanted to be, four games behind the Red Sox. A sweep would leave them in a first-place tie.

BUCKY DENT: We had a lot of injuries early in the season. Catfish was hurt. Mickey Rivers was out. I was out. There were a bunch of guys who were hurt. Then, all of a sudden, we started getting one guy back, then another. This guy came back, that guy came back, and Boston's team started getting hurt a little bit.

It's hard to explain, the 1978 team had a tremendous drive to be successful. Those guys just did not want to lose. As we started getting closer, we'd pick up one or two games, guys were saying, "We've got to win every series, and if we pick up one game a week until September when we play the Red Sox—because we play them seven times—we've got a shot."

So what happened, they started getting hurt. Burleson got hurt, Lynn got hurt, and it was the opposite, we started getting momentum. Catfish came back and won six games in a row. We started getting closer, and, as we got closer, everybody knew then that we had a shot at catching them.

And then the big series, when we went to Boston for four games. We went in there on a Thursday, and it was the weirdest feeling. We were four games back, and there was a different intensity about how our club came out, the way they went about their business. You could feel it, and you could sense it.

It was called the Boston Massacre and it started immediately, the Yankees spraying hits all over Fenway Park. They started hitting in the first inning of the first game and never stopped. In the first game, Mickey Rivers, Willie Randolph, Thurman Munson, and Reggie Jackson all batted three times before the Red Sox's number nine hitter batted once. The Yankees went on to a 15–3 rout in Game 1 and followed it up with a 13–2 blowout in Game 2, a 7–0 shutout behind Ron Guidry in Game 3, and completed the four-game sweep with a 7–4 victory. For the four games, the Yankees outscored the Red Sox 42–9 and outhit them 67–21.

On July 19 they were 14 games behind. When Bob Lemon took over a week later, they were $10^{1}/_{2}$ games behind. Now they had tied the Red Sox. Maybe it was Lemon's calm, settling leadership. But the Yankees had won five in a row before Billy Martin resigned.

Another defining moment of the decade: New Yorker Bucky Dent's home run on October 2, 1978, against the Boston Red Sox, which propelled the Yankees over the Bosox in their one-game playoff to decide the winner of the American League East. Dent also won the World Series MVP in 1978, hitting .417.

BUCKY DENT: When we swept them, it was like, here, we're going to beat these guys. We got it now. We knew we were going to win.

––––––––––

The Yankees had moved into a tie with the Red Sox for first place, but there were still 20 games to play.

A week after the Boston Massacre, the teams met in a three-game series at Yankee Stadium. For the second time in six days, Ron Guidry shut out the Red Sox to win the first game of the series, 4–0. When Catfish Hunter beat Mike Torrez, now with Boston, in the second game, the Yankees suddenly had a three-and-a-half-game lead. Now it was Boston's turn to come back. They salvaged the final game of the series.

A week later, the Yankees' lead was down to one game with seven games remaining. They went on a six-game winning streak, but the Red Sox matched them win for win and went into the final three games of the regular season trailing the Yankees by one game.

––––––––––

BOB STANLEY: We played Toronto, and they played Cleveland. We both won the first two games, so we went into the final day still behind by a game. Then Rick Waits beat them, and Tiant beat Toronto. We were listening to the Yankees game on the radio in the bullpen.

THE BOSTON STRANGLER

For only the second time in American League history, two teams finished the regular season tied for first. In 1948 the Cleveland Indians and Boston Red Sox tied for first. While National League rules called for a three-game series in the event of a tie (Brooklyn and St. Louis in 1946, Brooklyn and New York in 1951, Los Angeles and Milwaukee in 1959, Los Angeles and San Francisco in 1962), the American League opted for a one-game, sudden-death, winner-take-all playoff.

It had been previously determined, by a coin flip, that Boston would be the home team in the event of a one-game playoff, and the game would be played on the day after the final game of the regular season.

Monday, October 2 came up crisp and sunny in New England. Ron Guidry, with a record of 24–3 and two consecutive shutouts of the Red Sox, started for the Yankees on three days' rest. Mike Torrez, a star for the Yankees in the 1977 World Series who had signed with the Red Sox as a free agent the previous November, started for Boston. His record was 16–12.

The Red Sox reached Guidry for a run in the second and another in the sixth, and the Yankees were helpless against Torrez, who had won only one game in six weeks but was being a big-game pitcher once more.

Going into the top of the seventh, with time running out on them, the Yankees trailed 2–0. With one out, Chris Chambliss and Roy White hit back-to-back singles and Jim Spencer batted for Brian Doyle, who was playing because of a hamstring injury to the Yankees' regular second baseman, Willie Randolph. Spencer flied out for the second out. That brought up Bucky Dent, the Yankees' ninth-place hitter, hitless for the day.

In the press box, New York writers looked to the dugout, expecting to see a pinch-hitter for Dent. But that wasn't Bob Lemon's style. He had gotten the team this far by letting the players play and staying "out of the way," and he wasn't about to change now.

Dent took Torrez's first pitch, then fouled the second pitch right down on his foot and dropped to the ground in pain. While Yankees trainer Gene Monahan came out to spray the injured area with ethyl chloride to deaden the pain, the on-deck batter, Mickey Rivers, had picked up Dent's bat and was examining it.

BUCKY DENT: Mickey and I had only taken a couple of bats up there, so I was using one of his bats in batting practice and I broke it. Right under the tape. It was a hairline crack, you could hardly see it. When I went up for that at-bat, I mistakenly pulled that bat out of the bat rack, so when I fouled the ball off my foot and I went back and Monahan was spraying the stuff on my ankle, Mickey came over to me and said, "Hey, homey, you're using the wrong bat, man. That bat's cracked." And he gave me the other bat that he had.

Not even thinking about it because my leg was hurting, I just took it, and I went back up there and the next pitch he threw a fastball. He tried to get it in on me, but he got it down.

Lem

Bob Lemon had come up to the Cleveland Indians in 1941 as a third baseman/outfielder. He had been the center fielder and caught the fly ball for the final out of Bob Feller's no-hitter against the Yankees on April 30, 1946. That year, the Indians began using Lemon as a pitcher. By 1948 he was a pitcher exclusively and posted a record of 20–14. He would win 20 games or more seven times in his career, finish with a career record of 207–128, and be elected to the Hall of Fame.

It was at the suggestion of Yankees president Al Rosen, who played alongside Lemon with those Indians teams in the late forties and early fifties, that Lemon was chosen to replace Billy Martin. Lemon was the ideal man for the job, thought Rosen. He had served as Yankees pitching coach under Martin in 1976, so he was familiar with most of the Yankees players. He had managing experience, with the Royals and the White Sox. And he was available, having been fired by the White Sox 26 days earlier.

What's more, he was the perfect antidote to Martin. Where Martin was fiery, feisty, and intense, Lemon was laid-back and low-key. Where Martin created tension in the clubhouse, Lemon brought a relaxed atmosphere. Where Martin was suspicious, Lemon was friendly, outgoing, and likable. He called everybody "Meat," and everybody called him "Meat," or "Lem."

Lemon wasn't one for rah-rah speeches, rules, throwing things, or disciplining players, whom he treated as adults, not children. His idea of strategy was to write the names of his players on the lineup card, then just sit and watch. He set the tone of his regime in his first meeting with the team.

"You guys won last year, which means you must have been doing something right," he said. "So what do you say you go out and play just like you did last year, and I'll try to stay out of the way."

MIKE TORREZ: I pitched a great game. I have nothing to be ashamed of. I wished he hadn't fouled that ball off his foot, because I had great concentration, but the three or four minutes, whatever it took for him to do whatever he had to do, freezing it, knocked my concentration off.

It really wasn't a bad pitch, but I didn't get it where I wanted to. I could have thrown him the slider because I was ahead of him, two strikes and no balls. What I was going to do was come in on him to knock him off the plate, then come back with a slider away. It was a fastball that tailed back over the plate. It was going to be more of a waste pitch, but I didn't really throw the ball. It was the difference between throwing a ball because that's what you want to do and guiding it. I guided it instead of throwing it, and I didn't get the ball in deep enough. It caught too much of the plate. Bucky had a tendency to go in the bucket a little bit, and it got right in his wheelhouse.

BUCKY DENT: When I hit the ball, I never did see it go into the net. I knew it was on a line, I didn't know if it was high enough. I thought it was going to hit off the wall. I knew I was the lead run, so I was trying to get to second base. When I rounded the bag at first, the umpire signaled it was a home run.

MIKE TORREZ: When he hit it, I didn't think it was going out because I saw Yaz pop his glove, and anytime you see him pop his glove, the ball is catchable. So I said, "Good, I'm out of the inning." Then he kind of backed up, he backed up, and then he hit the wall, and I'm going, "Oh, shit," and the ball went over the wall. Yaz dropped his head, and I said, "Damn."

BUCKY DENT: As I rounded second and third and was trotting toward home, Fenway was dead silent. You could hear a pin drop, except for the few Yankees fans. You could hear them clapping. After the game, my friend Joe Illigasch said to me, "Do you know what you just did?" I said, "I hit a home run." He said, "No, it's going to change your life," and he was right.

The Yankees tacked on another run in the seventh on a walk to Rivers and Thurman Munson's double and one in the eighth on Reggie Jackson's home run to make it 5-2, but the Red Sox weren't done yet.

Pitching on guts and heart, Guidry began to wear out in the bottom of the seventh, when Goose Gossage replaced him and put down a Boston rally. But in the eighth, the Red Sox scored two, and they batted in the bottom of the ninth trailing 5–4.

The tension in Fenway Park was suffocating as Rick Burleson walked with one out and Jerry Remy hit a wicked line drive to right. Later, right fielder Lou Piniella would say, "I didn't see the damn thing until it landed about 10 feet in front of me."

The late-afternoon sun, descending over the stands behind home plate, had temporarily blinded Piniella. The ball could easily have skipped past him, scoring Burleson and sending the winning run to second or third. Piniella fought the sun and groped for the ball, his arms outstretched as if he were stopping traffic. Actually, he was hoping the ball would hit him somewhere. It hit him right in the glove. The runners held on first and second.

Now Gossage had to face the Red Sox's two most dangerous hitters, Jim Rice, who would finish the season with a .315 average and a league-leading 46 homers and 139 RBIs, and the veteran Hall of Famer–to-be, Carl Yastrzemski, who had already homered in the game.

Rice drove one deep to right that brought the crowd to its feet, but Piniella caught it just a few steps from the low right-field fence as Burleson tagged up and went to third. If Burleson had not hesitated between first and second on Remy's hit, thinking Piniella was going to catch the ball, he would have made it to third and then scored the tying run on Rice's drive.

So it came down to Gossage against Yaz, power against power. And Gossage was not going to get cute now. He simply reared back and fired nothing but heat.

GOOSE GOSSAGE: That whole game was unbelievable. I went to bed the night before thinking, "Oh, man, I'll probably end up facing Yaz for the final out," and sure enough, here it was.

Up until that point, I was so nervous and scared to death. My legs were banging together, so if somebody had come out there to talk to me, I wouldn't even have known they were there. I was that nervous and that scared. I'd never come close to playing in a game of that magnitude.

When Yaz came up to the plate, it was 5–4, I had two runners on, and essentially, this is it. This is the game. I was holding a conversation with myself on the mound. I was asking myself questions and I was answering them.

I was saying, "Why are you so nervous?" And I answered, "I don't know." I said, "What's the worst thing that can happen to you?" I said, "The worst thing that can happen to me is I'll be home in Colorado tomorrow hunting elk."

And it was like the weight of the world was taken off my shoulders and this calm came over me. It was weird. What happened was I put the game in perspective. That it was just a game. I was pitching like if I don't get these guys out, I'm going to face the firing squad after the game. But I put it into perspective of what was going to happen if I didn't get these guys out.

400 Total Bases

Jim Rice's second-inning single off Toronto's Jim Clancy on October 1, 1978, made Rice the first player with 400 total bases in a season since Joe DiMaggio did it with the 1937 Yankees.

When I got Yaz to pop up—Nettles tells me this story, he said, "Pop it up, pop it up, pop it up, oh, shit, not to me."

BUCKY DENT: Gossage threw a fastball right down the middle, and Yastrzemski popped it up. As the ball went up over toward third base, I felt something go down my arm like a bug. Nettles caught the ball for the last out, and everybody rushed out of our dugout to jump on him. I was the closest one to him, but I never went to jump on him.

What happened was, my Saint Christopher medal broke and went down my arm. I was looking at the ball and I felt this thing, so I looked down and I saw my chain. I pulled the chain, and I looked back up. Nettles caught the ball and everybody was running on the field, and I was looking on the ground for my medal. I couldn't find it, so I figured I'd come back later and look for it. I went over and joined the crowd, then I went into the clubhouse, but I realized I still hadn't found my medal. I went back out to shortstop and I was looking and looking, and I still couldn't find it. I finally found it when I undressed. It had fallen down into my pants.

GOOSE GOSSAGE: Munson came in after the game. I was sitting in the training room, and Thurman said, "Where in the hell did you get that fastball?" He said, "That ball had another foot and a half on it."

I don't know if it was the hardest ball I ever threw, but it rode in on Yaz's hands and he couldn't get the bat head out and he popped it up.

BOB STANLEY: Nobody remembers it, but I replaced Torrez in the game. I had pitched Friday against Toronto and pitched seven innings and beat them, 11–0. When the playoff game came, Don Zimmer put me in the bullpen.

If we were tied going into the last game, we were going to save Tiant for the playoff. But we needed to win our last game, so we had to pitch Tiant.

When I came in, Mickey Rivers was on base and Munson hit a bloop double for another run. In the next inning, Reggie hit a home run off me that just cleared the center-field fence. I shouldn't have been in the game. I had only two days' rest, but Zim was the type of manager who went with the guy who was hot.

The big play was Piniella in right field. He just stuck his glove up and the ball went in. It was meant to be, I guess.

After the game, we were down, but we had a good year. We kind of blew it. We definitely should have won that year. I always said if we had played that game in Yankee Stadium, we would have won. Bucky Dent's home run would have been a can of corn, and all our runs didn't have anything to do with Fenway Park.

The Yankees were in the American League Championship Series for the third straight year, and for the third straight year, they would face the Kansas City Royals, who finished five games ahead of the California Angels in the American League West.

GEORGE BRETT: Let's put it this way, when the Red Sox and Yankees had that playoff, I was pulling for the Red Sox. I think everybody on our team was, because we went to battle with the Yankees in 1976 and again in 1977 and lost both times. So when 1978 came around and all of a sudden they have one game, I think everybody in Kansas City was pulling for the Red Sox because we hadn't had any success against the Yankees in the playoffs.

When a team comes from so many games behind and wins, like the Yankees did, and then they won that game in Boston, when something like that happens, you have to feel it's in the cards for them to win.

Not that we went into the playoffs with a defeatist attitude, but that's the most unlikely guy to hit a home run for the Yankees. Bucky Dent hits the home run, the game-winner. It's not that he wasn't a good player—he was a very, very good player—but he's not the type of guy you expect to hit a home run to win the pennant for you.

I was pulling for the Red Sox and all of a sudden the Red Sox lost, and now you go into it saying, "Oh, shit, we're playing the Yankees."

BLEEDING DODGER BLUE

In the National League, the Phillies won the East by one and a half games over the Pirates. In the Western Division, the Dodgers stole a page from the Yankees' book. Down by six and a half games in midseason, the Dodgers turned it on and finished two and a half games ahead of the Reds.

SPARKY ANDERSON: We won in 1975 and 1976 and those guys never cheat you a minute, but I don't believe it's a question of cheating you, I think it's a question of "Tomorrow, we get 'em."

And you had to give Tommy Lasorda tremendous credit. He was selling a bill of goods and selling it well. I saw him sell for two years, 1977 and 1978, as well as somebody can sell something. He sold the product and made the Dodgers believe it.

I thought it was two things. I didn't think we were hungry enough, and, the other thing, I thought Tommy did a great job. I thought that was his two greatest years of doing an unbelievable job.

THE L.A. ZOO?

Coincidentally, the Dodgers' comeback began just about the time Don Sutton and Steve Garvey, longtime adversaries, were involved in a clubhouse scuffle.

TOMMY JOHN: The thing that ticked me off, I was signing All-Star baseballs for the Mets. I had a big bunch of baseballs, about nine or ten dozen, and they fought and they fell in my locker and they knocked all the balls all over the clubhouse. It took me 20 minutes to pick those balls up.

It was a catfight. It was like two women fighting in the locker room over some guy. Sutton made a comment about Garve's wife, and Garve took exception to it. They didn't like each other anyway.

Somebody said, "Stop the fight, they'll kill each other." And Joe Ferguson said, "Good."

The Kansas City Royals had won the American League West in 1976 and 1977. Both times, however, the Yankees had beaten them in the tightly played league championship series. George Brett's three homers in Game 3 of the 1978 American League Championship Series were not enough to rewrite the script. The Yankees dispatched the Royals in four games to advance to their third straight World Series.

Al Campanis was on the trip, and he kept saying, "Oh, my God, what are we going to do? What are we going to tell the press?" They were on the phone back to Los Angeles to Fred Claire, who was director of media relations. "Fred, how are we going to handle this? Oh, God." You would have thought he was on the line with Schwarzkopf and Colin Powell talking about Desert Storm, trying to figure out how they were going to preserve the Dodgers family, Dodgers harmony.

Lasorda came out and said, "Only one guy's in the fight? Shoot, I used to fight with my teammates all the time." Tommy didn't make a big thing of it.

I went out to the field, and Monty Basgall, a coach, asked what happened. I said, "Sutton and Garvey got into it." He said, "Were there any good punches?" I said, "Nah, they were just scratching, and they were just wrestling around." Monty said, "That's a shame. We have a good ballclub, and I hope this doesn't do something to keep us from winning," and it didn't.

The Dodgers kept their differences in the clubhouse and banded together on the field to win the National League West, then won the first game of the National League Championship Series from the Phillies, 9–5, with Steve Garvey hitting a pair of homers and a triple and Davey Lopes and Steve Yeager also homering. In the second game, John pitched a 4–0 four-hitter that gave the Dodgers a two-games-to-nothing lead.

Back in Dodger Stadium for the third game, Steve Carlton went all the way and hit a three-run homer and a sacrifice fly in a 9–4 Phillies win. But the Dodgers wrapped it up in the fourth game, 4–3, on Bill Russell's game-winning RBI single in the tenth, and, for the second straight year, Tommy Lasorda's first two years as manager, the Dodgers were going to the World Series.

K.C. CAN'T BREAK THROUGH

Having lost to the Yankees in the American League Championship Series two straight years, the Kansas City Royals were determined to change things, buoyed by the fact that they would not have to face Ron Guidry, who had pitched the playoff game in Boston, until Game 3 at the earliest.

The Yankees started Jim Beattie, a rookie who had won six and lost nine, in the first game in Kansas City. Beattie pitched five scoreless innings and worked into the sixth, staked to an early lead by Reggie Jackson, who scored twice and drove in three.

BUCKY DENT: Al Hrabosky was really talking it up: "We want to play the Yankees, I want Reggie." And the first time he faced Reggie with two on in the eighth, he did all that stuff behind the mound, walked up on the mound, and Reggie hit it over the fence in right field. I told Hrabosky, "Yeah, you really tricked him, Al."

Hrabosky, known as "the Mad Hungarian," had a ritual. Before each pitch, he would walk behind the mound, turn his back to the batter, bow his head, and talk to himself, then he would slam the ball into his glove and turn around with a flourish to face the hitter.

AL HRABOSKY: That came about because I was going back to the minor leagues. Kind of failure and frustration. I had always done a variation of it as a starting pitcher in the minor leagues, in between innings. As you made your final warm-up toss and they were throwing the ball around the horn, I kind of went back there and started pumping myself up, "Hey, one, two, three," this and that.

I felt I needed something special, something to motivate me to get a little something extra on a pitch, so I went back there and started doing that. I know I pissed people off, but I did it with my pitching style. But it wasn't like if I struck you out, I started making gestures and pumping my arm. I didn't show hitters up.

Before I started doing it, I was having a terrible season. I was the Cardinals' closer, and I had a seven ERA when you weren't supposed to have anything above four. I was on borrowed time, and GM Bing Devine apparently had mentioned something to catcher Ted Simmons. "Hey, what's going on? We're thinking about sending him down." And Simmons said, "Something's bothering him, but don't worry about it. He'll work it out."

So I knew I had to do something. It was either going to accelerate my exit or keep me in the big leagues.

It was kind of a lopsided game (7–1). I was shocked as to why I was in that game. The only thing I can surmise is that since it was my first postseason game, maybe Whitey Herzog wanted to bring me in so I could relax.

The next day, it was not a save situation, but I struck Reggie out to end the game.

As a relief pitcher, the perfect matchup to me is me and Reggie, so if I said something, it would probably be in the vein of "Hey, let's bring on the show."

The Royals came back to win the second game, 10–4, then the two teams headed for New York for the final three games.

Game 3 belonged to the remarkable George Brett, who did his best to beat the Yankees single-handedly. Brett was in a gang fight, but he was the only one in his gang. He belted three homers, all with the bases empty.

The Yankees matched Brett, and then some, with a two-run homer from Jackson and a tremendous two-run homer from Munson into the left-field bullpen in the eighth to win it, 6–5.

GEORGE BRETT: Normally, when your team hits three home runs in a game, it's a win. When one guy does, you figure that's a win. Unfortunately, that day I was batting leadoff, and every time I came up, I was the first batter in the inning. My first three at-bats, three solo home runs off Catfish, in the first, third, and fifth innings, and the last one tied the score, 3–3.

Chambliss' home run [in the 1976 playoffs] wasn't the end of the world. Thurman's home run [in the eighth inning of Game 4 in the 1978 playoffs] *was* the end of the world for a lot of us.

Now the Royals had to face Ron Guidry, pitching with his normal four days' rest and with a chance to close out the series.

"Ron Guidry isn't God," said George Brett. "He can be beaten."

The Royals reached Guidry for a run in the first, then Louisiana Lightning held them scoreless through the eighth. Graig Nettles' home run in the bottom of the second tied it, and Roy White's home run in the bottom of the sixth put the Yankees ahead 2–1, which is how the game ended. Goose Gossage pitched a scoreless ninth for the save, and the Yankees were on their way to their third straight World Series, their second straight against the Los Angeles Dodgers.

Third baseman Graig Nettles was an integral part of the Yankees' three World Series teams from 1976 to 1978, playing stellar defense and hitting for power. He is shown here in action during the 1978 World Series against the Dodgers.

Farewell, Lyman

The California Angels team, wearing black armbands on their uniform sleeves, mourn the senseless, accidental death of outfielder Lyman Bostock, killed by a shotgun blast in Gary, Indiana, on September 23, 1978. Bostock batted .311 in his four years in the majors, was 27 years old, and had gotten two hits earlier that day in a game against the White Sox.

GEORGE BRETT: They were great series, they were a lot of fun to play in, but unfortunately we came up on the short end those three years, but then we finally got revenge in 1980.

It was fun, it was exciting. When you play in any championship and that championship is located in New York City, I mean, the electricity and the excitement level, it's just incredible. It was really amazing.

I'll never forget one of the games we played there in 1976 and sitting behind the Yankees' dugout was Telly Savalas, and I'm going, "God, that's Kojak. Kojak is out here." It was neat.

YANKEES VS. DODGERS—ONE MORE TIME

It wouldn't be the Yankees without controversy, which is how the 1978 World Series started. Reggie Jackson was angry at Graig Nettles for some unknown reason; Mickey Rivers had engaged in a shouting match with the team's traveling secretary, Bill Kane; and word leaked out that the Yankees had voted Bob Lemon only a half share of the World Series pie because he did not join the team until midseason.

The Dodgers jumped all over Ed Figueroa in the second inning of Game 1, scoring three runs, two of them on Davey Lopes' two-run homer, then continued the assault with three more in the fourth on Lopes' second homer, a three-run shot off Ken Clay.

It was 7–0 Dodgers with Tommy John sailing along when Reggie Jackson led off the top of the seventh with a homer.

TOMMY JOHN: I had pretty good luck with Reggie. I tried to throw him curve-balls. I thought Reggie was an off-speed hitter, a slider-speed hitter. A good fastball Reggie would have a hard time catching up with unless it was out over the plate. The medium-speed fastball or a hanging breaking ball, Reggie just hammered.

So he hit this home run off me, and later he said, "I got you there." I said, "Reggie, what was the score when you hit the home run? You couldn't hit a seven-run homer to beat me." The count was 3–1 and I threw him a fastball right there, and he hit the tar out of the ball.

The Dodgers won the opener, 11–5, and the second game, 4–3. Ron Cey singled in one run and hit a three-run homer, and the game ended when Bob Welch dueled Reggie Jackson with two on and two out in the top of the ninth. The count went to 3–2. The Dodger Stadium crowd of 55,982 was on its feet as Welch kept firing his fastball at Jackson. Reggie fouled off four straight pitches with vicious swings. He took one more vicious swing and missed, and the Dodgers had swept the first two games at home.

Two days later, in Yankee Stadium, the Dodgers ran into Ron Guidry and Graig Nettles' glove. In a performance reminiscent of, and equal to, Brooks Robinson's in the third game of the 1970 World Series, Nettles made four brilliant, unbelievable plays at third base, probably taking five runs away from the Dodgers.

"They can stop shooting," said Davey Lopes. "They have enough high-lights for the film already."

Guidry went the distance in a 5–1 win that, including the playoff against the Red Sox and the ALCS, was his 27th win of the year.

Game 4 produced the most unusual and the most pivotal play of the Series. It came in the bottom of the sixth, with Tommy John again handcuff-ing the Yankees and leading 3–0. With one out, Roy White singled, Thurman Munson walked, and Reggie Jackson singled home the Yankees' first run.

Outfielder Lou Piniella, known more for his bat than fielding, crashes into the wall in Game 5 of the 1978 World Series to make a great catch.

Lou Piniella then hit a perfect double-play ball to shortstop Bill Russell, who stepped on second and fired to first for what would have been the inning-ending double play.

REGGIE JACKSON: It was a perfect double-play ball. I was too far away to break it up, so I kind of swiveled my hip, hoping the ball would hit me, and it did.

The ball hit Reggie in the hip and ricocheted into right field, Munson scoring to make it a 3–2 game.

The Yankees tied it in the eighth on Munson's RBI double and won it in the tenth on Piniella's RBI single, evening the Series at two games each.

The Yankees exploded in Game 5, an 18-hit attack off three Dodgers pitchers for a 12–2 rout. Mickey Rivers, Thurman Munson, playoff hero Bucky Dent, and Brian Doyle, filling in at second base for the injured Willie Randolph, each had three hits. Jim Beattie pitched his first major league complete game.

Needing one more win to clinch their second straight world championship, the Yankees sent veteran Catfish Hunter to the mound in Game 6. Hunter, injured much of the season, had won only 12 games, but he returned to be a vital part of the stretch run, winning 9 of his last 11 decisions with a 6–0 record in August. He held the Dodgers to six hits through seven innings and left leading, 7–2, which is how it ended.

Jackson hit his second home run of the Series, his seventh in two World Series against the Dodgers. He batted .391 and drove in eight runs for the Series. Doyle had three more hits in the final game and ended up hitting a remarkable .438, 246 points over his season's average. Dent, a .243 hitter for the regular season, also had three hits in the sixth game, batted .417 for the World Series, and was named Series Most Valuable Player.

GOOSE GOSSAGE: The thing I remember most about that World Series is I was so excited because it was the first time that I had been there. But everybody else had been there. And had done it. They'd been there, done that, and it was kind of anticlimactic for us to win it after the playoff game with Boston.

A ticker-tape parade in New York City salutes the champion Yankees, who won back-to-back World Series for the first time since 1961–1962.

As great as it was, it wasn't as great as I thought it would be. The club-house was very subdued afterward. We sat in the training room, just kind of hanging out with ourselves, drinking a couple of beers in the clubhouse after the final game.

After that Boston game it was like, "We're going to win this thing." It wasn't a real cocky attitude, no bragging, but it was kind of a silent thing. We won it in L.A., and I thought, "God, I've seen these clubhouses, everybody's jumping on one another and champagne and stuff," and there was none of that. It was very, very quiet. It was almost as if we won the World Series when we won in Boston.

Almost overlooked was Thurman Munson's .320 batting average and seven runs batted in. With no Johnny Bench to overshadow him, the Yankees catcher finally got his long-overdue recognition as a star. To put an exclamation point to his brilliant season, Munson caught the final out of the World Series, a foul pop by Ron Cey, completing the Yankees' miracle comeback.

CHAPTER 10

THE TENTH INNING

1979

Having won three American League pennants and two world championships in the past three years, with all their major players in place, and with the addition of free agent signees Tommy John and Luis Tiant, the Yankees were sending out unmistakable signs that they were in the midst of another dynasty, one to parallel their successes of the thirties, forties, and fifties. The signs were not dismissed lightly by their fearful rivals.

The Yankees lost their first two games of the season to the Milwaukee Brewers. But not even those two losses, hung on their two 20-game winners, Ron Guidry and Ed Figueroa, could dampen their enthusiasm, shake their faith, or give aid and comfort to the enemy. When the Yankees reeled off seven wins in their next nine games, it was business as usual at the big ballpark in the south Bronx.

By Thursday morning, April 19, the Yankees had closed to a half game behind Baltimore as they prepared to meet the Orioles in an afternoon game at Yankee Stadium, looking for a sweep of their three-game series. Guidry and Tommy John had held the powerful Birds to one run each in winning the first two games of the series. A sweep would put the Yankees into first place in the American League East on their way to what surely would be their fourth straight pennant.

It was hardly cause for alarm when Jim Palmer beat the Yanks, 6–3, to salvage the final game of the series for Baltimore. But an incident in the Yankees' shower room after the game would have more wide-ranging ramifications.

INJURIES

It started with the sort of good-natured needling that had marked this Yankees team.

Yer Out!

The season began with major league umpires on strike, and they would not return until May 19, six weeks into the season. Major league baseball filled the void with replacement umps, amateurs, former professional umpires, and college and high school officials. A handful of these replacements were given full-time jobs as major league umpires, but they were shunned by the regular umps as "scabs." In time, however, the replacement umps were accepted.

GOOSE GOSSAGE: Cliff Johnson wasn't catching, and he thought he should have been in the game that day. We were playing Baltimore. So he was in a bad mood. He bitched and moaned and cried the whole day down in the bullpen. He wouldn't catch. Just being a lazy ass.

I didn't pitch that day, and we came into the clubhouse after the game and I had tape on my socks to keep my socks up. I unrolled the tape and rolled it up in my hand and balled it up. Cliff's locker was right straight across from me, and I winged this tape over his head and it went into his locker, missed him. Just as I threw it, Reggie was walking by and he said, "Hey, Goose, how'd Cliff do against you in the National League?"

And I said, "Well, he couldn't hit what he couldn't see." Just joking. It was not meant as a knock on Cliff, it was just that I threw so hard, he couldn't see it. It was no knock on Cliff's ability, but he took it wrong.

I continued to undress and I was ready to go in and take a shower and I stopped at the urinal. Next thing I knew, Cliff was standing next to me on my right and he said, "Hey, do you think you can back that shit up?"

I looked at him and I thought, "God, this guy's serious." Then he took my head and he kind of slapped and shoved it real hard. I came back and hit him in the chest with my elbow, then I hit him about six or seven times. I had him backed up against the first stall in the bathroom. I kind of quit hitting him and he came back and hit me. I ducked and he hit me on the top of the head a couple of times, and I had a couple of goose eggs on top of my head.

Brian Doyle was right there and he tried to break it up, but he couldn't, so he went and got a couple of other guys, and everybody came in and finally broke it up.

I was standing there and I said, "You know, Cliff, you're just a lazy bleep," or something like that, and as I said it, I was kind of walking away and he tackled me and we fell against the wall. I was completely naked except for my shower shoes. He still had his whole uniform on. I fell against the wall, and then I fell down and I put my hand down to break my fall and we both landed on it. Cliff weighed 235 or 240 and I weighed 230, and all that weight was on my thumb. My thumb had no chance.

Gossage suffered a tear of the ulnar collateral ligament in the joint of his right thumb. He would undergo surgery three days later and would not pitch again until July 12.

BUCKY DENT: Cliff used to joke around all the time. He was one of those happy-go-lucky guys, and I think he caught Goose in a wrong moment. He kind of slapped him on the head, and Goose, who usually just kidded back and let it go, went after him and they got into it.

Goose was another fun-loving, happy-go-lucky guy who was always kidding around. I remember another time in 1978. We had about seven or eight games to go, and the guys used to go into the sauna after a game, joke around, drink a beer. That was a big thing.

This one night, there was only me and Thurman. And Thurman used to stand up, and he'd walk and talk about the game and chirp. And we were sitting in the sauna talking and Gossage came up and put his face up to the window. And Munson said, "Look at this great big old pie face." He turned around and he slapped the window. And when he hit it, it exploded, and it laid Thurman's knuckle open.

Goose yelled, "Oh, my God, there goes the pennant."

They kept it quiet, but he wound up getting about eight stitches. And they had to pick glass out of Goose's face.

As fate would have it, just five months earlier, the Yankees had finally traded their other relief ace, Sparky Lyle, to the Texas Rangers in a 10-player deal that brought left-handed pitcher Dave Righetti to New York.

There was to be more bad karma for the Yankees. On June 2, while jogging in from the outfield after the top of the ninth, Reggie Jackson suffered a partial tear of the sheath of muscle in his left calf area and would miss almost a month. A series of minor injuries would reduce Graig Nettles, the fielding hero of the 1978 World Series, to a shell of his former self. And Guidry was hard-pressed to match his incredible 25–3, 1.74 ERA, 248-strikeout, nine-shutout season of the year before.

After splitting his first four decisions, Guidry volunteered to go to the bullpen to fill the closer role left vacant by Gossage's injury. In his first two relief appearances in a span of three days, Guidry won one game and saved another, but when he went seven days without getting a chance to pitch, it was decided to return him to the starting rotation.

On May 16 Guidry beat the Tigers with a complete-game 6–2 win, but then lost five of his next seven decisions. He was 6–7 on July 21, when he beat the Oakland A's and took off on an 11-game winning streak.

BILLY II

On June 18, with the Yankees struggling with a record of 34–31 and in fourth place, eight games out of first, George Steinbrenner fired Bob Lemon and replaced him with Billy Martin. It had already been announced that Martin was to return in 1980, so, Steinbrenner reasoned, why not bring him back six months earlier in the hope that brash Billy could light a fire under his sagging ballclub?

Billy II, however, did not produce the quick fix Steinbrenner had hoped it would. Although the team played better under Martin (55–40 for the remainder of the season), the Yankees were buried too far behind and beset with too many problems to pose a serious challenge to the runaway Orioles.

Not the least of Martin's problems was what to do with the Yankees' captain, their heart and soul, Thurman Munson, who was suffering with painful knees. The years of squatting behind the plate had taken their toll on Munson, and it was becoming increasingly apparent that his days as a full-time catcher were behind him.

The idea of Munson not being able to catch again was disturbing to his teammates, who relied heavily on his leadership.

RON GUIDRY: Having him there, everybody kind of revolved around him. You could take me out and they could still play and win. You could take anybody else out and they would probably still play and win. But if you took Thurman out, our chances of winning were cut in half.

Pitching was made easier because I got to throw to a guy like Thurman. He made pitchers who were average good. He made them win a lot of games because of his ability to take all the pressure and call the game. And we all felt that's the best pitch to throw. I'm not going to second-guess him and say it's not. I could have thrown a guy 20 sliders and made him look foolish, but if he called for a fastball, that's what I threw. If I threw a pitch that a guy hit out of the ballpark, he took the responsibility. He'd say, "Hey, I called for it."

Everybody looked at him, and looked up to him, to say where we were going, and if he said we're going to retreat and run, we ran. If he said we're going forward, we went forward.

THURMAN

Though Munson's physical problems weighed heavily on his mind, he was distracted by other thoughts. He preferred not to disrupt his children's schooling by moving them to his home during the season in New Jersey. His wife, Diane, daughters Kelly and Tracy, and son Michael—who needed special care because of his hyperactiveness—remained back home in Ohio, and Munson knew his place was with them. He took advantage of every opportunity to go home to be with his family, if only for a few hours.

He had begun taking flying lessons during the winter between the 1977 and 1978 seasons. Then he purchased a small plane, a Cessna Citation, with one objective in mind.

WILLIE RANDOLPH: He wanted to be close to his family. His son and his daughters were growing up, and I think it always bothered him that he wasn't there to share that. Most ballplayers go through that. I understood he was getting more involved in flying. It's a passion. He loved to do it.

DIANE MUNSON: He realized he needed to spend some time with the kids. Our son was having some problems at the time. He was hyperactive. It takes some special parenting, and I think Thurman felt that he could add a dimension to Michael's life that was lacking with him playing in New York. So one

The Friendly Confines

The scoreboard tells it all. With the wind blowing out at Chicago's Wrigley Field, the Philadelphia Phillies defeated the Cubs in a 23–22 slugfest on May 17, 1979. The wild game featured eleven homers, including two by Mike Schmidt for the Phils (one was the game-winner in the tenth inning), three by Dave Kingman for the Cubbies, and one by Phillies pitcher Randy Lerch. There were also 50 hits. Rawly Eastwick was the winning pitcher, and Bruce Sutter took the loss. In a way, one could say the Phillies got their revenge on the Cubs, but it was a long time coming. This game was the highest-scoring affair since the Cubs beat Philadelphia 26–23 back on August 25, 1922. Guess where that game was played.

of the reasons for him purchasing the airplane was that he could spend more time with the kids.

As a rule, teams frowned on players commuting to out-of-town cities, especially on game days, and ordinarily they would forbid a player to fly his own plane during the season. But Thurman was a special case to the Yankees, and they looked the other way to accommodate him.

During spring training Munson was asked about his flying in a television interview with former-Yankee-turned-sportscaster Tony Kubek. He replied, "I think it's great, the feeling of being alone for an hour or two by yourself. You're up there, and nobody asks any questions. You don't have to put on any kind of an act. You just go up there and enjoy yourself. You have to be on your toes, but it's just a kind of relaxation when you spend a lot of time by yourself, and I need that. I also need to get home a lot, so I love to fly."

As July approached, Munson began taking fly balls in the outfield. The plan was for him to turn over the regular catching duties to a committee of replacements, veteran Cliff Johnson and youngsters Jerry Narron and Brad

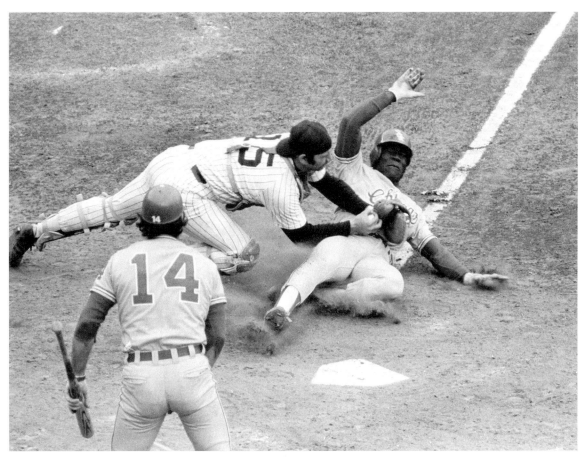

Yankees catcher Thurman Munson tags out Jorge Orta of the White Sox. Munson died in a plane crash in the middle of the 1979 season.

Gulden, and for Munson to play right field while Reggie Jackson became the full-time DH, a plan that was certain to displease Jackson.

Of the Yankees' first 106 games of the 1979 season, Munson would catch in only 88 (he played three games at first base and five games as DH). Not only had his bad knees hurt his defensive skills, but his hitting was also affected. In 97 games, he had only three home runs and 39 RBIs.

On July 26 the Yankees, with Ron Guidry, beat the California Angels 2–0 in an afternoon game at Yankee Stadium, their 100th game of the season. They had completed their first homestand after the All-Star break with six wins in eight games, putting them ten games over .500, but this still left them in fourth place, twelve games behind, as they prepared to embark on a six-game trip, three in Milwaukee, three in Chicago.

The day after the final game in Chicago—Thursday, August 2—was an off day on the Yankees' schedule, and Thurman Munson had already made his plans. After the final game of the homestand, he would fly his plane to Chicago, where it would be waiting for him when the three-game Chicago series ended. Then he would fly to Canton and spend the off day with his family before flying back for the start of a homestand against Baltimore on Friday night, August 3.

PHIL PEPE: As the Yankees' beat writer for the *Daily News*, I had made the Milwaukee-Chicago trip, and, like Munson, I was looking forward to the day off to catch up on some personal business, do my laundry. We had arrived home late after the final game in Chicago, and I slept late the next morning before tackling the chore of paying some bills. It was about 1:00 P.M. when my telephone rang and the voice on the other end said, "Did you hear the news?"

"What news?" I asked.

"Thurman Munson was killed in an airplane crash."

I felt chills run up and down my body. Just three weeks earlier, in Anaheim, I had spent hours talking with him. I had arrived back at the team hotel about 11:00 P.M. and saw Munson in the snack shop, picking out bags of potato chips, Fritos, pretzels.

"What are you doing?" I asked.

"Oh, I missed dinner," he said.

"Don't eat that junk," I said. "There's a hamburger place up the street. Why don't you go there?"

"I hate to eat alone," he said.

"I'll sit with you," I offered.

"You will?" he replied in a surprised voice.

We talked for hours, about family, about things apart from baseball. Eventually, the subject of his flying came up and he talked animatedly of his love for his new hobby and even invited me to go up with him someday.

"No way," I said. "I'm not going to fly with you."

"Hey, you don't have to worry," he said. "It's safe. I don't care if you live or die, but I certainly do care if I live or die."

Moments after I hung up the phone, it rang again. It was my office, calling to give me the details. Munson was practicing takeoffs and landings at the Canton-Akron Airport. Coming in for a landing, he apparently lost control and the Cessna Citation crashed a thousand feet short of the runway. Rescuers were unable to free Munson from the burning wreckage.

"We need you to get reactions from the players," my editor said.

My first call was to Roy White. He had not heard the news. When I told him, he couldn't talk. He turned the phone over to his wife, Linda, until he could gather his emotions and talk about his late teammate and friend.

I called several other Yankees. Graig Nettles. Lou Piniella. Fred Stanley. Each of them had heard the tragic news. They cried. They spoke in hushed tones, their voices cracking with emotion. To a man, they were in a state of shock.

WILLIE RANDOLPH: It was total shock . . . stunned. You hear what people were saying to you, but you don't believe it. No, there's no way this happened. I was just with him the other night. We were sitting there joking, playing cards. It was total shock. Disbelief. I broke down and cried.

CHRIS CHAMBLISS: Audry [Chris' wife] and I were in a car going to get some ice cream, not far from our house in New Jersey. We were driving down the street, and the guy said over the radio, "Thurman Munson just died . . . crash . . ." and Audry and I just looked at each other and didn't say a word for I don't know how long. We were just stunned . . . quiet . . . . We didn't say anything to each other for a long, long time. . . . We were both so shocked.

The next day, that's a meeting I'll never forget when Billy had to talk to everybody and he couldn't hold himself from talking about it. Everybody was crying in there. That was in the clubhouse the next day.

BILL WHITE: I was driving to New York when I heard it, outside a little place called Sergeantsville, New Jersey, and I just yelled and cussed out loud when I heard it. It's something that you don't expect. I think many times we athletes think we can do anything and we're invincible and will go on and on. It was a tough period for the family, because he left a wife and kids.

BUCKY DENT: The last time I saw Thurman, we played a game in Comiskey Park, and I was sitting on the bus, real early. I saw Thurman and Bobby Murcer and his wife come walking out in front of the bus. They went to their car.

The next day, I was gone all day, then I went to the Twin Towers for dinner, and I came down after dinner and I was going to get my car and some guy said, "Aren't you Bucky Dent?" I said, "Yeah." He said, "Isn't it a shame what happened to Thurman?" I said, "What are you talking about?" He said, "He got killed in a plane crash."

It stunned me. I kind of fell back on the car. I said, "No, that's not true." He said it was, and I asked him, "Was there anybody with him?" He said, "Yeah, there were two other people in the plane."

My first reaction was I thought it was Bobby Murcer and his wife, because they walked out with Thurman in Chicago. I thought maybe Bobby and Kay were flying to Canton with him.

The weird thing is that one of the people in the plane with Thurman when he crashed was my partner in my baseball school. I had met him through Thurman. He was a flying instructor from Canton, and his son was a baseball player. He used to bring teams down to my school. We became friends and we hooked up and we became partners.

His name is Jerry Anderson, and he and Thurman were in some businesses together. He told me Thurman was going to do some touch-and-goes, and Thurman asked Jerry if he wanted to go up with him. Jerry and his buddy were going to do some flying, so they said they'd go with Thurman.

They were up, and Thurman was doing some landings on an elevated runway. He was coming in and he put the landing gear down and dropped his airspeed, and the plane hit and spun up on top of the road and burst into flames. They kicked out the side door, and he and the other guy got out. Jerry got burned in the flames, but he said when the plane hit on Thurman's side, it jammed Thurman up and broke his neck and he couldn't move. That's why he didn't get out and the two other guys did.

I got interested in flying that year. I was learning how to fly. I used to fly out of Teterboro. I used to fly with Thurman all the time. He used to park his plane in Boca Raton and we'd be playing in spring training and Thurman would say, "Do you want to go flying?" I'd say, "Sure," and we'd go to Boca and get in his plane and fly to West Palm or down to Miami, land and come back. He was big into it.

After Thurman got killed, that made me stop flying.

The Yankees director of public relations at the time of Munson's death was Mickey Morabito. He was in his office on the morning of August 2, when he, along with other Yankees employees, were summoned to George Steinbrenner's office. Ordinarily, a summons from "the Boss" was an indication that Morabito was about to be reprimanded for some newspaper article that was unfavorable to Steinbrenner.

MICKEY MORABITO: When I walked into George's office, he was in a somber mood. He waited until everybody had gathered—there were about five or six of us—then he said, "I've got some bad news. We lost Thurman today."

Somebody said, "What do you mean we lost Thurman?"

Then George explained about the plane crash. I was shocked, but George said to me, "Go find Billy Martin and give him the news."

I knew Billy was fishing somewhere on the Jersey shore. I didn't know where exactly, but I had a phone number for the harbormaster. I walked out of George's office and right outside his office is the receptionist's desk and switchboard, and I just picked up her phone and made a call.

I got the harbormaster and told him to get Billy off the boat, it was an emergency. I waited a long time, and then I heard Billy's voice on the line and I told him the news. At first, he didn't believe me. "No," he said, "it's not true."

I convinced him that it was by telling him all the details, and Billy just started to sob. He was crying like a baby. Billy was such an emotional guy, and he loved Thurman. I think in Thurman, Billy figured he had an ally in his battles with Reggie and George.

I don't ever remember Billy saying good-bye. He just kind of ended the conversation by hanging up the phone without a word, that's how broken up he was.

The next night, the Yankees were scheduled to open a four-game series at the stadium against the Orioles.

Oh, Brother

Three days after Lou Brock set his stolen-base record, Atlanta beat Houston, 9–4. The winning pitcher was Phil Niekro. It was his 20th win of the season. He would finish the season with a record of 21–20, the first pitcher since Wilbur Wood of the Chicago White Sox in 1973, and the first National League pitcher since Irv Young of the 1905 Boston Braves, to win 20 and lose 20 in the same season. The losing pitcher for the Astros was Joe Niekro, Phil's younger brother, baseball's only other 20-game winner that season. That made the Niekros only the second pair of brothers to win 20 games in the same season. In 1970 the Perrys—Jim for the Minnesota Twins, Gaylord for the San Francisco Giants—were both 20-game winners.

EARL WEAVER: The ballplayers didn't want to play, and I said anybody who really didn't want to play didn't have to play. Some of my guys had been his teammates. We were going to play because you have to play, but if we didn't have enough players then we'd forfeit the game.

I was asked about it, and I said whatever they wanted to do was fine with me. I was concerned about my ballplayers who might not want to play, but why wouldn't they want to play?

The game was played, but the Yankees were lifeless. They lost, 1–0, to Scott McGregor, a former Yankee. They lost the next night, too, but managed to win the third game of the series, Sunday afternoon, as Tommy John outpitched Mike Flanagan.

Monday afternoon, August 6, was to be Thurman Munson's funeral. Steinbrenner had arranged for a charter plane to fly the Yankees, their wives, manager, coaches, executives, trainers, clubhouse attendants, front-office workers, and members of the press from Newark Airport to Canton for the funeral. Players and former players, teammates and opponents, umpires and baseball executives came from all over the country to say their last good-byes to a player who was universally respected for his competitiveness and his desire to win.

DIANE MUNSON: *Numb* would be the word I would use. I saw my friends, men who I'd always see laugh and tell jokes and cutting each other on the bus. These men who were so different, and here they were getting off a bus and coming to a cemetery in order to see their teammate and their friend. It was heartbreaking. It was heartbreaking for all of us.

In the little church, a couple of Yankees said eulogies to their fallen captain, including Lou Piniella.

> We don't know why God took Thurman away from us. Nobody really knows that. But we all know that as long as we wear a Yankees uniform . . . Thurman will never be too far from us. . . . He'll be right with us. . . . Diane, I hope God gives you the strength, the courage, and the conviction to carry on just the way Thurman wanted you to carry on and raise your family just the way Thurman would have wanted you to raise them. God bless you, Thurman, wherever you are, and God be with you and by your side forever.

The flight back to New York was solemn; the entire day had been emotionally wrenching and exhausting, but there was a game to play that night. First, there was a pregame memorial to the Yankees captain.

The Yankees took the field, and the area behind home plate, Thurman Munson's customary position, was left vacant during the ceremony. Munson's image flashed on the huge message board in right-center field, superimposed by these words: "Our captain and leader has not left us—today, tomorrow, this year, next . . . Our endeavors will reflect our love and admiration for him." Yankees stood at their respective positions, hats removed, heads bowed. Reggie Jackson, in right field, brushed tears from his eyes.

Terence Cardinal Cooke of New York led the huge crowd in prayer.

WILLIE RANDOLPH: I never really felt as close or as one with the team as I did at that particular moment. The feeling of togetherness. Knowing that here we are at a tough time, but we've got to go out tonight and play, and play for the man because when we looked up at the scoreboard and we saw that picture of Thurman, we knew that he was on the field with us. And, in essence, he was.

It was as emotional and as heart-wrenching a moment in Yankee Stadium as the one almost exactly 40 years earlier, when a dying Lou Gehrig made his famous farewell speech, the last Yankees captain before Munson coming to a tragic, premature end, just like his successor.

The crowd of 36,314 stood in silence during the ceremony; then, as one, they began to applaud and chant Munson's name.

DIANE MUNSON: I think it was New York's way of bidding farewell to their captain, their hero. Heroes don't die. This was unbelievable to have happened, period, but to happen during the season is even more amazing, and you looked at those ballplayers, tough, tough men, men who have to go out and fight, and be rough and tough all the time, and then you look at them on the field and you see them all crying, heads bowed. It was heartbreaking. I don't know. I give credit to them for being able to play, because I don't know how they did it.

Somehow they did. The Orioles went out to a 4–0 lead; then, in the seventh inning, with two runners on, up to bat for the Yankees came Bobby Murcer. He had been there 11 years earlier when Munson joined the team, a brash, cocky, tough rookie. Murcer was traded after the 1974 season and was away for five years until he returned to the Yankees just six weeks earlier. He remained close to Munson and had been one of the eulogists earlier in the day, and now he belted a three-run homer that cut the Orioles' lead to 4–3.

Then, in the bottom of the ninth, Murcer batted again with runners on second and third and ripped a two-run single that gave the Yankees a 5–4 victory. He didn't have to say a word. Everyone knew that Bobby Murcer did it for his buddy, Thurman.

Murcer's game-winning single against the Orioles would be the Yankees' last shining moment of 1979. They were not the same team without their captain, their heart and their soul, and they floundered the rest of the season. They did manage to win their last eight games, but by then it was too late. They finished fourth, 13½ games behind the Baltimore Orioles.

Carl Yastrzemski replaced Ted Williams in the outfield for Boston in 1961. Nineteen seasons later he collected his 3,000th hit, on September 12, 1979.

YAZ

On September 12 in Boston, Carl Yastrzemski singled past Willie Randolph for his 3,000th hit and became the first American League player in history with 3,000 hits and 400 home runs.

BOB STANLEY: It was off Jim Beattie. Willie Randolph looked like he was saying, "Ah, let's get it over with," and the ball went past him into right field.

THE ART OF THE STEAL

Eleven days later, with the days dwindling down on another season, Lou Brock of the St. Louis Cardinals stole the 938th base of his magnificent career. It would be the last stolen base for the man who made the steal an art form. Two seasons before, he had passed Ty Cobb for the modern all-time record for steals.

Brock had arrived in the major leagues with the Chicago Cubs in 1961, a remarkably strong man for one so small—5'11", 170 pounds. The following season, he became one of only three batters to hit a ball into the center-field bleachers in New York's Polo Grounds, some 510 feet from home plate. Joe Adcock and Hank Aaron were the other two.

In 1964 the St. Louis Cardinals acquired Brock from the Cubs in exchange for pitcher Ernie Broglio, who had won 21 games in 1960, to replace the recently retired Stan Musial in left field.

"The reason they won the pennant in 1964," Musial would say, "is because they got rid of me and got Brock."

Brock would help the Cards win two more pennants. He would retire after the 1979 season with 3,023 hits, a career batting average of .293, and the all-time record for stolen bases at the time. In 1985 he was inducted into the Hall of Fame.

WE ARE FAMILY

Early in the season, the Pittsburgh Pirates hit upon a theme, "We Are Family," the hit recording by the R&B/soul group Sister Sledge. Someone brought the record to the clubhouse and played it, and it became their rallying cry for the rest of the season.

***

RENNIE STENNETT: That was the closeness of our team. We were that type of team where guys looked out for each other. That song came out, and we used to play it in the clubhouse. We could lose a game and if you came in there 10 minutes after the game, you would think we won because we had such a loose club. We knew that we did everything we could, but tomorrow somebody's going to suffer. That's the attitude we had so you wouldn't know that we lost the game. And we used to play that song "We Are Family."

***

If the Pirates were family, their patriarch was Wilver Dornel "Willie" Stargell. They called him "Pops." He was the soul of the team, a big teddy bear of a man, and the rest of the Pirates looked to him for leadership and counsel. They brought their problems to him, and he showed them how to win.

It took a few years for Stargell to crawl out of the shadow of Roberto Clemente. He did it by hitting prodigious home runs, twice leading the National League in homers, with 48 in 1971 and 44 in 1973, once leading the league in runs batted in, with 119 in 1973.

By 1979 Stargell was in the twilight of an illustrious career in which he would play 21 seasons (all with Pittsburgh), get 2,232 hits, hit 475 home runs, drive in 1,540 runs, and be elected to the Hall of Fame. Even at age 39, there was still thunder in his bat as he belted 32 homers and knocked in 82 runs in what would be his last hurrah.

RENNIE STENNETT: We used to call Willie "Pops" Stargell. Willie was the type who was a silent leader. On the field, I was the leader on defense. The main guy was Stargell, but we really didn't need a leader. Everybody motivated each other. For instance, if you go out and have a bad day at the plate, the guys would talk about it. "Man, that was some time up. You must have been hitting with the *Daily News* or something." And everybody would laugh.

We just had a lot of fun playing ball. We'd be at the ballpark at 1:00 for a 7:00 game sometimes. I'd be coming to the ballpark and I'd stop and buy $10 worth of corned beef or something. Stargell would bring fried chicken. We'd go to the ballpark and we'd play cards; some guys would go out and take extra batting practice. If you came out early, you were there, hanging out with the guys, talking baseball. It was great.

It was always that way with the Pirates club. It started with Danny Murtaugh. If we had a slump, lost four games in a row, we considered that a slump and it was time to get together. Especially on the road. Everybody put in 20 bucks, and we'd buy some food and meet in a suite in the hotel, just the players, to talk about why we were losing. It always worked.

One time, in 1971, Murtaugh was the manager and we fielded the first all-black lineup in baseball. Richie Hebner was sick. Somebody else was hurt, and Murtaugh made out his lineup. First base, Al Oliver. Second base, me. Shortstop, Jackie Hernandez. Third base, Dave Cash. Left field, Stargell.

Center field, Gene Clines. Right field, Roberto. Catcher, Manny Sanguillen. Pitcher, Dock Ellis. Murtaugh signed the lineup card, and somebody said, "Hey, that's nine black players out there." Murtaugh said, "I didn't even realize it. I just put my nine best players available out there." Ellis got knocked out in the second inning.

Our mentality with the Pirates was that if we were 0 for 3 and we came up in the ninth inning with the winning run on base and knocked in that run, it was like having a 4 for 4 day. We felt we couldn't lose.

Supporting Stargell were Bill Madlock and Dave Parker, both .300 hitters; Bill Robinson, who combined with Stargell and Parker to form a trio that accounted for 81 home runs; and infielder Phil Garner, whose hell-for-leather style of play earned him the nickname "Scrap Iron."

The Pirates finished two games ahead of the surprising Montreal Expos to bring the sixth National League East title in the decade to Three Rivers Stadium, situated at the confluence where the Monongahela and the Allegheny Rivers form the Ohio River.

THE REDS, AGAIN

Downriver on the Ohio was Riverfront Stadium, home of the Cincinnati Reds, who also won their sixth division title of the seventies by finishing a game and a half ahead of the Houston Astros. The two rivals would meet to decide the National League pennant for the fourth time in the decade.

On paper, the Reds appeared to have the upper hand. Although they had lost Tony Perez to the Expos and Pete Rose to the Phillies by way of free agency, most of the Big Red Machine was intact—Joe Morgan; Johnny Bench, who had 22 homers and 80 RBIs; George Foster, with 30 homers and 98 RBIs; and Ken Griffey, a .316 hitter. In addition, Tom Seaver, who had come over from the Mets in 1977 to become the ace of the Reds' pitching staff, posted a record of 16–6.

SPARKY ANDERSON: I had managed seven years, but that [getting Seaver] was a big thrill for me. I'll never forget, he pitched in Montreal, and I was seeing for

Disco Sox!

Disco Demolition Night at Chicago's Comiskey Park was among the nuttiest promotional events ever dreamed up. In conjunction with local radio disc jockey Steve Dahl, Mike Veeck—the son of Bill Veeck—decreed that any fan bringing a disco record to the ballpark got in for 98 cents. The albums were to be blown up between games of a White Sox–Tigers twin bill. The Tigers won the first game, 4–1, despite albums being flung onto the field by rowdy fans.

About fifty thousand teenagers had shown up, ready to make "burn, baby, burn, disco inferno!" a reality. But thousands refused to leave the field, and after a delay of more than an hour and 15 minutes, umpire Dave Phillips awarded the second game to the Tigers in a 9–0 forfeit. For the White Sox, disco really did suck.

Promotional wizard Mike Veeck got more than he bargained for when the White Sox put on Disco Demolition Night on July 12, 1979—a riot on the field between games of a doubleheader and a forfeit loss to the Tigers.

myself one of the greatest pitchers of our time. He was very professional how he did everything. And he was a character. He always played games.

I had a long talk with him, and he said, "Just watch." There were a couple of things he wanted me to watch. Where he was landing. He said, "Just keep your eye on where I'm landing, because if I'm going to be off, it'll be there." So I always watched his lead foot.

Everything he did, his work habits. You never had to mess with that.

PIRATE TIME

Seaver started the first game of the NLCS against John Candelaria, pitched eight innings, and left with the score tied 2–2. In the eleventh inning Stargell belted a three-run homer and the Pirates took an early lead in the series.

The next day, the Pirates won again, and again in extra innings, pushing across a run in the top of the tenth for a 3–2 victory and a sweep of the first two games in Cincinnati.

Back in Pittsburgh for Game 3, Bert Blyleven pitched a complete-game eight-hitter, Stargell hit another home run, and the Pirates won, 7–1, for a three-game sweep of the Reds and their second National League pennant of the decade. The vaunted Big Red Machine scored only five runs in the three games.

TOM SEAVER: That was a real disappointment. We pitched pretty well, but we just didn't hit. It was like they were a team of destiny. They did what they had to do to win.

FOR THE BIRDS

In the American League, the Baltimore Orioles easily outdistanced the field in the East after the Yankees dropped out of the running with Goose Gossage's thumb injury and Thurman Munson's tragic death. In the West, the California Angels made it to postseason play for the first time in their history, led by Don Baylor (36 homers, 139 RBIs) and Nolan Ryan (16 wins, 223 strikeouts). The Championship Series started in Baltimore with another Earl Weaver–Jim Palmer disagreement.

EARL WEAVER: He didn't want to pitch the first game of the playoffs, because [23-game winner] Mike Flanagan was going to be the Cy Young Award winner and he deserved to start. I said, "Mike Flanagan has never started a playoff game," and he said something about, "I wouldn't be able to come back." Well, if you win the first game and Flanagan wins the second game, you might not have to come back. He didn't like the manager to have the final word.

Earl Weaver (right) won 1,480 games in 17 seasons for the Baltimore Orioles, including six division wins, four pennants, and one championship. He also had a habit of getting ejected, as he was in this game on August 16, 1979.

But Weaver had the final word. He wrote out the lineup card, and he wrote in Jim Palmer's name for Game 1. It was Palmer against Nolan Ryan, a dream matchup.

Neither was around at the end, and neither was involved in the decision. Ryan left after seven innings, Palmer after nine, with the score tied 3–3. In the tenth, pinch-hitter John Lowenstein belted a three-run homer to give the Birds a 6–3 win.

As he planned, Weaver pitched Flanagan in the second game and got a 2–0 lead in the series, although it wasn't pretty. The Orioles jumped out to a 9–1 lead after three innings. The Angels came back to score seven times in the last four innings, but fell a run short, 9–8.

The Pirates reemerged as postseason threats with the help of Dave Parker, who twice led the National League in both hitting and doubles.

Dennis Martinez, a 15-game winner, started the third game for the Orioles in Anaheim and took a 3–2 lead into the bottom of the ninth, three outs away from the pennant. When the Angels rallied, Weaver sent for his relief ace, Don Stanhouse. He was nicknamed "Full Pack," because he had a tendency to always pitch into trouble, then have to wiggle his way out. Weaver, a habitual smoker who used to duck into the corner of the dugout for a cigarette in stressful situations, would go through a full pack when Stanhouse was on the mound.

The Angels rallied for two runs off Stanhouse for a 4–3 win and stayed alive for another day. But in Game 4, Scott McGregor hurled a complete-game, six-hit shutout. The Orioles won, 8–0, and were on their way to the World Series for the first time since 1971.

IT'S 1971 ALL OVER AGAIN

Mike Flanagan was the Orioles' starter in the first game of the World Series in Baltimore and was treated to five runs in the first, which he managed just barely to protect. The Pirates scored one in the fourth, two in the sixth, and one in the eighth. In the ninth, Dave Parker singled with one out, was caught off first by Flanagan, but reached second safely when shortstop Mark Belanger dropped first baseman Eddie Murray's throw. Parker moved to third on Bill Robinson's grounder to the right side.

With the tying run on third, Pops Stargell, who had homered against Flanagan the inning before, came to the plate. Weaver stayed with his starter, and Flanagan vindicated his manager's faith in him by getting Stargell to pop to short left for the final out.

The Pirates evened the Series by taking Game 2, 3–2, on a pinch-hit RBI single in the ninth by Manny Sanguillen off Full Pack Stanhouse, wasting a big day for Orioles first baseman Eddie Murray, who had three hits, including a home run.

In Pittsburgh the Orioles won the third game, 8–4, and came back from a 6–3 deficit to score six runs in the eighth and take the fourth game, 9–6, for a three-games-to-one lead in the Series. It was reminiscent of the last time these two teams met in the World Series, in 1971. The Orioles won the first two games, but the Pirates, sparked by the play of Roberto Clemente, came back to win the Series in seven games.

All-Star Break

Seattle's Kingdome hosted the All-Star Game on July 17. The American League jumped out to an early lead, scoring three in the first and single runs in the second and third. Going into the eighth, the American League clung to a 6–5 lead when Lee Mazzilli of the Mets was sent up to pinch hit. In his first All-Star at-bat, Mazzilli hit a game-tying home run off Jim Kern of the Texas Rangers.

Mazzilli stayed in the game and batted again in the ninth. With the bases full, he drew a walk that forced in the winning run in a 7–6 victory for the National League, its eighth straight win.

At the All-Star break, the surprise teams in the National League were the Houston Astros, who had finished fifth in 1978, and the Montreal Expos, who had never finished higher than fourth in their 10-year history.

But the Astros, under manager Bill Virdon and with National League strikeout sensation J.R. Richard, and the Expos, under manager Dick Williams (who had won championships in Boston and Oakland), were making a serious run at division championships.

In the American League, Baltimore continued to set the pace in the East, while the California Angels, led by free agent signees Don Baylor and Bobby Grich, seemed ready to unseat defending champion Kansas City.

RENNIE STENNETT: We were down three games to one, and we had a meeting. Willie Stargell brought Dick Gregory to the meeting, and we talked until 2:00 in the morning and Gregory was telling us about positive thinking and believing in ourselves. He was trying to put us in the right frame of mind for the rest of the Series. We came out of that meeting, and we felt we were going to win. We had the confidence to come back, because we did it all year.

It was déjà vu for Earl Weaver and the Orioles. The Pirates won the fifth game, 7–1, and back in Baltimore won Game 6, 4–0, to even the Series at three games apiece.

For the deciding seventh game, Weaver chose Scott McGregor, who had won a game each in the ALCS and the World Series without losing. McGregor took a 1–0 lead into the sixth when, once again, Pops Stargell ignited the Pirates with his third home run of the Series, a two-run shot that put the

Pirates ahead. They tacked on two more runs in the ninth, and the Pirates used four pitchers to hold the Orioles to four hits for a 4–1 victory and another world championship.

EARL WEAVER: We were up three games to one and Pittsburgh was out of pitching, and I had Palmer, Flanagan, and McGregor all on proper rest. Eddie Murray quit hitting. We didn't score any runs. The last game, we were losing 2–1 in the eighth, we had the bases loaded, and Eddie hit a rocket that went right at Dave Parker [the Pirates right fielder]. Why we quit hitting, I don't know. But it happens.

RENNIE STENNETT: Earl Weaver didn't know the Buccos.

After getting 24 runs and 37 hits in the first four games, the Orioles scored two runs and had 17 hits in the last three. Eddie Murray, who had four hits in five at-bats in the first two games, went hitless in 21 at-bats over the last five games, and Earl Weaver relived his 1971 nightmare.

BRING ON THE EIGHTIES

On the last day of the decade, the Basic Agreement between players and owners expired, setting the stage for another prolonged labor dispute that would drag on through the 1980 season, which was played without a Basic Agreement between players and owners. It would lead to a devastating midseason strike in 1981.

The seventies began with labor strife (the Curt Flood suit), and it ended with labor strife (the imminent strike of 1981).

The seventies began with the Baltimore Orioles disappointed at having lost the World Series to the New York Mets in 1969 and determined to get back, and it ended with the Orioles disappointed at having lost the World Series to the Pittsburgh Pirates in 1979 and determined to get back.

In between, baseball underwent the most sweeping changes in the history of the game.

BOWIE KUHN: The things I'm proudest of are opening baseball up to new and different ways of marketing itself, which turned the game around on the national level and the local level, and baseball showing the United States that we were color-blind. That, too, was good marketing. Not only was it good marketing, but it was morally right.

The end of the seventies in baseball also brought with it the end of our age of innocence. Free agency was in full swing, and it brought player greed and strikes. In the next decade, baseball would be plagued by an epidemic of drug use among players. In the 1980 World Series between the Phillies and the Royals, who finally made it—it was also the first all-AstroTurf Series— policemen in riot gear and police dogs circled the field as the Phillies were about to clinch their first World Series in their 98-year history.

While the nation was going through sociological changes, so was baseball—and the game, and our perception of it, would never be the same.

THE SEVENTH-INNING STRETCH

Most Valuable Players

Year	National League	American League
1970	Johnny Bench, Reds	Boog Powell, Orioles
1971	Joe Torre, Cardinals	Vida Blue, A's
1972	Johnny Bench, Reds	Dick Allen, White Sox
1973	Pete Rose, Reds	Reggie Jackson, A's
1974	Steve Garvey, Dodgers	Jeff Burroughs, Rangers
1975	Joe Morgan, Reds	Fred Lynn, Red Sox
1976	Joe Morgan, Reds	Thurman Munson, Yankees
1977	George Foster, Reds	Rod Carew, Twins
1978	Dave Parker, Pirates	Jim Rice, Red Sox
1979	Keith Hernandez, Cardinals	Don Baylor, Angels
	Willie Stargell, Pirates (tie)	

Cy Young Award Winners

Year	National League	American League
1970	Bob Gibson, Cardinals	Jim Perry, Twins
1971	Ferguson Jenkins, Cubs	Vida Blue, A's
1972	Steve Carlton, Phillies	Gaylord Perry, Indians
1973	Tom Seaver, Mets	Jim Palmer, Orioles
1974	Mike Marshall, Dodgers	Catfish Hunter, A's
1975	Tom Seaver, Mets	Jim Palmer, Orioles
1976	Randy Jones, Padres	Jim Palmer, Orioles
1977	Steve Carlton, Phillies	Sparky Lyle, Yankees
1978	Gaylord Perry, Padres	Ron Guidry, Yankees
1979	Bruce Sutter, Cubs	Mike Flanagan, Orioles

Rookies of the Year

Year	National League	American League
1970	Carl Morton, Expos	Thurman Munson, Yankees
1971	Earl Williams, Braves	Chris Chambliss, Indians
1972	Jon Matlack, Mets	Carlton Fisk, Red Sox
1973	Gary Matthews, Giants	Al Bumbry, Orioles
1974	Bake McBride, Cardinals	Mike Hargrove, Rangers
1975	John Montefusco, Giants	Fred Lynn, Red Sox
1976	Pat Zachry, Reds	Mark Fidrych, Tigers
	Butch Metzger, Padres (tie)	
1977	Andre Dawson, Expos	Eddie Murray, Orioles
1978	Bob Horner, Braves	Lou Whitaker, Tigers
1979	Rick Sutcliffe, Dodgers	Alfredo Griffin, Blue Jays
		John Castino, Twins (tie)

Batting Champions in the Seventies

Rod Carew (5)
Bill Madlock (2)
Dave Parker (2)
Fred Lynn (2)
Rico Carty
Alex Johnson
Joe Torre
Tony Oliva
Billy Williams
Pete Rose
Ralph Garr
George Brett
Keith Hernandez

Top 10 Leading Hitters in the Seventies*

1. Rod Carew, .343
2. Bill Madlock, .320
3. Dave Parker, .316
4. Pete Rose, .313
5. Jim Rice, .30964
6. George Brett, .30958
7. Ken Griffey, .30956
8. Fred Lynn, .3094
9. Ralph Garr, .3072
10. Joe Torre, .3071

*Minimum of 2,000 at-bats

Most Home Runs
in the Seventies

1. Willie Stargell, 296
2. Reggie Jackson, 292
3. Johnny Bench, 290
4. Lee May, 270
5. Dave Kingman, 252
6. Mike Schmidt, 235
7. Graig Nettles, 232
8. Tony Perez, 226
9. Willie McCovey, 207
10. Reggie Smith, 205

Most Wins
in the Seventies

1. Jim Palmer, 186
2. Gaylord Perry, 184
3. Steve Carlton, 178*t*
4. Tom Seaver, 178*t*
5. Catfish Hunter, 169
6. Don Sutton, 166
7. Phil Niekro, 164
8. Ferguson Jenkins, 158
9. Vida Blue, 155*t*
10. Nolan Ryan, 155*t*

Most RBIs
in the Seventies

1. Willie Stargell, 1,100
2. Johnny Bench, 1,013
3. Tony Perez, 954
4. Lee May, 936
5. Reggie Jackson, 922
6. Graig Nettles, 913
7. Rusty Staub, 860
8. Bobby Bonds, 856
9. Carl Yastrzemski, 846
10. Bobby Murcer, 840

Most Saves
in the Seventies

1. Rollie Fingers, 209
2. Sparky Lyle, 190
3. Mike Marshall, 177
4. Dave Giusti, 140
5. Tug McGraw, 132
6. John Hiller, 115
7. Gene Garber, 110
8. Bruce Sutter, 105*t*
9. Clay Carroll, 105*t*
10. Dave LaRoche, 102

NICKNAMES OF THE SEVENTIES

"Hammerin' Hank" Aaron
Bob "Beetle" Bailey
Paul "Motor Mouth" Blair
Larvell "Sugar Bear" Blanks
Ron "Boomer" Blomberg
"Downtown" Ollie Brown
"Gates" Brown
Rick "the Rooster" Burleson
John "the Candy Man" Candelaria
"Buzz" Capra
Steve "Lefty" Carlton
Gary "Kid" Carter
Orlando "Cha Cha" Cepeda
Ron "the Penguin" Cey
Andre "the Hawk" Dawson
"Boots" Day (an outfielder, not a promotional giveaway)
Mark "the Bird" Fidrych
Carlton "Pudge" Fisk
"Disco" Dan Ford
Leo "Bananas" Foster
"Kiko" Garcia
Phil "Scrap Iron" Garner
Ralph "the Road Runner" Garr
"Goose" Gossage
Jim "Mudcat" Grant
Ron "Gator" Guidry (aka "Louisiana Lightning")
Tom "the Blade" Hall
Mike "the Human Rain Delay" Hargrove
Ken "Hawk" Harrelson
Dave "Kojak" Heaverlo
Frank "Hondo" Howard

Al "the Mad Hungarian" Hrabosky
"Catfish" Hunter
Reggie "Mr. October" Jackson
Jim "Kitty" Kaat
Dave "Kong" Kingman
"Coco" Laboy
Bill "the Spaceman" Lee
Greg "the Bull" Luzinski
Albert "Sparky" Lyle
Bill "Mad Dog" Madlock
Gary "Sarge" Matthews
Willie "Say Hey" Mays
"Bake" McBride
Willie "Stretch" McCovey
"Sudden" Sam McDowell
Gene "Stick" Michael
John "the Hammer" Milner
John "the Count" Montefusco
Graig "Puff" Nettles
Phil "Knucksie" Niekro
John "Blue Moon" Odom
Dave "the Cobra" Parker
Fred "the Flea" Patek
Tony "Big Dog" Perez
"Sweet" Lou Piniella
"Boog" Powell
Doug "the Rooster" Rader
"Bombo" Rivera
"Mick the Quick" Rivers
Aurelio "Chi Chi" Rodriguez
Pete "Charlie Hustle" Rose
Nolan Ryan "the Ryan Express"
George "Boomer" Scott
Tom "the Franchise" Seaver

Roy "Linus" Staiger
Don "Full Pack" Stanhouse
Fred "Chicken" Stanley
Willie "Pops" Stargell
Rusty "Le Grande Orange" Staub
John "the Dude" Stearns
"Champ" Summers
George "the Stork" Theodore
Luis "El Tiante" Tiant
Bob "the Bull" Watson
"Sweet" Lou Whitaker
Walt "No Neck" Williams
"Bump" Wills
Jimmy "the Toy Cannon" Wynn
Carl "Yaz" Yastrzemski
The Big Red Machine
The Mendoza Line*

*Mario Mendoza was a good-fielding, no-hit shortstop for Pittsburgh, Seattle, and Texas who fought an ongoing battle to keep his average above .200. In nine seasons, he finished under .200 five times and had a lifetime batting average of .215. When a batter's average fell below .200, he was said to have fallen "below the Mendoza Line," a phrase attributed to George Brett.

STYLE OF THE SEVENTIES

Best Beard
Gene Garber
Tommy Harper
Bobby Tolan
Bill North

Best Goatee
Dave Cash
Claudell Washington
Willie Horton
Frank Taveras

Best Fu Manchu
Al Hrabosky
Bobby Grich
Luis Tiant
Dick Tidrow
Mike Marshall

Best Walrus
Don Stanhouse
Sparky Lyle
Phil Garner
Ramon Hernandez
Dennis Leonard

Best Handlebar
Rollie Fingers

Best Mutton Chops
Garry Maddox
Johnny Briggs
Jack Heidemann
George Scott
Nate Colbert

Honorable Mentions
Dick Allen
Gene Clines
John Milner

Longest Hair
John Lowenstein
Ted Simmons
Billy Champion
Ross Grimsley
John Candelaria
Brian Downing

Biggest Afro
Oscar Gamble
Jose Cardenal
Nino Espinosa
Jesse Jefferson
Jim Bibby

Honorable Mentions
Reggie Smith
Mike Cuellar
Bake McBride

Best Perm
Wayne Garland
Randy Jones
Bernie Carbo
Dick Bosman
Charlie Williams

No Hair
Dave Heaverlo

Hairpieces
Joe Pepitone
Luis Tiant

Loudest Uniforms
Pittsburgh Pirates
Oakland A's
Cleveland Indians
San Diego Padres
Baltimore Orioles
Houston Astros

Candlestick Park, San
Francisco, CA, 46, 157, *157*
Cannon, Robert, 6
Cappadoccia, Ron, 264
Capra, Buzz, 115–16, 132, 222,
224
Carbo, Bernie, 26, 147–52, 160–
63, 170, 173–74, 176, 177–78
Carew, Rod, 96–97, 102, 109, 163,
207, 208
Carlton, Steve, 48, 72, *73*, 205–6,
241, 244, 290
Carpenter, Ruly, 205
Carroll, Clay, 79
Carroll, Lou, 15
Carty, Rico, 41, 55–56
Cash, Dave, 315
Cash, Norm, 101
catchers, Steve Yeager accident,
202, 204
CBS television, 86, 87, 88, 213,
220
Cepeda, Orlando, 44, 95, 96
Cey, Ron, 106, 249, 295, 298
Chambliss, Chris, 126, 195,
209–10, *210*, 216, 249, 252, 253,
254, 282, 292, 307–8
Chance, Frank, 165
Chandler, Happy, 185
Chaney, Darrel, 78, 224
Charles, Ed, 53, 54
Chicago Cubs, 65, 112, 142, 157,
158, 304
Chicago White Sox, 4, 43, 53, 68,
69, 71, 85, 104, 220
Bill Veeck's purchase of,
184–87, *185*
Disco Demolition Night,
Comiskey Park, 317, *317*
Cincinnati Reds, 8, 21, *21*, 22,
23–29, *23*, 49, 66, 72, *75*, 105,
316–17
Bernie Carbo and, 147–50
George Foster's home-run
records, 241, 242, *243*,
244
and Henry Aaron's home-
run record, 127–29
in 1973 National League
Championship Series,
112–18, 152
during 1975 season, 156–57
in 1976 National League
Championship Series,
209
in 1979 National League
Championship Series,
318
vs. Oakland A's in 1972
World Series, 67, 76–80,
76
vs. Orioles in 1970 World
Series, 29, *30*, *31*, *32*,
33–34, 149–50

Pete Rose's 3,000 hits,
275–76, *277*, 278
vs. Red Sox in 1975 World
Series, 159, *163*, 167–68,
169, 170, *171*, *172*,
173–74, *175*, 176–78, *178*
Tom Seaver trade to, 227,
228, 229–32
vs. Yankees in 1976 World
Series, 211–12, *212*
Claire, Fred, 290
Clancy, Jim, 286
Clemente, Roberto, 35, 40–42,
315, 323
with Brooklyn Dodgers,
37–38
death of, 81–84
election to Hall of Fame,
83–84
in 1970 All-Star Game, 26
in 1971 All-Star Game, 44,
45, 46
in 1971 World Series, 50, *51*,
52, 53
with Pirates, 21, *36*, 41–42,
65
3,000th hit, *65*, 72, 74
Cleveland Indians, 26–27, 87, 88,
93, 144–45, 153, 184, 240, 283
first black manager with,
154–55, *154*
first black player with, 153,
186
tied games, 281
Cleveland Pipers, 88
Cline, Ty, 148, 149
Clines, Gene, 316
Cloninger, Tony, 150
Clyde, David, 98, 109
Cobb, Ty, 314
Colbert, Nate, 130
Coleman, Joe, 16, 72, 194, 195,
196
collective bargaining, 7, 181
Comiskey Park, Chicago, IL, 317,
317
Concepcion, Dave, 168, 176
Cooper, Irving Ben, 15, 16
County Stadium, Milwaukee,
156, 202
Cowens, Al, 205, 209
Crawford, Jim, 194
Cronin, Joe, 2, 4, 86, 125
Crosetti, Frankie, 218
Cuellar, Mike, 19, *32*, 33, 34, 43,
44, 46, 48, 52, 150
Cy Young Award winners, 141,
205, 206, 227, 229, 241, 260,
266, 318, 325

Dahl, Steve, 317
Dallas Cowboys, 177
Darcy, Pat, 176
Dark, Alvin, 143
Davis, Willie, 137

de Roulet, Lorinda, 229–30
Dedeaux, Rod, 24
Dent, Russell Earl "Bucky," 186,
220–22, 234–35, 260, 268, 279,
280, 281, 282, 284–85, 286, 287,
291, 297, 301–2, 308–9
designated hitter (DH) rule,
85–86, 104
first DH, 93–97, *95*
Frank Robinson as DH,
154, 155
Reggie Jackson as DH, 305
in World Series, 118
Detroit Tigers, 3, 16, *70*, 72,
74–75, 165, 261–63
at Disco Demolition Night,
Comiskey Park, 317, *317*
Mark Fidrych and, 191–92,
193, 194–97, 199–201
in 1984 World Series, 263
Devine, Bing, 291
DiMaggio, Joe, 242, 271, 272, 286
Dobson, Pat, 43, 126, 195
Doby, Larry, 153, 186
Dodger Stadium, Los Angeles, CA,
132, 144, 191, 290, 295
Donovan, William E. "Wild Bill,"
165
Downing, Al, 130, 131, 133
Doyle, Brian, 282, 297, 300
Doyle, Denny, 20, 178
Drago, Dick, 168, 201
Dressen, Charlie, 40
Driessen, Dan, 117–18, 121, 174
drugs and alcohol, 147, 150, 324
Duncan, Dave, 76
Durocher, Leo, 27, 65
Dyer, Duffy, 115
dynasties, baseball, 1

East and West divisions, Ameri-
can League/National League
creation of, 2–3
Eastwick, Rawly, 170, 174, 259,
304
Eckert, William, 7
Ellis, Dock, 42, 44, 45, 68, 74, 82,
191, 195, 213, 316
Ermer, Cal, 164
Erskine, Carl, 40
Estrada, Francisco, 53
Etchebarren, Andy, 31
Evans, Aaron, 112
Evans, Dwight, 170, 173, 178

facial hair, 66–68, *67*, 78, 240, 329
Feeney, Charles "Chub," 2, 86, 116,
182–83, 224, 245
Fenway Park, Boston, MA, 160,
161, 166, 167–68, *169*, 173, 176,
239, 279, 284
Ferguson, Joe, 131, 288
Fidrych, Mark "the Bird," 191–92,
193, 194–97, 199–201, 261

Figueroa, Ed, 195, 214, 219, 250,
270, 294, 299
Fingers, Rollie, 77, 78–79, *78*, 118,
143–44, 198, 213
Finley, Charles O., 66, 67, *67*, 86,
105, 119, 121, 125, 126, 142,
143, 146, 188–89, *189*, 190,
198–99
Fishel, Bob, 90
Fisk, Carlton, 27, 160, 170, *171*,
176, 177, 178
Fitzgerald, Ed, 15
Flanagan, Mike, 268, 310, 318,
319, 321, 323
Flood, Curt, 4, 6, 8–18, 69, 149,
323
Flood v. Bowie Kuhn et al., 15
Flynn, Doug, 229
Foli, Tim, 81, 111, 122
Ford, Gerald, 129
Ford, Whitey, 127, 164, 271
Forsch, Bob, 143
Fosse, Ray, 26–29, 66–67, 119,
121, 144–46, *145*
Foster, George, 129, 156, 157, 168,
170, 173, 176–77, 209, 241,
278, 316
Fowler, Art, 72
Fox, Charlie, 48, 64
Foxx, Jimmie, 242
Foy, Joe, 53
Francis, Bevo, 88
free agency, 324
and Curt Flood case, 15
first class of free agents,
213, 259
and Messersmith arbitra-
tion case, 179–84
players as free agents, 143,
146, 166, 189, 282, 299,
316
Freehan, Bill, 192, 194
Fregosi, Jim, 53, 55, 56, 65
Friend, Bob, 6
Froemming, Bruce, 245
Fuchs, Emil, 222

Gaedel, Eddie, 184–85
Gamble, Oscar, 68, 195
gambling, 3
Gantner, Jim, 202
Garber, Gene, 278
Garland, Wayne, 190
Garner, Phil, 316
Garr, Ralph, 50, 112, 128
Garrett, Wayne, 110–11, 117
Garvey, Steve, 105–6, 141, 249,
251, 288, 290
Gaston, Cito, 130, 222
Gehrig, Lou, 242, 312
Gentry, Gary, 19, 21, 55
Geronimo, Cesar, 77–78, 168, 170,
173, 174
Gibson, Bob, 142, 143, 151–52
Giles, Warren, 2